Muslim Hausa Women in Nigeria

Muslim Hausa Women in Nigeria

Tradition and Change

BARBARA J. CALLAWAY

Foreword and Photographs by
ENID SCHILDKROUT

SYRACUSE UNIVERSITY PRESS

First Edition

91 90 89 88 87 5 4 3 2 1

The paper used in this publication meets the minimum requirements of American National Standard for Information Sciences—Permanence of Paper for Printed Library Materials, ANSI Z39.48-1984. ∞™

Library of Congress Cataloging-in-Publication Data

Callaway, Barbara.
Muslim Hausa women in Nigeria.

Bibliography: p.
Includes index.
1. Women, Hausa—Nigeria—Kano. 2. Women, Muslim—Nigeria—Kano. 3. Kano (Nigeria)—Social conditions.
I. Title.
DT515.45.H38C35 1987 305.4'88937'06695 87-6464
ISBN 0-8156-2406-9 (alk. paper)

MANUFACTURED IN THE UNITED STATES OF AMERICA

For Alhaji Baba dan Bappa

BARBARA CALLAWAY is Professor of Political Science at Rutgers University in New Brunswick, New Jersey, where she is Director of the graduate programs in Political Science and in Women's Studies. Her early research was on processes of change and development in African societies, and her field research was conducted in Nigeria and Ghana. In recent years she has focused on women and social change. During 1981–83 she was Visiting Fulbright Professor of Political Science at Bayero University in Kano, Nigeria. Her articles have appeared in the *Journal of Modern African Studies, Comparative Politics, African Studies Review* and the *Journal of Politics.*

Contents

LIST OF TABLES

Foreword

ENID SCHILDKROUT

SEVERAL years ago, when Barbara Callaway and I first discussed her plans to go to Kano, Nigeria, we spoke of the possibility of doing research and writing a book together. That never happened, although one joint paper did emerge from these discussions. Instead, she built upon my research, and that of many others, and took on the formidable task of integrating the concerns and methodologies of social scientists with those of humanists and feminists. This is a courageous book. It dares to ask questions and broach subjects that many of us, as scholars, prefer to sidestep. We describe an alien reality, but attempt to leave aside our personal indignation, particularly while we are doing fieldwork and gathering data. We may be feminists at home, but we try not to impose this point of view on our research, even if we do come to terms with it in our analysis.

Anthropologists and other social scientists who adopt the method of participant observation are inevitably grounded in cultural relativism, so much so that for many field research can be extremely disconcerting. We attempt to share the lives of the women we study, but we can only visit them because we are not of them. We attempt to understand what it is like to see adulthood as inseparable from marriage—though some of us are unmarried and therefore in Hausa eyes still children. The Hausa term for a woman who has never been married, ***buduruwa,*** is the same as that for virgin. Many of us have worked among the Hausa before having children, and some of us have seen our careers as alternatives to marriage and childrearing. These lifestyles are inconceivable for Hausa women, and being with them is a constant reminder of the choices one has made or is free to make. I will never forget the young girl who exclaimed, upon hearing that I was thirty-five years old and had still not had children, "But you are old enough to be my grandmother!" I remember my closest informant, who was exactly my age. The last time I saw her she had borne thirteen children and had eight living children and three grandchildren. My first children (twins) were born the same year as her fourth grandchild; she died that same year, having lived a full life in her own terms. Had she lived, she would have had the status of an old woman —widowed, poor, yet with many children and grandchildren—whereas I was in the middle of a career and just beginning a family. The conclusions that this contrast suggests are too momentous and painful to face while one is in the midst of doing field research, while one is attempting to be "objective."

Because Hausa society is so sexually segregated, most of the studies of Hausa women—with a few important exceptions—have been done by women, women who clearly have been able to act in a totally alien way in Hausa terms as they profess to do "participant observation." In our freedom of mobility we have not had the privileges of men (for within that culture men, too, must observe the barriers that seclude women), but rather we have had a peculiar status as outsiders. Our status has been much more like that of young children, for only children (and some elderly women) are free to bridge the barrier that separates men and women in this gender-split society.

The dichotomy between the world of men and that of women in northern Nigeria has shaped the research and careers of many scholars who have come from outside to study this society. For the most part men have studied men and women have studied women, though there are classic works by M. G. Smith and Polly Hill which have in some ways bridged this chasm and to some extent integrated data from the worlds of men and women into a single analytic framework. Smith and Hill did this primarily in their studies of the Hausa economy. In this book, Barbara Callaway looks at both men and women in a political framework. She shows that while politics is undoubtedly a male business in Kano, it has current implications for the status of women. She shows that men are aware of these implications and not hesitant about harnessing the latent power of women for political ends. The voting statistics she has gathered from official records—in which the numbers of female (as well as male) voters *far* exceed the available figures for the total local population—show how the political significance of enfranchising women was not lost upon those who were involved in election politics.

Another major chasm that runs through this society is that symbolized by the mud brick walls surrounding the *birni,* or old city, of Kano and the modern metropolis outside. Situated in the university setting, Barbara Callaway also attempted to bridge this gap, comparing the worlds of women behind the old city walls and the worlds of women in the university. This is one of the unique and most fascinating sections of this book. Jean Trevor's work with schoolgirls pointed early on to some of the problems Hausa girls developed when they were given the exceedingly rare opportunity of gaining some Western-style education. At the time this study began, the oil boom had led to an outburst of interest in Western education in northern Nigeria which swept women into the tide. Important consequences flowed from this, such as instances of delaying the age of marriage and the substitution of education for other forms of bridewealth. This book deals head on with the implications of these changes both for individual women and for the society as a whole. Right now the oil economy is on the wane and retrenchment is inevitably going on, but it is conceivable that some of the changes that occurred during the 1970s will have a more permanent effect.

Unabashedly, change and progress are being defined here in Western terms—in terms that not even all Western women would accept. I share with Barbara Callaway a commitment to women's liberation, to equal rights and opportunities for women and men, to freedom of choice over all aspects of one's life. These are values that are not yet accepted throughout Western society—either in the United States, or even in all of western Europe. We are dismayed when we see the outright denial of rights of women in Nigeria, and we applaud our own relative progress. But it is only relative, and we have only reached a plateau. What makes it so easy to talk about the predicament of women in northern Nigeria is its blatancy. In relation to a society where even the notion of equality is openly rejected, we can hold ourselves up as an ideal. Yet the indignation which we as observers feel about the position of women in northern Nigeria is in part an expression of the anger we feel about aspects of our own condition.

At the conclusion of this book one comes away with the thought that there are two developments which could occur to change the lives of Muslim Hausa women significantly. One of these—a kind of deus ex machina—is the emergence of a charismatic leader of relatively liberal persuasion, as was Malam Amino Kano. What this book does not dwell on is the more likely emergence of a reactionary charismatic leader who could harness the most conservative forces in the northern Nigerian psyche.

The other precondition for women's liberation in northern Nigeria is a profound change in the way men and women perceive and interact with each other. This must occur in the public domain in order to give women opportunities equal to those of men, and it needs to occur as well in the most private social arenas. The crucial element, I venture to suggest, is the development of intimacy and empathy in male/female relations. Hausa women do not seek intimacy in marriage. The ritual of respect, tied as it is to patterns of inequality, dictates that women do not even address their husbands directly by name, but use honorifics instead. Until women can share with men the deep aspirations so clearly described in this book, the walls that seclude them and shut them out of the halls of power will remain. Autonomy, even a degree of economic and psychic independence, are conceivable for Hausa women even now. But equality and authority outside the circumscription of the home are quite another matter. In the final analysis, intimacy between men and women is therefore a political issue, whether it is a precondition of liberation or a result of it. If we acknowledge the urgency of the plight of women as described in this book, we also must go further and admit that the same problems exist, albeit in different forms and to different degrees, in our own lives.

Preface

THIS book explores pressure for change in the status of women in a deeply conservative, Islamic society in West Africa. Its focus is the interplay between significant forces for change and the prescriptions of an entrenched traditional culture, which together create the intricate path Muslim women must tread in their emergence from the seclusion of the household into a public and less subservient role.

Kano, Nigeria, is the setting for the study. The selection of Kano is partly due to the importance of Kano City as an urban center in West Africa and partly due to the religious and political significance of Kano State in Nigeria. It is both the largest state in the Nigerian Federation and the only one with a homogeneous indigenous population (Hausa/Fulani). Throughout its history, Kano has served as a predominant force for political and social change in this part of the world.

Modern Kano is the scene of changing political realities—only recently have any Kano women voted, been appointed to government positions, or been permitted to form organizations—and rising educational opportunities—girls have begun to go to school in large numbers since the introduction of Universal Primary Education in 1976. In tracing the emergence of these changes and their problematic impact on traditional social roles, I hope to provide some foundation for predicting the probable effects of various efforts toward modernization in women's roles both in Kano and in the wider Islamic context.

Both radical politics, which enhance women's awareness of issues affecting them, and education, which expands knowledge of rights and obligations of women in other societies, are beginning to alter Hausa women's perceptions and interpretations of Islamic teachings concerning women's roles generally and their perceptions of appropriate behavior in particular. If so, we should expect to see an impact upon the structure of the Hausa household, the institution of wife seclusion (*kulle*), the economic activities of women in and out of seclusion, and the marital responsibilities of both men and women. At the same time, the deep determination of both men and women to preserve the Islamic way of life will necessarily inform and temper Hausa women's response and adaptation to changes wrought through education and public policy.

In Kano today the emphasis of traditional Hausa culture remains on inherited family status, stratification of classes, ascription of roles, continuity of institutions, and conformity of behavior to prevailing interpretations of Islamic doctrine. In this culture women are positioned in effect as the minor wards of their fathers and husbands; they are induced to marry early, to confine their activities to the domestic sphere of social relationships and functions, and to observe postures of deference and service toward men. Girls marry young, generally at the onset of puberty. Upon marriage, most women enter *kulle* or seclusion: they do not go out to shop, to trade, or to attend the market. Because they cannot go out, their opportunity for paid work is severely limited. Most engage in some sort of small-scale trade, especially the preparation of cooked food for sale by their children, but the profits are small. Life expectancy is forty-five years for men. For women it is thirty-six, which is in part the consequence of high mortality during childbirth; this in turn is related to the fact that most girls in Kano will be married by age twelve (Interview #33, Kano, May 3, 1983). Infant mortality is still about fifty percent. In addition to seclusion and their consequent absence from sophisticated forms of economic life, women are further handicapped by the fact that Kano State is the most educationally disadvantaged state in Nigeria. A system of Islamic education and Qur'anic learning has long existed, but the little secular education available has been, until recently, theoretically reserved for the sons of traditional elites. (In fact, traditional rulers sent sons of retainers rather than their own sons to such schools during the colonial era.) Because most men, whether commoners or traditional ruling elites, have not been exposed to secular teaching, they have had little opportunity to develop an awareness of modern or enlightened attitudes concerning women. And, as the study will suggest, the progress of women in Kano is necessarily highly dependent on the perceptions and wishes of men. A primary task of analysis in this study is to assess the salience and efficacy of both activist politics and new educational opportunities as sources of reorientation and emancipation for women in a society that has long resisted change in social values generally, and with respect to women particularly.

The study begins with an historical overview of women's positions of authority in the Hausa states at the time of their founding and briefly summarizes the evolution of women's public roles to the present time. Throughout, the study explores aspects of the attempts of feminist theory to explain the nature of female subordination. One predominant theme in such theory posits that because women generally both bear and raise children and depend on men for support, they of necessity define their psychological needs more in relation to others than do men. This consequent dependency is then reinforced in adult life, as men are treated more as independent and fully responsible human beings and women are treated as dependent and less than fully responsible adults. Hence, women's motherhood and mothering functions become a critically important factor in accounting for their universally subordinate status. The development of psychological qualities in women who are dependent on men for support reinforces this dependency and is central to the perpetuation of women's "proper" role. Contrasting male and female experiences throughout childhood do, indeed, result in different male and female psyches in adult life. The thorough socialization of Hausa girls to become wives and mothers will be reviewed in chapters two and three in order to suggest how pervasive these dynamics are in Kano.

In contrast, chapters four and five focus on the attempts of a self-proclaimed radical state government in Kano State to initiate changes in the social status of women. Through political activity (recruiting women to active party politics, encouraging them to vote, and appointing them to public positions) and educational reform, the People's Redemption Party (PRP) (which won elections in Kano State in 1979 and again in 1983) tried to frame public policies that would permit women to emerge from the seclusion of the household into legitimate participation in the public domain. In this vein, chapters six and seven will investigate the impact of the exhortation to send girls to school that accompanied the introduction of Universal Primary Education in 1976 on attitudes toward early marriage, family size, career expectations, occupational choice, differential sex roles, and the participation of women in public affairs. The impact of these radical political orientations on the popular perception of women's proper role in an Islamic society and on women's perceptions of themselves and their own life prospects is the central theme explored throughout this book.

This study builds primarily on data collected in Kano by the author and her students during the period 1981–1983. To a lesser degree, it was informed from published and unpublished written sources (many of the latter in the form of studies conducted by other scholars working in northern Nigeria). As a whole, the data base consists of personal interviews, university and secondary school student surveys, and surveys of teachers and illiterate urban and rural parents of girls in school in Kano State.

During the course of the two years, I personally conducted fifty-four unstructured interviews with both men and women recognized as prominent in Kano society. In the context of this culture, the information sought was very sensitive; thus, most of those interviewed wished to remain unnamed, and most interviews are cited only by date and place. I also conducted structured interviews with eighty-eight women living in two wards of Kano City (Kurawa and Kofar Mazugal), building on the prior work of Dr. Enid Schildkrout, an American anthropologist who conducted research on women and children in Kano from 1976–1978 and again in 1981. A third set of interviews, of ninety-two women in Gwagwarwa ward, was facilitated by one of my students whose father was the *mai unguwa* (ward head) and who gave permission and sanction for the work. Finally, I developed and administered a survey questionnaire to 686 university students and 144 female secondary school students.

During the first year in Kano, I collected as much general information as possible about the life experiences of Hausa women through conversation, observation, and preliminary free interviews. I investigated what sources were available in the University library concerning Kano political history and the history of education. During the summer of 1982, I left Kano for several months. My return in October of that year seemed to establish my standing as a serious person doing "some research on our womenfolk." I suddenly found myself warmly accepted and greeted in the communities where I had established my presence and begun preliminary structured interviewing. Originally confined to women from families of my acquaintances at the University, this enterprise eventually was extended to women in the surrounding compounds. From this point the research activities seemed to flow easily and naturally. During October, November, and December 1982, I was assisted by students whose research I was supervising at Bayero University. Through them, the data base was extended to include 183 teachers in rural and urban girls' secondary schools, 275 students in these schools, 138 illiterate mothers with daughters in school, 292 illiterate men with daughters in school, and 294 women in the village of Malumfashi.

At this time, I was also able to secure the help of two female research assistants with whom I worked throughout the remainder of the study. With their assistance, the interview schedules written in English were administered in Hausa. Formal interviews based upon these schedules were carried out simultaneously with the administration of questionnaires to secondary school students and teachers and to parents, both in the city and the countryside near Kano. Coding of my own interview schedule, which had been administered to 686 university students and 144 secondary students over the two-year period, was accomplished in May 1983. At the end of that month the program on this material (SPSS) was run on the University computer, and the data were cross-checked.

Information on three aspects of women's lives was gathered from the data: first, the norms by which Hausa women defined their roles; second, their expectations for and ideas about changing roles for their daughters and themselves and the extent to which these ideas conformed or conflicted with these norms; and third, their actual behavior in response to expanding educational opportunities and political exhortations.

Social contacts that followed from my work brought many new acquaintances and the opportunity to attend seemingly continuous events—marriages, naming ceremonies, and condoling or mourning functions—in homes in the city. By the end of the two years I felt comfortable and accepted in those parts of the city where I had worked and spent many afternoons simply sitting in women's quarters or visiting, helping with children or cooking, as seemed appropriate.

Thus, during the time of the study my participation in local social life steadily increased. *Allah ya ba ki hakuri* was the phrase I heard most often from women as I went into and out of their houses and compounds in the capacity of interviewer or guest. No matter how long I stayed, I always appeared, unlike them, to be rushing away—rushing to go shopping, or to return to my own home and husband, or to the University for a meeting or a class. *Allah ya ba ki hakuri*—"Allah calm you." The admonition to be patient, to be calm, to accept whatever Allah gives was the seemingly universal advice given by women to other women. These women normally did not dwell on the past or focus on the future. They lived in the present, dealing with joy and tragedy as it occurred. Whether planning a wedding, preparing for the arrival of a new wife, caring for a sick child or watching it die, they did indeed remain calm. While all around them prevailing norms were challenged and behavior patterns altered, their lives remained anchored in traditional tasks and attitudes. Living in mud-walled compounds in an area of dense population that lacks a reliable supply of water or sewage facilities, they own radios, videos, and color television sets. Many of their husbands and sons work in the civil service, serve in the military or police forces, or hold positions in commercial institutions that have grown up in the last fifteen years. Most of their children are attending secular schools, at least to the primary level. And yet, in their own lives, they allege that nothing changes unless "it is the will of Allah."

To paraphrase the words of Professor Richard L. Sklar of over a decade ago, this study is deliberately cast in narrative form as it seeks to reveal the interplay between the persistence of Hausa cultural particularism, the thrust of specific Islamic beliefs, and the crystallization of emerging women's consciousness as part of a wider, worldwide movement for women's liberation. I have set forth the pertinent data and documentary evidence (such as exist) in the hope that they will survive the test of further scholarship and eventually be expanded upon and subsumed in more extensive projects by other researchers.

During the course of the past five years, I have incurred a considerable number of debts of warm gratitude to those who have sustained me through these sometimes difficult years of research and writing: Abena Busia, Lucy Creevey, Richard Mansbach, Jean Parrish, and Carol Nackenoff have given unlimited personal support and moral encouragement. Susan Broadhead, Louise Haberman, Martin Kilson, Enid Schildkrout, and Dennis and Cynthia Sunal have offered personal encouragement, insightful scholarly comment and constructive criticism; Larry Diamond graciously shared his impressive files of clippings from Nigerian newspapers with me. Omar Ibrahim Farouk, Jennifer Klot and Kevin Canada, my students at Rutgers, have lent critical intelligence and an attention to details that have gone far to make completion of this manuscript possible. Enid Schildkrout graciously read the entire text, generously sharing much of her own work. Earlier, she took me to Kurawa and Kofar Mazugal Wards and introduced me to her informants there. Chapters 2 and 3 in particular build upon her work. In Nigeria itself my work could not have been done, nor could I personally have sustained my efforts, without the help, support, and hospitality of friends and acquaintances, both at Bayero University and in the city of Kano. I hope I may be forgiven for offering particular appreciation to the following: Alhaji Baba and Mrs. Betty Dan Bappa, Mrs. Priscilla Starratt (Galadanci), Alhaji Husseini Adamu, Dr. Isa Hashim, Hajiya Magagiya Adamu, Rabi Es Hak, Dr. Ahmed Es Hak, Eva and Yolamu Barongo, Hajiya Rabi Ilyiasu, Amina Mai Kano, Hafsa Ibrahim, Zainab Mohammed, Deja Yahaya, Amina Bature, Bilkisu Mohammed, and Binta Baturia.

Finally, I owe a profound debt of professional appreciation to three scholars whose early work laid the foundation for an understanding of Nigerian politics for those of us who have followed in their path over the course of the past twenty-five years—James S. Coleman, Richard L. Sklar, and C. S. Whitaker.

I am grateful to Carmela Hermann, Betty McCoy, and Phyllis Moditz of the Political Science Department at Rutgers University, who corrected parts of the manuscript, typed tables, and produced the final document. In addition, together and individually, they made the Word Processing Center an enjoyable place to spend seemingly endless hours.

Muslim Hausa Women in Nigeria

1

The Historical Setting and the Place of Women

INTRODUCTION

With an estimated ten million inhabitants, Kano State is the most populous state in Nigeria, which is itself Africa's largest and richest independent black nation. One out of every four Africans is a Nigerian and one of every ten Nigerians lives in Kano State. The people of Kano are overwhelmingly Hausa speaking and Muslim.[1] The Hausa are the largest of Nigeria's several hundred ethnic groups, and Kano is recognized as the most important of the old Hausa emirates (city-states) that predated the nineteenth- and twentieth-century Fulani and British conquests (Hogben and Kirk-Greene 1966; M.G. Smith 1960; Whitaker 1970). Kano has long been a center of religious learning and continues to be viewed as an important center of Nigerian Islam. A plurality of Nigeria's peoples is Muslim, and Islamic consciousness is an increasingly important theme in Nigerian politics.

Kano City has been a commercial center since the twelfth century. For thousands of years it was at the southern end of the trans-Saharan trade routes. Since the early 1900s, it has been at the northern end of an internal economy introduced and developed by the British, who entered Nigeria as a colonial power in 1900 and remained until 1960. Today Kano City is not only a major commercial center, but boasts a level of industrialization second only to that of Lagos, the federal capital. Crumbling mud walls built at the end of the tenth century still separate it from the newer sections of the metropolitan area ("The Town"), which have grown up around it. The Town boasts some five million inhabitants, while the walls of old Kano City—a place devoid of sanitation systems, restaurants, or other modern conveniences—enclose some one and a half million. Within the walls of this city, women

A view of present-day Kano above the city's main gate (Kofar Nassarawa). Most women live in traditional compounds like that in the foreground. Even the more modern two-story cement dwellings nearby are surrounded by walls from which women do not venture alone.

between the ages of twelve and forty-five are rarely seen during the daylight hours.

Kano's large and homogeneous population, its long history and standing as an important traditional city, its development as a leading commercial and industrial city, and its central place in the development of Islam in Nigeria render it an appropriate site for a study of social change. In addition, the fact that the Hausa, most of whom live in northern Nigeria and adjacent territories, are the largest subnational ethnic group in West Africa makes this study of the interaction between pressures for change, Hausa culture, and Islamic beliefs relevant to gaining an understanding of the status of Islamic women in much of Africa. Because many non-Hausa Muslims in Nigeria and areas adjacent to it look to Hausa/Fulani Muslim scholars for their interpretations of Islamic law, the Hausa case can be viewed as representing a model or paradigm of Islamic life in this region.

As one of the original Hausa states in the region that today encompasses northern Nigeria and southern Niger, Kano's history is intricately related to that of the surrounding area. At the same time, however, it is somewhat distinct in that information on the historical role of women is uniquely missing. The following section traces women's historical visibility in the area.

HISTORY AND LEGEND: GLIMPSES OF WOMEN

Attempts at reconstruction of the public role of women in earlier periods of Hausa history is difficult, although some indication of roles assumed by women who were part of the ruling classes may be glimpsed from secondary historical information (Hiskett 1960, 1973; Hogben and Kirk-Greene 1966; Last 1967; Palmer 1936, 1928; H. F. C. Smith 1975; M. G. Smith 1960, 1978). Anthropological studies of those Hausa areas less directly affected by the Fulani-led Islamic jihad (holy war) of Usman dan Fodio (1804–1812) (Hiskett 1973) also give some indication of important roles played by women in times past.[2]

It is clear that in early Hausa history there were queens and there was a preeminent female title, *magajiya.* When a king (*sarki*) ruled, his mother was called *magajiya.* The title *magajiya* was not confined to the biological mother of the *sarki* however, but designated the most important female title-holder who could advise the *sarki* against any action (Hogben and Kirk-Greene 1966, 147; M. G. Smith 1978, 57). In Daura, the original Hausa state, the title *Magajiya* was translated as "Queen Mother"; although not necessarily the mother of the reigning king, she was always of high royal descent. She selected three important female title-holders: the *Yar Kunta, Dan Gawa,* and *Magajiya Karya.* She had her own compound near the *sarki*'s palace and was usually a widow or wife of a leading *mallam* (an Islamic learned man or teacher). All girls of royal descent were required to undergo a week-long preparation for marriage in her compound. She could on occasion countermand the *sarki*'s instruction and even depose him. She received part of the *kudin sarauta* (royal money) and was entitled to wear ostrich feather shoes, a sign of the highest-ranking authority. She could grant pardons to offenders and was adorned with distinctive facial markings (M. G. Smith 1978, 120–22).

The next most senior title for a woman of royal lineage was *iya.* She, too, had her own compound. The *iya* supervised the ritual preparation of princes for marriage and, more important, was in charge of the magicians and the initiates of Bori, the pre-Islamic Hausa religion. She, too, commanded a portion of the *kudin sarauta.* She received all visiting herbalists, magicians, and Bori initiates and supervised the election of a new *magajiya* (M. G. Smith 1978, 124).

The importance of female power-holders in the early history of Hausaland is also exemplified in the state creation myths and the king lists or royal chronicles, which provide histories of the rulers of the original seven Hausa states. It is best portrayed (and perhaps exaggerated) in the "Bayajidda legend" of Daura, which is cited by Hausa people in validating the legitimacy of the seven original Hausa states known as the Hausa *bakwai.* Daura, the first of the seven states according to the legend, clearly established a precedent for female rule as manifested by the names of seventeen queens given as its earliest rulers (Palmer 1928, vol. 3, 142–43; Hogben and Kirk-Greene 1966, 145–54). The suggestion by A.E.V. Walwyn (Palmer 1928, vol. 3, 136–37) that the queen list is more a description of matrilineal descent than of the institutionalization of female rule is unconvincing, given the evidence that queens ruled elsewhere in the savannah (Pitten 1979, app. 1) and the strong supportive Hausa mythology and history. The historical sources suggest the existence of a pattern of women rulers that subsequently gave way to exclusively male rule, but with exceptions that permitted the temporary resumption of power by royal women over both men and women. The seven "legitimate" Hausa states share the traditions of Daura and the Bayajidda legend, and at least five of these states also share a history of political power exercised by women. Kano, however, is not one of these five (Hogben and Kirk-Greene 1966, 118, 484).

In explaining the origin of the Hausa states and in documenting the dramatic change in the perception of proper roles for women in Hausa culture, the Bayajidda legend of Daura is critical. The people of Daura believe that their ancestors migrated from Canaan to Palestine to Libya. Toward the middle of the tenth century, Abdul Dar, unsuccessful in his attempt to succeed his father as king of Tripoli, fled toward the oasis of Kusugu in what is now northern Nigeria. He settled in the area of present-day Daura. His offspring were all female; the ninth daughter, Daura, had the title *Magajiya.* Upon her father's death, she moved her people to a new well, which she called Kusugu, and the town built around it was named after her in her honor (Palmer 1928, 135; M. G. Smith 1978, 53–54). During this part of her reign, a snake took possession of the well and permitted the people to use it only on Fridays.

Meanwhile in Baghdad, Abu Yazidu, the son of Abdullahi, the ruler of the city, led an unsuccessful revolt, and he too fled across the Sahara toward present-day Bornu (Palmer and Smith, *ibid.*). He later traveled to Kano, where he purchased a knife at Dala Rock (which was famous for its blacksmith community) and went on to Daura. Arriving at night, Abu Yazidu wanted a drink of water and so lowered his bucket into the well. Pulling up a snake, he quickly cut off its head with his knife. He then retired for the evening. The next morning Daura began a search for the slayer of the snake and eventually found Abu Yazidu (who later became known as Bayajidda) in the house where he had slept. Immediately falling into love with each other, they were married, whereupon Daura gave Bayajidda half of the town as his own. Because she was childless and believed herself unable to conceive, she gave him a slave girl to be his concubine and bear his children. The concubine produced a male child, after which Daura herself conceived a son, Bawo. Bawo then sired six sons, by three wives. The father and his six sons each established or conquered a Hausa state, and these became known as the Hausa *bakwai* or seven: Daura, Katsina, Zazzau or Zaria, Gobir, Rano, Hadeija, and Kano. Bawo's half-brother, Karbogari ("the son of the slave wife"), also had seven sons, and they in turn founded the *banza bakwai* or "worthless seven."

Whether or not the legend is based on fact, it is clear that it represents something significant in the development of Hausa historical and political identity. Many historical commentators agree with Walwyn and hypothesize that the Bayajidda legend represents the transition of Hausaland from matrilineal to patrilineal descent and succession patterns (M. G. Smith 1978, 56–57; Palmer 1936, 137; Last 1967, 12; Hogben and Kirk-Greene 1966, 92–93). The Daura "King's List" or *girgim* lists seventeen queens, of whom Daura was the last, followed by forty-seven kings. The fact that Abdul Dar had only daughters and that Bayajidda had only sons is seen as being symbolic of a profound change in the Sudanic matrilineal descent patterns existing before the tenth century.[3] Also of significance is the fact that in Hausa lore snakes are female. In the legend, the snake is slain by a noble stranger whom the queen then marries and to whom she gives half her kingdom. In Hausa, the title *sare-kia* ("snake slayer") was shortened to *sarki* and is today translated as king or chief (Hogben and Kirk-Greene 1966, 148). According to M. G. Smith, the slaying of the (female) snake that held the well assertedly legitimates agnatic descent and masculine rule (M. G. Smith 1978, 57). As there is evidence that snakes were worshipped in Hausa lore, the slaying may also have represented the replacement of snake rites by new forms of worship (Palmer 1936, 136).

That more than an end to matrilineal descent is suggested in the Bayajidda legend is borne out by several factors. First, the fact that royal women were politically significant in the Hausa states is supported by myths of origin, the existence of female offices and titles such as *magajiya* (or queen) in the various states, and evidence of actual women rulers. Second, the political place once held by women of this class was closely allied with and validated by pre-Islamic socioreligious conventions and institutions reflected in the Bori cult, which was, in effect, a state religion led by a woman or women of the ruling class. The continued success of the state was held to be dependent in large measure on the efficacy of the Bori rites performed, with responsibility ultimately assigned to the ruler, usually but not always a king (Greenberg 1966). Third, even after queens ceased to rule in Daura, the *magajiya* continued to be important and to countermand orders of the *sarki.* M. G. Smith (1978) suggests that during the Middle Ages the Sarki Daura functioned as a sort of executive agent of the *Magajiya* (p. 57).

In several Hausa states the title *magajiya* continued to represent a remnant of female authority and sometimes considerable responsibility up until the Islamic jihad in 1804. Today, where it exists, it is only symbolic. In Daura to the present day female children of the traditional elite families are sent to the *Magajiya* (a title given to a female member of the royal family by the emir—the successor title to the *Sarki*) in order to be prepared for marriage, and sons are sent to the *iya,* who is now a male advisor to the emir. To this day, during the *Salla* (the days of feasting and celebration marking the end of the Muslim Ramadan or fasting period) the *Sarki* (emir) pays a ceremonial visit to the *Magajiya* (Interview #34, Kano, April 1, 1983). In Bornu, a traditional state to the northeast of Kano, the title was retained as *Magira,* and its holder today retains influence in the political structure of Kanuri court society. In Kano, the present emir pays a similar ceremonial visit to his first wife (*uwar soro*) in her rooms, the *babban daki.*

It is clear that between the tenth and thirteenth centuries, the pattern of matrilineal descent was replaced by a patrilineal one, but deference to the mother, sister, and wife of the ruler was maintained. The titles of *magajiya, magaram,* and *gumsu* were retained. Palmer, who cites praise songs to the Magajiya of Zaria (Palmer 1936, 315; 1927, 233), also records a legend attesting that in the twelfth century the Sarkin Zazzau, driven out of his kingdom and electing to take the Magajiya with him, traveled with her as far as the village of Kumboda where, since she could go no further, he left her as ruler. "Until recently at any rate," Palmer concluded, "the ruler of this town was still a woman" appointed by Sarkin Abuja (Palmer 1936, 137).

After the thirteenth century, the influence of Islam became ever more pervasive and women's public roles, titles, and offices disappeared or were transferred to or assumed by men. This gradual erosion of royal women's status was compounded by a series of major upheavals over the past two hundred years that, together with Islam, further diminished the public voice of women. The political roles of royal women in early Hausa history are still recognized symbolically in some Hausa states (Daura, Katsina, and Zaria), but not in Kano.

THE EARLY HISTORICAL RECORD IN HAUSALAND

Most of what is known of the early history of Kano is gleaned from the *Kano Chronicle,* which is essentially an annotated list of kings. The *Chronicle* records the reigns of forty-eight kings who ruled from approximately A.D. 999 to 1892. The author is unknown but is assumed to be from across the Sahara because much of the original script was in Arabic.[4] This record suggests that between A.D. 900 and 1000 the area of what is now the Hausa states was occupied by Berber races coming from east and north (from Songhai and Bornu). Kano is believed to have been founded at that time by a blacksmith named Dala, who built a house on Dala Rock, in the heart of present-day Kano City.

The *Chronicle* relates that during the reign of Barbushe, the great, great grandson of Dala, strangers arrived who introduced the horse to Kano. It is widely believed that the leader of these strangers was Bagauda, the son of Bawo of the Bayajidda legend of Daura (Palmer 1928, vol. 3, 92). Bagauda became the first Hausa king of Kano, where he reigned for sixty-six years, until his death in 1063; his nickname was Yakano (Son of Kano) and from him the city, the emirate, and the state take their names. Bagauda is credited with starting the walls of Kano about A.D. 1050 and building the inner part of the present emir's palace in Kurawa Ward of the present city (Hogben and Kirk-Greene 1966, 185). His title was *Sarki* and he is said to have had 1000 wives (Palmer 1928, 112).

Hence, while the historical record as recorded by the *Chronicle* contains no allusion to female rulers in Kano, it does show a direct lineal descent between the kings of Kano and Daura, where there was an explicit account of female rulers. Because of the direct link of Kano to the Bayajidda legend, the absence of a tradition of public roles for women in Kano is intriguing. It may be supposed, however, that the establishment of a strong Islamic presence in Kano is responsible. According to the *Kano Chronicle,* the first Muslims came to Kano some hundred years after Bagauda's reign, about 1150, from Mali. Two centuries later, the fifth Hausa king, Yusa, received forty Muslim missionaries (c. 1380), built a mosque, and ordered the people to pray five times a day (Hogben and Kirk-Greene 1966, p. 188). Kano was one of the first Hausa states to be affected by Islam, which came to be more deeply entrenched there than anywhere else in present-day Nigeria. Hence, while even in Bagauda's reign there is no mention of a Magajiya or Iya in Kano, this may be evidence of the early influence of Islam in this basically pre-Islamic area.

For several centuries Kano was subjected to internecine wars, and its outskirts were raided by various armies seeking slaves. By the early 1400s,

Bornu (a non-Hausa state to the northeast) had established domination over Kano, bringing new trade and a reaffirmation of Islam.

Under Mohammad Rumfa (1463–99), the city reached its "golden age." Rumfa established wide trade connections and brought Muslim missionaries directly from the holy city of Medina to Kano. The missionaries found the soil of Kano to be "the same" as that of Medina, thus establishing a special and mystical connection between it and Kano. Rumfa extended the walls of the city and established the Kurmi market, which still functions as the main market inside the city. Rumfa also began the practice of requiring all first-born females in Kano to be brought to him for their first sexual experience, introduced seclusion for women (or *kulle* in the Hausa language), and decreed that his 1000 concubines be secluded in the enlarged palace that still occupies the center of the city (Hogben and Kirk-Greene 1966, pp. 190–93; Palmer 1928, pp. 111–12). Thus, by the end of the reign of Rumfa, Islam was firmly established in Kano, and women of high social standing (both wives and concubines) were secluded. If ever there had been public roles or official titles for such women in Kano, they are not recorded. Whether or not Kano was an exception among the Hausa states, or whether, if so, the early establishment of Islam there explains this fact, cannot be known.

As late as the fifteenth or sixteenth century, instances of women in important public roles were recorded in the history of the Hausa states surrounding Kano. The most striking and impressive evidence of this is written in the history of Zazzau, or Zaria, which was ruled by the most illustrious of Hausa queens, Amina. School children in present-day Kano, as well as throughout Hausaland, cite Queen Amina as one of the greatest of all Hausa rulers. The most frequently quoted information about her is taken from Sultan Muhammad Bello of Sokoto's *Infak al Maisuri* (translated into English in Hogben and Kirk-Greene 1966, 217; and Heath 1952, 5; and reprinted in Kirk-Greene 1972, 8).[5] Sultan Bello observed:

> Strange things have happened in the history of the seven Hausa states, and the most strange of these is the extent of the possessions which God gave to Aminatu, daughter of the ruler of Zazzau. She waged war in the Hausa lands and took them all, so that the men of Katsina and the men of Kano brought her tribute (Hogben and Kirk-Greene 1966, 217).

Hogben and Kirk-Greene date her accession to the throne of Zazzau at 1576 (216–18). According to the *Kano Chronicle,* Amina conquered Kano and Katsina and "all the towns as far as Kwararafa and Nupe" by 1580.

Amina was the daughter of Bakwa Turunku, the twenty-second ruler of Zazzau. (He had another daughter, Zaria, after whom the present city and emirate are named). At age sixteen, Amina assumed the title of Magajiya and was given forty female slaves. After her father died, she loved riding into battle with the Sarki. When he died in 1576, Amina became queen. She extended her rule throughout the land by successive victories on the battlefield, conquering the south and west all the way to the banks of the Niger (Hogben and Kirk-Greene 1966, 216–17). She was known for these conquests and built walled camps wherever she went. Today the walls of many Hausa towns are still called *ganuwar Amina,* "Amina's walls." Whether or not Amina ever married is disputed. According to Sultan Bello's *Infak al Maisuri,* Amina took a lover in every town she conquered and had him beheaded the next morning. She was the first ruler in Hausaland to use eunuchs and the Sarkin Nupe sent forty eunuchs and 10,000 kola nuts to her. It is not clear how her reign of thirty-four years ended, but she had become perhaps the best known of the Hausa rulers. "Every town" paid tribute to her. Today a song is still sung: "Amina . . . a woman as capable as a man" (*Kallabi tsakanin rawuna*), or literally, "a head-tie among the turbans" (*Kano Chronicle* in Palmer 1928, vol. 3, 109). Thus, although there is no enduring legacy of any public role for women in its affairs, there is a recognition in Kano's historical tradition of the existence of a Hausa queen to whom the state succumbed.

Another instance of a woman ruler in Hausaland comes from Gobirawa, or people of Gobir, who preserve a history of a queen who ruled during the period of settlement at Birnin Lalle in the present-day Republic of Niger, northwest of Sokoto. The time of this settlement is given by Hogben and Kirk-Greene as early eighteenth century (p. 369) and by Nicolas as some time around or shortly after the fifteenth century (1975, 203). The tomb of this queen, Tawa, is still visited by the inhabitants of the area, and from the time of her reign the Gobirawa assumed the sobriquet "sons of Tawa."

The Empire of Bornu provides yet a further instance of a political role for women throughout the states of the Nigerian savannah before the Fulani jihad of the early nineteenth century. "The lady of the great white horse, *Me Aisa,* a princess of the blood, daughter of Danama" reigned in the sixteenth century; she was, however, regent rather than queen (Palmer 1913, 79). Further, *Magira, Magaram,* and *Gumsu,* all women's offices and titles, were traditionally associated with control of property and the exercise of power. Thus, whatever may have been the initial factors responsible for women's high status in Bornu society, it is clear that women held recognized positions of power for nearly a millennium (Hogben and Kirk-Greene 1966, 92–93, 314–15; Palmer 1950, 162–63).[6]

In the Hausa states then, a system of women's titles and offices, conferring specific authority on the holders, appeared to be widespread and to be supported by strong religious authority. Information concerning women's titles and offices other than queen is sketchy partly because the holders, not being rulers, do not appear on king lists, partly because of a lack of an enduring historical significance to these offices, and perhaps partly because of a conscious effort in the states conquered in the jihad to minimize the former political significance of women. But such material as is available gives an idea of the role of some women of wealth, ability, and influence. Women exercising institutional political power included the "queen mother," who was not necessarily the mother of the incumbent king, but rather a woman (called the Magira in Bornu, the Iya in Habe Abuja and Katsina, and the Magajiya in Daura and Zaria) with authority and influence over him and the sisters and/or daughters of the ruler. The royal sister or daughter was called Magajiya in Katsina, Zaria and Kebbi; Magaram in Bornu; and Sarauniya or Mardanni in Abuja. The kingdoms of Damagaram (present-day Zinder in the Republic of Niger), Gobir, and Daura appear to have maintained a single royal female title (respectively, *Magaram, Inna,* and *Magajiya*) (Pitten 1979, app. 1). Kanta, ruler of Kebbi, is said to have given eighty-four towns of Yauri to his daughter when she was Magajiya Kebbi at Silame in the nineteenth century (Hogben and Kirk-Greene 1966, 246). In Zazzau, during Hausa rule, certain "fiefs" were traditionally administered by the *Iya, Sarauniya,* and *Mardanni*—all female titles, While none of the women was eligible for succession to the kingship, the Sarauniya and Iya in particular were consulted by the king on matters concerning royal women and other women (mostly slaves and concubines) within the walls of the palace (Pitten 1979).

In many of the smaller states as well, a tradition of women in political power is reflected in the mythology of the states and of the groups who, through migration and/or conquest, became associated with larger political entities; however, the position of head of state appears to have been only infrequently held by a woman and is perhaps selectively recorded. Women in political power probably reached their zenith around the sixteenth century, when the titular heads of some Hausa states and Bornu were women.

After this time, ruling class Hausa women experienced a steady diminution in their influence and were systematically deprived of their authority and autonomy. The traditional titles and offices relating to authority over women and redress of their grievances have now become nominal or have been discarded altogether. In Kano they do not exist, and no memory survives of their ever having existed, even in legend. The Hausa people offer no explanation why Kano should have been different from the other Hausa states in this regard. Binta, who claimed to be 103 years old in 1983 and who lived all her life in the slave quarters at the back of the emir's palace, stated categorically that there is no legend, tradition, or knowledge of women having authority or responsibility over men or women in Kano. She asserts that any grievances on the part of women were always taken directly to the emir through a woman messenger, who was always of slave lineage. Binta and the other women in her compound knew of Queen Amina and of Daura of the Bayajidda legend but were quite adamant that no such person could have emerged in Kano itself. Such an event was unimaginable to them (Interview #24, Kano, February 26, 1983).

THE MODERN HISTORICAL RECORD: WOMEN DISAPPEAR

As we have seen, there is enough in the record to suggest that through the decades and over the centuries, ruling-class Hausa women have been systematically and increasingly deprived of whatever authority they once held. Traditional titles and offices relating to the authority of women over the community at large, or over other women for the redressing of grievances, have become nominal or nonexistent. While this apparently happened earliest in Kano, by the twentieth century it was generally true throughout the Hausa-speaking areas.

By the sixteenth century, the erosion of the standing, influence, and authority of women title-holders coincided with the growing influence of Islam, which, appearing as a significant force first in Kano, had become an established presence in the area of the Hausa states by the end of the fifteenth century. Kano's desert commerce with North Africa brought Arab traders who settled in the city and in turn became the nucleus of a small Islamic community; by the end of the fifteenth century, Kano had become a key trading center with a growing urban culture and was becoming a center of religious learning as well. While the ruling lineages and their followers increasingly identified with Islam, they continued to participate in the rites of Bori, the spirit possession cult that had acquired the status of a more or less official state religion (Palmer 1914). Hence during the sixteenth century, Islam coexisted with animist practices and rites and individuals participated in both without perceived conflict (Greenberg 1966). Because we have no evidence to suggest that Bori was different in Kano from elsewhere in Hausaland, we must assume, despite the absence of record, that titled women played important religious, and hence political roles in Kano.

Under the influence of the North African Arabs, a few of whom settled permanently in the city, a small number of Kano men became literate in Arabic and knowledgeable about the *Qur'an.* They formed a tiny literate minority in a preliterate Hausa-speaking area. Because they were associated with the

Muslim strangers (Arabs) and were becoming quite wealthy, they gained increasing influence and a growing number of converts. Some of them became scholars, who were usually attached to the emir's palace, where they served as religious teachers, scribes, advisors, and even physicians. It was a comfortable relationship in that neither the Arabs nor the Hausa Muslim scholars objected to local custom, including the mixing of Islam with Bori. These men studied books brought to them from North Africa and began to write on their own, producing a small body of literature c. 1700–1750 (Hiskett 1973, 6–7).

According to the *Kano Chronicle,* by the time of the reign of Yakubu (1452–1463) Fulani traders had become a significant presence in Kano and had begun to settle there permanently and to intermarry with the Hausa. During the eighteenth century, many thousands of nomadic Fulani herdsmen (the "cattle Fulani" as opposed to the "town Fulani") moved into the area of the Hausa states from present-day Mali. The Fulani were Muslims and greatly expanded the Islamic presence.

The Muslim teachers or *mallams* (most of whom by this time were Fulani rather than Arab or Hausa) began to voice their disapproval of those portions of the surrounding Hausa culture that were not yet fully Islamic. In particular, they protested the passing of inheritance through the female line, the "nakedness of women," and the mingling of the sexes in public—all of which according to them defied Islamic law (Bivar and Hiskett 1962, 142f.).

As devout Muslims became increasingly dissatisfied with the contrast between daily Hausa life and the Islamic ideal, the stage was set for the Fulani reformer, Shehu Usman dan Fodio. During his childhood Usman dan Fodio had begun the life of a scholar, totally submerging himself in memorizing the *Qur'an* and learning the *Fiqh,* or Islamic legal theory. By the time he was a young man, he was well-versed in the laws of personal status and had become an expert on the Sharia (Islamic law) and the application of Islamic legal codes and social regulations to civil and criminal cases as prescribed by the Qadiriyya brotherhood, a Sufi mystic sect. Dan Fodio came under the tutelage of Shaikh Jibril b. 'Umar, a Sudanese mystic particularly critical of Islam as practiced in Hausaland. Between 1789 and 1804, dan Fodio experienced visions in which the "Sword of Truth" instructed him to launch a holy war in order to purify the area of the Hausa states for Islam (Hiskett 1973, 8–17). He returned to the desert and became a teacher and preacher among the Fulani, who continued to immigrate and settle in Hausaland. As he met with continuing frustration in reforming Hausa society by word, the Shehu decided to use force.

The Fulani jihad (or holy war) erupted during the reign of Mohammad Alwali, the forty-second king of Kano. Alwali was killed in 1807, and the Shehu appointed Sulemanu, "the most learned man in Kano," as his flag-bearer; the flag represented authority from the Shehu to rule in his name (Hogben and Kirk-Greene 1966, 198). The appointment of Sulemanu as emir completed the Islamization of Kano Emirate, a process that had been occurring peacefully in Kano, as throughout Hausaland, over the course of several centuries. In his *Kitab al Farq,* the Shehu listed various accusations concerning pagan practices and sins against religious teachings among the Hausa. (*Kitab al Farq* has been translated by Hiskett, 1960.) The political authority of women over women was seen by him as one of the fundamental manifestations of the un-Islamic nature of Hausa society: "One of the ways of their governments is that [a man] put the affairs of his women into the hands of the oldest one, and every one [of the others] is like a slave-woman under her" (Hiskett 1960, 67).

The Shehu's second son, Muhammad Bello, founded the town of Sokoto, which became the Fulani capital, and Kano came at least nominally under the control of Sokoto as did Daura, Zaria, Katsina, and the other Hausa states. The Fulani rulers established the Sharia, or Islamic law, as a uniform code throughout the empire and ruled "in the name of Allah." They freely intermarried with the Hausa (Habe) and made wives of the Hausa (Habe) slave women, thereby assuring a great deal of Hausa-Fulani and Fulani-Hausa assimilation.

While the Shehu denounced the inappropriate roles of royal women in the Hausa states, he deplored the virtually universal ignorance of common women (i.e., ignorance of the *Qur'an*) and advocated that they be taught basic Arabic literacy and Islamic religious doctrine. As an example, he taught his own daughter, Asma, the *Qur'an* in Arabic (dan Shehu 1971, 77).

It is likely that most of the Hausa population did not understand the nature of the Islamic jihad, perceiving only that they had been conquered by the Fulani who were now establishing an empire. But, the *Qur'an* and the Muslim religion provided a new identity and were especially a boon for that part of the populace subject to constant slave-raiding by the Hausa kings; intervention by the Fulani provided relief from this particular source of oppression. Slavery was widely practiced in Kano as in the rest of Hausaland, and most people who were not of royal lineage were subject to enslavement. Hence, although there was no overt warfare or rebellion, a substantial undercurrent of discontent was available for the Shehu to tap. Women in particular had been taken away from their homes at random and forced into harems; although women in the royal families could attain position and influence, common women were viewed as objects, bearing no rights whatsoever. The Shehu objected to this, warning that women should be protected as specified in the *Qur'an.* Thus, while highly placed women lost status dramatically under the imposition of Fulani or Islamic rule, common women gained status and protections unknown to them before.

The Shehu increasingly was viewed in Hausaland as a leader of great knowledge who was bringing into the light much that was only vaguely understood about Islam. He constantly traveled and preached, revealing to his listeners rights of which they were ignorant (e.g., equality before Allah and therefore equal protections as members of the Muslim community or *umma*) as well as duties (such as praying five times a day) demanding performance. The Shehu traveled with a group of scholarly followers who had been farmers and nomads, not rulers, and in so doing, touched a foundation of both discontent and Islamic acculturation that had been developing for seven centuries (Hiskett 1973, 76–77).

The jihad was fought between 1804 and 1812, during which time Fulani rule was superimposed over Hausa, and Hausa titles transferred to the holders of new Fulani-sanctioned offices. The jihad itself was more a reformist movement than one aimed at bringing about fundamental changes in the society. The Fulani political system that evolved during the next century was essentially the original Hausa system with a strong Fulani and Islamic overlay. (For an elaboration of these points, see M.G. Smith 1960, and Whitaker 1970.) The jihad centralized power in Sokoto, and the Shehu designated an emir in each of the Hausa states, including Kano, as his representative and sole authority. Based on a system of fief-holding and patronage, the authority of the emirs was maintained through the institutionalization and extension of Islamic courts, a complex system of taxation, and an elaborate administrative machinery. The emirs levied taxes and other fees and paid tribute to Sokoto; power was delegated from Sokoto to the emirates. Each emir was charged with ensuring the proper conduct of religious affairs and waging holy war against non-Muslims (Hiskett 1973, 140–41; Whitaker 1970).

For royal women, the most important consequence of the successful waging of the jihad was the loss of their ritual religious authority and with it, the primary foundation of their political influence. The ascendance of Islam, which had hitherto coexisted with the cult of Bori, forced Bori into eclipse; Bori lost its political legitimacy, and its adepts lost their influence. Still, the process of withdrawing titles and offices from women in states affected by the jihad was often a matter of realizing short-term goals rather than of making a political statement about the status of women. Thus, in Zaria women's titles, such as Magajiya, Sarauniya and Mardanni, were bestowed upon the daughters of the first emir, but were subsequently removed from women and either retired or assumed by men, or in one case, retained at a wholly formal level (M.G. Smith 1960, 131).

Nevertheless, women in present-day Katsina, the Hausa state immediately to the north of Kano, are reported to claim that even after the jihad some women retained political authority: the wives of district heads are believed to have heard and judged controversies concerning women under their husbands' authority and even to have traveled around the district settling disputes. Men disagree, however, claiming that no women had any such authority either before or after the jihad (Pittin 1979, 465–66). It is interesting to note that in both Daura and Katsina the title of Iya—still the highest-ranking member of the traditional hierarchy after the emir in Katsina and the senior member of the emir's council in Daura—is now bestowed upon men. From the time of the jihad until 1979, no women anywhere in the Hausa-Fulani north were in public positions even remotely political, although there is some indication of residual influence as late as 1893 (Fika 1978, 58). At that time Emir Muhammad Bello died in Kano, which was subsequently plunged into a civil war over the question of succession. The Sultan of Sokoto favored one faction, but his chief legal advisor, the Waziri, favored another, "whereupon Nana, the daughter of Shehu Mujaddadi, proposed Bello [a nephew of Muhammad Bello] as the compromise candidate" (quoted from the *Kano Chronicle* by Hogben and Kirk-Greene 1966, 202). The traditions of the present palace, however, do not admit of any such past influence for women.

The title of Magajiya has been retained within the ruling class of some Hausa states (emirates), but has been shorn of any political significance. Because of extensive intermarriage between royal families, women who themselves hold the title or whose mothers once held it live in the palaces of all the emirs. But in Kano, these women were born in other palaces—it is not a title bestowed on girls who are born in Kano. In Daura, the original Hausa state, the title is sometimes conferred upon a daughter of the emir, but it is not automatic and has no special significance other than a routine acknowledgment of a somewhat special status. It is usually conferred upon a favorite daughter following the petition of her husband. One of the present emir's daughters is called Magajiya, but no authority attaches to the title (Interview #34, Daura, March 31, 1983).

Clearly, the political experience of ruling-class Hausa women has declined gradually but dramatically over the centuries, with a final and fatal break at the time of the jihad and shortly thereafter. That all women in the post-jihad north were already political minors when the British arrived is apparent from the dearth of reference to them in official documents, except for the inevitable mention of marriage and divorce patterns. Presumably the subordination of women accorded with British predilections for a male-controlled society.

Systematic exclusion of women from political authority and influence was a situation that did not offend British sensitivities. In the years following their arrival and until independence in 1960, the notion that women bore any interests that would warrant their having a political place in northern Nigeria had no relevance.

The early twentieth century brought another very sharp change in historical direction in the area of the Hausa states. Most of the Fulani empire, centered in Sokoto, came under the domination of the British. Kano fell to British-led troops in 1903, the same year that what is now the northern states of Nigeria were declared to be a British protectorate.

The leader of the British conquest and the first governor-general of the Protectorate of Northern Nigeria was Sir Frederick Lugard, the principal architect of the British colonial policy known as "indirect rule." The core of the policy of Indirect Rule was the conviction that traditional authorities in the colonies should be recognized wherever possible and that whenever possible, the metropolitan power should seek to rule through them in accordance with their own social and political institutions and mores (Lugard 1929). As part of the overall policy of Indirect Rule, virtually no Christian missionaries were allowed into the Muslim areas of Northern Nigeria, thus assuring that Islam there was protected from liberalizing forces at work in the south. Islam became ever more deeply entrenched, and the Shehu's legacy of ideas remains part of the ethos of the area to the present day.

It was the framework of the Fulani empire, not the pre-existing Hausa state structure, that was preserved by Lugard and the British under Indirect Rule. Under Fulani rule and British protection, the Islamic (or Sharia) courts were very much a part of this system. The colonial state provided the stable conditions necessary for Islamic culture to grow and develop. An elite, conservative, and orthodox class of Muslim teachers (*mallams*) flourished with considerable influence under the protections provided by Indirect Rule. To this day, when there is a conflict between Islamic orthodoxy and modern ideas, the *mallams,* who have considerable influence over their adherents, give evidence of a deep-seated hostility to change. Hence, any effort in this environment to enhance the rights of women without Islamic sanction is probably doomed to failure. The British did not try.

Under Indirect Rule, the emir's authority became formally delineated, his income was guaranteed and, with the protection of the British, his power was dramatically increased. In each emirate, the emir was designated sole native authority. In addition to the administration, he controlled the police, the judiciary, and the prisons. (For excellent discussions of the changing roles of emirs under British administration, see M. G. Smith 1960, and Whitaker 1970.)

The period of British colonial rule in Nigeria was very short. By the 1940s, a southern-based nationalist movement was already well underway, and demands for immediate and full independence could be heard. These circumstances made it inevitable that a nationalist movement would begin in the north to represent and protect northern interests; the Northern Elements Progressive Association (NEPA) soon emerged. The party was founded in 1945 by Raji Abdullah, Mallam Muhammadu Bida, and M. Abubakar Zukogi, all of whom were associated with the southern-based National Council of Nigeria and the Cameroons (Coleman 1960, 353–68).

By 1950, when political agitation and British acquiesence elsewhere in the country made the formation of a northern-based political party desirable, the NEPA had been replaced by the Northern Elements Progressive Union (NEPU). Like NEPA, it was founded in Kano, this time by a group of eight young men, mostly teachers. After initial confusion, uncertainties and anxiety over NEPU, the northern traditional elite decided in October 1951 to declare the Jamiyar Mutanen Arewa (JMA) (then ostensibly a northern cultural organization), a political party. It was called the Northern Peoples Congress (NPC); NPC later came under the leadership of the late Sardauna of Sokoto, Sir Ahmadu Bello.

Praise songs from that era link Ahmadu Bello to the founder of the Qadiriyya brotherhood of Islam:

> Sardauna, Ahmadu Bello, praise be to Allah,
> Descendant of the saint, Usuman, who does not sleep,
> The high-ranking one, Sir Ahmadu Bello, is the light,
> The Alhaji who removes the darkness of hypocrisy.
>
> We pray the Glorious God, the King in truth,
> NPC, may it have mastery over Nigeria,
> For the sake of Sidi 'Abd al-Qadir al-Jilani
> Your rule will last until the appearance of the Mahdi.
> (Hiskett 1973, 163)

Many Muslims believed the claim of the Sardauna that the genealogy linking him through his great, great grandfather, Shehu Usman dan Fodio, to the founder of the Qadiriyya brotherhood, went back to the Prophet himself (Ahmadu Bello 1962, 28; Paden 1973, 180–89). This claim was then used in the effort to legitimate unification of secular and religious authority under Fulani rule.

Nigeria became an independent state in 1960. The next five years brought tension and trouble for the civilian regime, culminating in a controversial and violence-plagued second election at the end of 1964. The intense struggle between regional elites and a central federal government that appeared too weak to check their excesses led to the demise of the First Republic by means of a violent military coup d'état in January, 1966. After waging a civil war in Nigeria, the military introduced changes that have had a profound and far-reaching impact. Perhaps one of the most important of these for the Hausa/Fulani emirates was the enfranchisement of women.

THE PRESENT: WOMEN REEMERGING

In 1967 Kano became a state within a reconstituted Nigeria without any alterations to its provincial boundaries. The first military governor of Kano State, the late Alhaji Audu Bako, founded five girls' secondary schools and two women's teacher training colleges. In 1976 the Federal Government introduced a scheme of Universal Primary Education (UPE) and all parents were urged to send their children to school. In 1978, the military government granted Muslim women the right to vote for the first time in the new elections called for 1979, which returned Nigeria to civilian rule for four more years. As a result of these innovations, the numbers of educated women and of girls in school in Kano increased manyfold, while the presence of women as teachers and as low-level administrators in various government agencies also grew steadily. By 1982 the Kano State Government had founded 130 new elementary schools and was actively urging parents to enroll their girls.

In the national elections of 1979, the People's Redemption Party (PRP) came to power in Kano State. The PRP was a "popularly based" mass political party that presented itself as "radical" and proclaimed a public commitment to the "emancipation" of women. (The efforts of the PRP and the Kano State Government to involve women in formulating government policy and serving in the public sphere will be reviewed in chapters four and five.)

Before he died in April 1983, Mallam Aminu Kano, the national leader of the PRP and its presidential candidate in the 1979 elections, announced that his vice-presidential running mate in the 1983 elections was to be a woman. Thus, after a long period of decline and virtual disappearance, women's political roles were being reconstituted, and at least one state government in the Islamic north was seeking to revive women's participation in the public domain. The real impact of these efforts is yet to be felt, but initial findings suggest a dramatic awakening of women's interest and participation in public affairs.

But, as will be discussed, Islam as practiced in Kano presents a major constraint upon any effort towards dramatic change in the public role of women, limiting freedom of choice and movement by gender and according privileges to men while defining restrictions for women. In spite of their right to vote, Muslim women are not generally afforded the protections of the Nigerian Constitution of 1979, which relegates to the states matters covered by "Islamic personal law." Hence, matters of vital concern to women (marriage, divorce, child custody, property) are regulated by the state according to Sharia (Islamic) law (Callaway and Schildkrout 1985). Wife seclusion (*kulle*) is widely practiced, and while this is an Islamic tradition, in Kano its practice takes the extreme form of actual physical seclusion rather than the more modified form of veiling as practiced in many other Muslim societies. Over the decades more and more women have entered *kulle;* at present, it is the general pattern of life for women in both urban and rural areas in Kano State.

As this chapter has noted, in the early nineteenth century the Fulani jihad replaced the Hausa hierarchy with a Fulani one, but continuity was maintained as the Fulani intermarried with the Habe, particularly among the ruling families. Beginning in 1903, the British threatened the social fabric of this highly stratified community by introducing a century of gradual social change through the slow importation of Western culture into this now overwhelmingly Muslim society. These tensions continue to exist.

For centuries Kano had reflected the religion and culture of North Africa. From the beginning of the twentieth century, Kano was also being pulled towards the southern coast with its Christian/European influences. Since 1952, when regionally based political parties were formed, Kano has been associated with radical and populist Islamic movements. It has retained its position, however, as the acknowledged seat of Hausa and Fulani tradition and culture and of Islamic learning. The juxtaposition of opposing currents represented by Islamic culture and traditions, on the one hand, and Western education and radical politics on the other hand, will be explored in this study.

In northern Nigeria, particularly in the geographical heartland of Hausa Islamic culture that is Kano State, the call for a fundamental reconsideration of the position of women has occasioned public controversy. The issue seems inseparable from a more general anxiety over the nature and direction of change. A sharpening perception of the claims and consequences of programs of social modernization goes hand in hand with a sensation of threat to a society that prides itself on its adherence to Islamic teachings.

The subordination of women to men and their exclusion from the world of men is central to the conception of Islam as practiced in Kano, where a sharp differentiation between male and female roles is maintained. Women live in seclusion, isolated in daily life from all but members of their immediate households. This physical seclusion of women from men and from the public at large is an extreme manifestation of a more general and universal asymmetrical structure of male and female roles found to some extent in all modern societies. These societies contain coherent, mutually reinforcing, and systemic patterns of culturally and religiously sanctioned perceptions, priorities, and institutional arrangements that imply the subordination of women to men. The case cited here is thus but one possible manifestation of a more general construct endorsing the notion of women's proper role and space.

The belief that the domestic unit must be more closely ministered to by females than by males in order to nurture the young is a part of this cultural conditioning. Thus, women face a multitude of restrictions: their sexual activities are circumscribed, their roles are more closely defined, and their access to social institutions are more limited than men's in order that their families may be the focus of their lives. Women are socialized to have more narrow and conservative attitudes than men—these attitudes are not inherently a part of the female psyche, they are learned. This book will explore some of the ways in which the limited social context of female adult life in Hausa society reinforces women's conservatism and traditionalism, undermining efforts towards social equality and encouraging women to accept or at least rationalize their subordination.

2

Hausa Women in Kano Society

REFLECTIONS ON THE NATURE OF FEMALE SUBORDINATION

"How is it that this world always belonged to the men and things have begun to change only recently? Is this change a good thing? Will it bring about an equal sharing of the world between men and women?" (de Beauvoir 1974, xxv).

This question, posed by Simone de Beauvoir over thirty years ago, remains a focus of concern for scholars of many cultures. In recent years, women in general and feminist scholars in particular have become increasingly articulate about the universality and the pervasiveness of a derogatory and/or constraining view of women that informs nearly every culture and every major religion. Some scholars have begun, in systematic fashion, to examine the basic assumptions that underlie notions about women and their "nature" in every field from psychology, biology and theology to history, political science, and sociology.

The subordination of women to men in Kano is not unique. Feminist perspectives, in attempting to explain such subordination in general and universal terms, help to clarify its manifestation in this particular case (Bardwick 1971; de Beauvoir 1974; Chodorow 1978; Deutsch 1949; Epstein 1970; Firestone 1970; Gornick and Moran 1971; Iglitzen and Ross 1976; Macoby and Jacklin 1974; Mead 1935; Millet 1971; Rosaldo and Lamphere 1974; Tiger 1969). It seems a dubious enterprise, however, to look for only one fundamental, constant, and universal theme. Any sound explanation is likely to entail a range of determinants, such as modes of economic organization (Engels 1972), contradictions intrinsic to specific forms of organized society (Lenin 1965), changing premises concerning the nature and substance of "female psychology" (Bardwick 1972), the perceived requirements of modern society (Parsons 1954), and evidence of physiological and biological differences and consequent "programming" (Tiger 1969). All of these factors are variable and relevant to an understanding of the social position and existence of women in Hausa society. In this study the focus is to conceptualize the relationship of a particular set of influences (religion and culture) and then to suggest their salience to the efforts of the state and individual reformers to affect the roles and social place of women.

A wide range of human behavior is culturally inspired; without doubt, behavior defined as male and female differs widely from culture to culture. The only role so far definitively limited by biology—and so, universal across cultures—is childbearing. But it is in this sense only that biology is destiny. In Kano, it is primarily the teachings of Islam and the norms of Hausa culture, not their anatomy, that confine women's activities.

For human beings, how biology is interpreted by the norms and expectations of the culture is critical. Tiger and Fox have drawn parallels between human and primate behavior and have speculated that biological determination is crucial to understanding the organization of human society (Tiger and Fox 1971). It might be objected, however, that since human beings have the capacity to interpret and even to alter their biology, the notion that we are subject to biological programming in the same way as the lesser species is questionable. It is the premise of this study that human culture, rather than biology, is critical in determining the *social* position of women, because human beings are governed by interaction between biological propensities and culturally specific expectations. While biological differences are a given, they do not inevitably carry social, cultural, and behavioral implications. Biology constrains but does not unambiguously determine behavior.

In Hausa society, as in most other societies, the reproduction of "masculine" and "feminine" personalities generation after generation has produced psychological and value commitments to sex differences that are tenaciously maintained and so deeply ingrained as to become central to a consistent sense of self. Because of different perceptions of male and female roles, boys and girls in Kano experience the same social environment differently as they develop and grow into adulthood. Girls learn early that they must be modest, demure, and maternal; boys are socialized early to know that they will be providers, heads of households, and the bearers of public responsibilities. This difference in social experience throughout childhood leads to what is perceived in adult life to be basic differences in personality.

As a result, Hausa Muslim women are often viewed by outsiders as being inherently conservative or passive if not overtly resistant to change (Cohen 1971; Dry 1950; Perham 1960). Too often this overt resistance to change is credited to female nature instead of to the life experiences of women, whose general powerlessness over their own lives and life choices may lead them to distrust new initiatives. They seek to preserve what they know rather than trust that change could make things better rather than worse for them.

ISLAM AND THE POSITION OF WOMEN

It has rightly been remarked that in Hausaland, as to a greater or lesser extent in other Islamic societies, "one could interpret the history of women in Islam as one long struggle on their part to maintain the rights enunciated by Mohammed in the face of a series of traditions hostile to women's rights in the various countries conquered by the Moslems" (Boulding 1976, 386).

Islam differs from other major world religions in the emphasis it explicitly places on the status of women and the protections it provides for them. Matters affecting women's status per se are either set forth in the *Qur'an* itself or in Islamic law (Sharia) derived from interpretations of the *Qur'an* and sayings of the Prophet.

The advent of Islamic law somewhat improved the social position of common women, who were subject to slave-raiding, in Hausa society and guaranteed to them certain rights brought into being only with the Islamic jihad in 1804. Still, Islamic law is interpreted within the traditions of Hausa society—a patriarchal society with patrilineal tendencies and clear class and status distinctions in which women are regarded as subordinate to men. Unless they are expressly superseded by the dictates of Islam, these cultural predispositions, some of which are described below, remain dominant. The life circumstances and patterns of socialization of Hausa women reflect the interplay between Islam and the local, indigenous Hausa culture. In order to understand the nature of the changes that Hausa Muslim women desire, we must look more closely at Islamic parameters.

In Islam, all of life is governed by the *Qur'an*. The *Qur'an* is regarded as God's final word and as such gives complete instructions for living good and godly lives. The *Qur'an* and laws that flow from it cannot be altered (except through reinterpretation). Therefore, in contemporary times, Islamic women are frozen into the expectations of an earlier reality and are today essentially limited by divine edict to the roles of wife and mother. Marriage and childbearing are believed to be religious duties, and celibacy for women is viewed as a deviation from the order created by God. These factors constitute serious constraints on possibilities for the emancipation of Hausa Muslim women.

Islamic law is believed to represent a divine contract between Allah (God) and individual Muslims. The Sharia is comprehensive in that it explicitly addresses and prescribes religion, morals, politics, commerce, and family life; because the family is believed to be at the center of the social order, Islamic law especially addresses itself to that topic. Approximately one-third of the *ahkam* (legal injunctions of the *Qur'an*) relate to the family and its proper regulation (Khurshid 1974, 16).

The Sharia is revealed law, revealed by Allah to his prophet Muhammad (A.D. 570–632) and recorded in the *Qur'an*; it also encompasses the *hadith* and *sunna.* The *hadith* are the words of the Prophet as recorded by his companions; the *sunna* encompass his acts as witnessed and recorded by his companions and constitute a set of instructions binding on Muslims although not recorded in the *Qur'an.* Much of Islamic scholarship concerns interpretations of the *sunna* and the *hadith* derived from study of nuances of meaning contained in the words of the Prophet. Islamic law does not distinguish betwen "religious" and "secular" law. All law comes directly from the *Qur'an* and the traditions associated with it and is interpreted by a consensus among religious teachers, the *mallams.* Most Muslims are Sunnis who adhere literally to the *sunna* and the Sharia. Sunni Muslims recognize four schools of jurisprudence—Hanbali, Hanafi, Shafi, and Maliki. Maliki is a conservative school of Islamic legal thought and is practiced primarily in the Maghreb (Berber North Africa), Senegal, and Nigeria. Only Shafi is more conservative and it is observed only in Saudi Arabia.

A potentially revolutionary notion in Islam held by some brotherhoods[1] is the belief in four sources of knowledge—revelation, interpretation, reason, and experience. The legitimacy of applying reason and experience to the interpretation of "revealed" knowledge allows room for reinterpretation and new understanding. Thus, although Islam is inherently conservative, in that knowledge may not be discovered but only better understood or more clearly "revealed," fresh interpretations offer the potential for reform or reinterpretation for some Muslims so as to reflect evolutionary changes in the structure and nature of society. This branch of Islam offers some possibility that more generous interpretations of the law might liberalize restrictions on women, should changes in society require such reform.

Islamic law thus may be subject to piecemeal reinterpretation by scholars, but it cannot be amended: "No government or assembly can make any amendment or change in the rights conferred by God. The rights which have been sanctioned by God are permanent, perpetual, and eternal. They are not subject to any alterations or modifications, and there is no scope for any change or abrogation" (Mawdudi 1976, 14). The *Qur'an* is very explicit concerning this matter: "Those who do not judge by what God has sent down are the disbelievers" (*Qur'an* 5:44).

Islamic political thought is based on the Sharia and is therefore also thought to be included in the divine contract between mortal men and Allah. Hence, Islamic social thought is inherently conservative in nature and recognizes no distinction between state and society or state and religion. In Islamic parts of Nigeria, the popular refrain "Islam is a total way of life" is often heard. Muslims believe that religion, moral codes, political behavior, and politics are mutually inclusive. What is legal is moral and vice versa. Thus, political disaffection is equal to religious dissent. In the Islamic state, the central function of government is the nurturing of Islam, the application of the Sharia, and the defense of Islamic orthodoxy against heresy.

Although Islam is widespread and exists in many different cultural contexts (Africa, the Middle East, Asia, and the Pacific), all Islamic cultures share basic understandings about women and their proper role and place in society. The revelation of the *Qur'an* to the Prophet Muhammad and the articulation of the Sharia through the ages by Islamic scholars have contributed to a basic understanding and unanimity of opinion concerning the rights and obligations of women. Muslim scholars maintain that the *Qur'an* explicitly demands the same standard for men and women and thus they are equal before God. "And whosoever does a righteous deed, be they male or female, and is a believer, we shall assuredly give them a goodly life to live; and we shall certainly reward them according to the best of what they did" (*Qur'an* 16:97).

Also, "Men who surrender to God and women who surrender to God, and men who believe and women who believe, and men who obey and women who obey, and men who persevere [in righteousness] and women who persevere, and men who are humble and women who are humble, and men who give alms and women who give alms, and men who fast and women who fast, and men who guard their modesty and women who guard their modesty, and men who remember God much and women who remember . . . God has prepared for them forgiveness and a mighty reward" (*Qur'an* 33:35). In commenting on these verses, Muslim teachers stress that these virtues are as necessary to women as to men and that the reward of the hereafter is provided for one as for the other.

Nevertheless, Muhammad revealed that Allah had ordained distinct but complementary roles for men and women with the overall injunction that in essence the "strong" should protect the "weak." Through the centuries, as scholars and judges further interpreted the words of the Prophet, they reflected the patriarchal customs and attitudes of their time and place.

In Islamic law, women are given explicit rights and protections, particularly in regard to inheritance, marriage, and support, but the general thrust of references to women in the *Qur'an* is that women are dependent on men and are fulfilled only through subordination to them. Although roles of wives and husbands are viewed as complementary rather than "unequal," it is quite clear that relationships within the family are hierarchichal and patriarchal in nature. The role of women is complementary to that of men, but it is not equal in any literal sense of the word. While "women have the same [rights in relation to their husbands] as is expected in all decency from them, men stand a step above them. God is mighty and wise" (*Qur'an* 2:228).

In Islam, men are to God as women are to men and as children are to women. According to the *Qur'an,* "All of you are guardians and responsible for your words and the things under your care. The Imam is the guardian of his people and is responsible for them. A man is guardian of his family and is responsible for them. A woman is guardian of her husband's house and is responsible for it" (quoted in Khurshid 1974, 17; Nasr 1966, 110).

Islamic teachers emphasize that a woman's primary concern is the family and that within it, she has both rights and duties. The fact that a woman's rights and duties are almost entirely restricted to the private realm does not imply that there is unequal status between men and women before Allah, they insist. Men and women are equally important and each will be judged by performance of his or her "proper" role. Men do have a role to play within the family, but their major obligations are related to responsibility in the "public" sphere.

The rights and duties of a woman within the family are related to stages in the development of her life cycle; her primary responsibilities occur during childbearing years and lessen with their passing. Until her childbearing years draw to a close, a woman is under the care and authority of the men in her life. A marriage guardian will ensure that her marriage is properly arranged and that appropriate bridewealth and/or dowry is set. The duty of a married woman is to be obedient, chaste, and modest. During this period her husband will provide for her while she produces and cares for children, who legally belong to him.

Most of the injunctions that seriously restrain a woman's freedom of movement and association are relaxed once she is postmenopausal, although continued modesty is encouraged. "As for women past childbearing, who have no hope of marriage, it is no sin for them if they discard their outer clothing in such a way as not to show adornment. But to refrain is better for them" (*Qur'an* 24:60).

The *Qur'an* treats a woman's identity from the point of view of a jealous husband. She cannot appear attractive outside the home, she cannot have friends beyond the family circle, she cannot have a life outside the supervision of her husband. On any occasion when men and women are together socially, women must stand aside and remain in the background.

Women have inheritance rights and own their own property. Female inheritance is generally one half that of male, with daughters inheriting one half the share of a son and a wife inheriting one eighth to one fourth of her husband's estate (*Qur'an* 4:11). In Maliki law, if a husband dies with descendent heirs (i.e., sons), his wife inherits one eighth of the estate. If there are no descendant heirs, she inherits one fourth of the estate. If a wife dies and leaves property, her husband inherits one half of it. If a man has more than one wife, the wives divide the one eighth or one fourth between them. Wills are not valid in Islamic law, and therefore should a man wish to increase his wife's share of his estate upon his death, he must give it to her as a gift before death (Hinchcliff 1975, 461). In practice, if a woman is widowed, she is allowed to keep her room in her late husband's house provided she has male sons in residence (Schildkrout 1986).

While Islam concerns itself with the property rights of women, those rights are not equal to those of men and there is a strong de-emphasis on conjugal property. Women do have specific property rights through inheritance, but this is not the same as actual control. The paternalistic thrust of Islam makes it clear that men are charged with providing the economic security of women: "Men are those who support women, since God has given some persons advantages over others, and because they expend their wealth on them. Men have authority over women because Allah has made the one superior to the other and because they spend their wealth to maintain them" (*Qur'an* 4:35). While women have access to property in that they inherit and technically own it and in that they can keep and spend or invest any income they might generate, in Kano actual managerial rights (particularly to land and real estate) usually belong to fathers, brothers, and husbands.

As outlined above, Islam gives certain protections to women. Many problems experienced by Hausa women in the northern parts of Nigeria are culturally imposed by such traditional conventions as patrilocality, child marriage, and polygamy. While Islamic women are not to be married against their will, for instance, Islamic sanction of marriage guardians and Hausa practices of child marriage combine to assure that guardians arrange marriages for most girls by age twelve. Hausa practices of polygamy reinforce the Islamic permission for four wives per man. As Islam has become more deeply entrenched, women have lost any independent right they may have had in Hausa society to engage in public trade, to work, to travel, or to assume public roles in either government or religion.

HAUSA SOCIALIZATION

The Hausa ethos of male domination and the Islamic emphasis on male supremacy combine to structure distinct conceptions of life for men and women. Perceptions of a woman's life cycle stress her current status in relation to men and her reproductive status as well as her approximate age—*jinjiniya* (female infant), *yarinya* (girl), *budurwa* (maiden or virgin), *mata* (woman or wife), *bazarawa* (divorced or widowed), or *tsohuwa* (old woman). The corresponding terms for males stress biological age—*jinjiri,* (infant), *yaro* (young boy), *miji* (young man), and *tsoho* (old man) (Schildkrout 1981, 96).

Married Muslim women in Hausaland live in seclusion (*kulle*). In Kano State—in contrast to other Islamic areas in West Africa—the practice appears to be increasing as the city and the countryside become more involved in the national cash economy (Abell 1962; Hill 1977; M. G. Smith 1955).

Hausa culture emphasizes siring large numbers of children, and in Kano the average number of living children per woman is seven.[2] Countries with Islamic majorities generally have the highest population growth rates in the world today. Nigeria has one of the highest (3.5 percent annually). While pro-natal tendencies are strong in all Nigerian societies, they are most evident in the Islamic north, where family planning is not considered a legitimate focus of public policy. In Kano, a metropolitan area of over five million people, no family planning office or publicly available information on either planning or birth control was available as late as 1983.[3]

The number of children born to a given woman is not necessarily indicative of the number for whom she is responsible. Widespread fostering and the practice of a woman's avoiding contact with her firstborn child (*kunya*) creates a great deal of fluidity in children's lives. Eighty percent of 500 Hausa children surveyed in Kano State for one study were not raised by their biological parents (Hake 1972, 23–24). Of these, 41.5 percent were raised by paternal grandmothers, 16.7 percent by stepmothers, 19.8 percent by other relatives, and 5.5 percent by "friends of the family." The giving of children for fostering indicates the strength of the bonds linking spatially dispersed kin. The firstborn child generally is given to an older woman who has no child currently living with her. A good daughter-in-law demonstrates that she is "polite" by giving her first child to her husband's mother, and in so doing strengthens ties between the two families (Interview #16, Kano, October, 1982).

Childhood is generally a mixture of good-natured freedom and harsh corporal punishment and deprivation. When 175 students at the Advanced Teachers College (male) and Women's Teachers College in Kano were asked if their childhoods had been happy or sad or both, 57.4 percent of the 102 men and 56.8 percent of the 73 women replied "both." One-third of these translated "sad" as referring to harsh punishment by parents or other adults. One-fifth complained of lack of sufficient food or clothing as children. "My brother was kind—but his wife was not good; she often gave me too little to eat." "I was not fed properly in my uncle's house where I went to live." "I lived with a stepmother, who had many children, and so I was neglected most of the time." Sixty percent of these students claimed never to have had a conversation with an adult while growing up. Eighty percent of the girls claimed to have been "often afraid" (questionnaire administered by Aisha Indo Yuguda, 1983).

While the birth of a new baby is cause for celebration in nearly all families, no matter what the economic status, the birth of a son is usually celebrated on a more lavish scale than that of a daughter. Among wealthier families, when a boy is born it is customary to slaughter *sa* or *sanuja* (a cow or an ox) for the *radin suna* (naming ceremony). When a girl is born, it is customary to slaughter a lesser animal, such as *tunkiya* (sheep) or *akuya* (goat) (Kabir 1981). In the home little girls are assigned domestic duties from about age five. By age six they are dressed in imitation of adult women and begin to be viewed as future wives. They go outside only for specific reasons, such as running errands for their mothers who cannot go out, selling food and handicrafts from bowls or baskets on top of their heads, and carrying messages; they do not go out to play. Little boys, at about age six, are sent out to play and sleep with other boys in the *zaures* or *soro* (entranceways) to their homes. They are ousted from their mother's rooms at night and virtually become visitors in her space during the day. By age ten, boys cross the line into female space less often. They eat with other boys, seldom with sisters or mothers. Boys whose fathers are artisans or traders may be apprenticed to their fathers or other adult men by age eleven or twelve. Even those going to school beyond the primary years spend little time "at home" and avoid contact with women as they approach adulthood. Adulthood means separation, even avoidance, between male and female. "The transition to manhood means moving out of the domain of female authority, into the world of men, and ultimately into marriage, where male dominance is as yet unchallenged" (Schildkrout 1978, 131).

As she grows up, a girl is made aware of her second-class status. In addition to housework, she is assigned child-care responsibilities, and she is made aware that her sex is a potential source of shame and dishonor. A girl's inferior status vis-à-vis her brothers, father, or male kin is early and constantly emphasized. She is told *ki dinga yin abu kamar mace,* "to behave like a woman." A girl should sit quietly, talk softly, cover her head, and never disagree with a male. *Ba ki ganin ke mace ce, she namiji ne,* meaning "Can't

Hausa girls dress like women from an early age. By three, a head tie is obligatory and girls begin to be taught the rules of feminine deportment.

you see you are a woman while he is a man?" (and thus superior) is a refrain repeated to her from her earliest years. She will also hear *ke mace ce, gidan wani zaki,* ("after all, you are a woman and you are going to someone else's house"), or "*komai abinki, gidan wani zaki*" ("No matter what you do you are going to someone else's house") (Kabir 1981).

When a girl shows signs of independence of character, she will be snubbed by her peers and told that *tunda ke mace ce, a karkashin wani kike,* "You are a woman and you are under someone's (male) authority." The girl seeking to join boys at play may be greeted with a popular children's song:

Mai wasa da maza karya
Tunda na gan ta na rena ta.

("She who plays with boys is a bitch
When I see her, I detest her.")

Finally, girls are repeatedly admonished that *Duk mace a bayan namiji take*—"Every woman is inferior to a man" (Interviews #6, Kano, January 20, 1982; and #21, Kano, February 24, 1983).

For the overwhelming majority of girls, it is almost inconceivable to aspire to anything other than the role of wife or mother. Normally, girls are expected to be married by the time they reach puberty. The widespread introduction of Western education (*boko*) is beginning to postpone the age of marriage for girls who go to school, but even in this event, there is great pressure to marry young, before age sixteen. Girls who are not married while in secondary school (all such noncommerical schools in Kano are single sex) are viewed with suspicion and it is said that *an gama da ita,* meaning "They have finished with her," implying that she is no longer a virgin and therefore not a good candidate for a first wife (Interviews #11 and 12, Kano, March 8 and March 12, 1982).

Although they may have heavy household responsibilities, girls are sent out to hawk wares for their mothers and are relatively free until they are abruptly married and secluded. After that, even though they are still very young, like adult women they can leave their houses only for naming ceremonies, marriages, funerals, and medical care. If they go out, it is usually at night and an older woman generally accompanies them as escorts. They must cover their heads and be accountable for their visits (Schildkrout 1979).

Since most girls are married by age twelve to fourteen, they are virtually confined to the female quarters of their compounds all their lives. If a girl is married as young as ten, she will not be expected to cook or have sexual

Childcare is one of the major responsibilities entrusted to young girls. As first births often still occur before age fifteen, whatever experience they get can be useful.

relations with her husband until puberty begins, but she enters *kulle* and loses the freedom associated with childhood. For all practical purposes, the house or compound is a woman's world. From the time she marries and enters *kulle* until after her childbearing years, a woman has virtually no freedom of movement or association. This socialization process is pervasive and thorough. Opportunities for broadening one's experiences or raising one's expectations are few.

Unlike girls, boys do not reach adult status until they become economically productive, usually in their late twenties or early thirties, because it is one of the requirements of Islam that men do not marry until they can provide shelter, clothing, and food for their wife or wives. While in 1982, ninety percent of the 92 Muslim women students at Bayero University were married, only fifteen percent of the 2000 men students were married (Bayero University 1982).

Even in matters of religion, a woman's inferiority is underscored. While all Muslims are equal before Allah, menstruating or pregnant women are considered "religiously impure." In addition, women cannot lead the community in prayer, do not officiate at religious festivals, and rarely attend mosque. Even at the mosque on the campus at Bayero University in Kano, women may attend only by standing in a separate room out of sight of the male worshippers and may not be in public areas of the mosque during Friday prayers. Hence, the thrust of socialization through religion is to emphasize a properly subordinate place for women.

Unlike other urban settings, Kano provides no specifically female organizations for Hausa women. The one exclusively women's club in Kano, the Corona Society, a British-based international service organization for women, had no Hausa Muslim Kano women as members. The National Association of Women's Societies of Nigeria (the federally recognized umbrella organization for women's associations) had no Kano chapter, although it asked the Corona Society to help organize one; no interest in affiliation with such an organization was expressed in Kano. Although interested in the idea of women's organizations, elite Kano women preferred to avoid the visibility entailed in membership. They seemed to perceive some advantage in their current status and not many advantages in radically changing it.

At Bayero University no northern Nigerian woman holds a position of regular faculty rank (there was one female teaching assistant in sociology), nor do women generally participate in University-sponsored conferences or symposia. As of 1983, the University had never sponsored a program dealing with women's issues or concerns; no course in the curriculum deals specifically with women's history or issues.

If women are absent from the public realm, within their own restricted but private world they enjoy considerable autonomy. Houses are a woman's domain. Women can enter virtually any house, but men can enter few and then they rarely go beyond the entranceway, or, in the case of wealthier homes, the man's sitting room. Women are secluded, but men are excluded from women's space. Even kinship does not open the door, for a man would not normally enter the house of a younger married sister or the female section of his younger brother's house. He might, with the husband's permission, enter the house of an older married sister (Schildkrout, 1978a, p. 115). "It shall be no crime in them as to their fathers, or their sons, or their brothers, or their brother's sons, or their sister's sons, or their women, or the slaves which their right hands possess, if they speak with them unveiled" (*Qur'an* 3:33 and

A woman in seclusion is not necessarily alone, for there is a constant stream of youthful female visitors in and out of most compounds. Women rely on these children for news of their relatives, friends, and neighbors.

33:55). Thus, young men and women are not thrown together in situations where they could form relationships that could lead to marriage; the system of arranged marriages, in which girls are married early and boys much later, means that relationships between unrelated young people of equal status but opposite sex are almost nonexistent. The fact that men and women live in separate and distinct worlds has profound psychological implications for women. While men's authority over women in the public domain is nearly complete, in the private domain, where interaction is highly limited and age differences between men and women are great, the differences in their interests are also great and thus the authority of men is quite precarious.

Hausa households are large and multigenerational abodes. Women are constantly surrounded by female consanguineal and affinal relatives and the children of all. The average number of persons in the households visited during the course of this study was twenty, but it was not unusual for fifty persons to be eating at a particular house or compound. Often, while fifteen to twenty people might actually be resident in a particular house, many others might be eating and sleeping there. In Kano it is exceedingly rare to visit a Hausa woman in her home and find her alone—women appear to be never alone. Thus, the large city does not provide the alleged anonymity and lower visibility attributed to urban life. Within seclusion, women maintain wide networks, through which news of the world and changing events moves in an unending flow. Marriages, naming ceremonies, and other rituals are constant. Goods, services, and money flow rapidly, and visiting of extended kin is incessant; large families ensure movement and wide-ranging networks of exchange. Nothing is as simple as it looks. Kano City, although rapidly industrializing, is nonetheless reminiscent of nonindustrial towns, where the sense of a small, face-to-face community is maintained in the midst of an urban area. When a woman leaves her compound or receives visitors to it, all her neighbors know; the many men standing outside their compounds speculate as to the identity of a stranger and the nature of his or her business.

To the casual observer, life behind the mud wall of the compound appears secure and peaceful, but time spent there brings hundreds of sad stories. Women complain of heavy labor, of marriages of young daughters against their wills, of child brides brought into the household, of forced sexual cohabitation at puberty regardless of mental or emotional development, of early motherhood and infant death. There is no sewage system, running water is unreliable, and animals roam freely. Illness, needless death, and especially female and infant mortality are commonplace. Said a mother of a twelve-year-old on her wedding day, "may the day be cursed when she was born a woman."

ON MARRIAGE

All Muslims are expected to marry; the family is the keystone of Islamic social order and, at least in Kano, there is no acceptable social place for unmarried women of childbearing age.[4] The Western notion of the evolution of the family as a social institution is considered blasphemy and is totally rejected in concept. Families are ordained by Allah; they do not evolve. Adult Hausa society is essentially a totally married society.

Marriage is both a social institution and a civil contract. Prior to marriage, terms of the arrangement are negotiated between a girl's guardian and representatives of the groom's family. Breach of contract is grounds for divorce. Normally there are witnesses to the terms and conditions of the contract and of its offer and acceptance by appropriate representatives. Under the contract, each party retains certain rights which, if violated, create grounds for divorce. The husband-to-be or his family makes appropriate gifts or payments to the bride's family and to the bride herself (brideprice). Such payment or gifts become her property (bridewealth) and are not refundable should the marriage end after having been consummated.

The experience of romantic love is not normally part of an Islamic marriage. In Kano, at least, it is unusual to find a Muslim woman disappointed in a marriage if her husband is a good provider. Nothing else is expected. Romantic love is not a concept that can be dealt with, since it is outside the experience of most women.

Generally, it is not up to a girl or a woman to decide whom and when to marry; these two of life's most significant decisions generally are made for her. Even if a woman is educated, her marriage most likely will be arranged while she is in school; her husband will decide whether or not she may work and what kind of job she may have and where. Only under most unusual conditions will she postpone or plan her childbearing. Often, there is an age gap of twenty years or more between a husband and a wife; a girl's first marriage is commonly made to an older man who may already have one or more wives. In this case, brideprice negotiations for her move from the home of her father or relatives to her husband's home may have gone on for years, and she may quite literally be raised in her husband's house.

Brideprice, given by the husband-to-be to the bride or her family, is to be used for the needs of the bride in setting up a household in her husband's house. During 1982 an effort was made in Sokoto State (Kano's next-door neighbor) to set limits on the amount of money that might be offered as brideprice, and a law was actually passed setting the amount at naira 200 ($350). It was widely reported in the Nigerian press that this law had no effect and was indeed unenforceable (*New Nigerian,* December 21, 1982; *The National Concord,* October 27, 1982; *The Sunday Herald,* November 14, 1982).

In addition to brideprice, the bride is given a dowry (*kayan daki*) by her own family. In Kano, the dowry consists almost entirely of brass and enamel pots, which are displayed in the bride's room while the marriage lasts and eventually pass on to her daughters. Marriage brings about business and political alliances between prominent families in most Islamic countries. Thus, marriage is a social or business, rather than a romantic, transaction.

While girls marry young, men often marry late because they must provide each wife with lodging of her own, separate from other wives or other members of the family. A husband, however, has the duty and responsibility to maintain and support a wife only so long as she is obedient. If she is dis-

Clapping and singing games are important among Hausa girls. The freedom of childhood ends abruptly by about twelve years of age for those who do not go to school. These two eleven-year-old girls were married the next year and thenceforth could see each other only on ceremonial occasions.

obedient, she forfeits support, and her husband is entitled to beat her (Hinchcliffe 1975, 257–58; *Qur'an* 4:34).

While a woman can have only one husband at a time, men can have up to four wives. A man does not need permission from an existing wife or wives to contract additional marriage(s), although such stipulations can be a part of the marriage contract.

Men are admonished to marry in order to fulfill their sexual urges: "Your wives are for you to cultivate; so go to your cultivation whenever you wish, and take care of what is for you, and heed God and know that you will meet him" (*Qur'an* 2:223). Sexual needs of women are not discussed. Marriage provides protection for a man's continuous sexual urges, "so marry them with their guardian's permission and give them their marriage portions as wives, they being chaste, not permitting fornication or having illicit friendships" (*Qur'an* 4:25). In a *hadith* transmitted by Abdullah ibn Mas'ud, the Prophet

Muhammad said, "Young men, those of you who can support a wife should marry, for it keeps you from looking at strange women and preserves you from immorality. But those who cannot, should devote themselves to fasting, for it is a means of suppressing sexual desire" (quoted in *New Nigerian,* March 25, 1983).

While among poorer people brideprice considerations are often persuasive, among wealthier families a girl's marriage guardian and her parents will seek families with whom they have much in common. The girl's parents want to assure that they have enough influence with the groom's family to be able to protect her interests; partly for this reason, alliances between children of brothers or first cousins are preferred for first marriages. Sometimes families will try to negotiate a limit to the number of wives a prospective bridegroom will take in order to limit the number of sons from different families who will inherit the wealth accumulated during the marriage.

Marriage guardians arrange marriages, and the bride's family determines the amount of dowry (*kayan daki*) to be brought into the marriage. Women are not to be made to marry against their wills or without their consent, except that "in the case of a minor girl, however, the father or grand-father is allowed to marry her without her consent, but it is most desirable to get the consent of even the minor girl, although she may not give her express consent" (*New Nigerian,* March 25, 1983). Maliki law holds that the consent of a guardian is required in the case of a *bik* (virgin), but is not essential in the case of a *thayyib* (widow or divorcée). There is a *hadith* according to Al-Bukhari which states that "a father, no more than anyone else, may give his virgin daughter in marriage without her consent. When a man forces his daughter into marriage, the marriage shall be null and void" (Charnay 1971, 61). This injunction is not observed in Kano. In Kano, the right of guardianship goes successively to the father, paternal grandfathers, brothers, and other paternal male relations in the order of inheritance. For each marriage, a new contract must be made. Should a woman be widowed, remarriage is encouraged, but it should not be a marriage forged against her will. Muslim women can only marry Muslim men, but Muslim men may marry "women of the book," i.e., Jewish or Christian women, as well as Islamic women (*Qur'an* 2:221). The pre-Islamic practice of inheriting women is forbidden. "Oh you who believe! You are forbidden to inherit [as chattels] the women against their will" (*Qur'an* 4:19).

Men are most interested in who their spouses will be. While family welfare comes first, men know much about girls under discussion, either from actual acquaintance (in the case of families already related) or from reports received regularly concerning the girl and her qualities. Many criteria are considered, including her personality; hence, her parents (and particularly her mother) put great emphasis on proper behavior and demeanor while she is growing up.

Women move in marriage in a complex pattern of status and patron-client relationships that defies simple analysis. The extended family is, in a very real sense, a corporate lineage. Families as units are ranked in relation to each other, and it is the family that gives status to individuals. Kinship and traditional status override economic considerations. Between such distinctions are vertical relationships based on patron-client traditions evolved over the centuries. Such relationships include etiquette and mutual obligations that do not resemble at all the categories that would emerge from a simple class analysis.

The preferred form of a first marriage in upper-class Fulani and Hausa families is kin marriage—*auren zumunci.* Since the children of marriage stay with the husband in the event of divorce, this at least assures that children stay in the family. First cousin (patrilineal and, less often, matrilineal), parallel and cross-cousin marriages are all common. Here, in the event of divorce, family relationships are not so fundamentally damaged as in other kinds of marriage. (*Auren zumunci* apparently does not affect the rate of divorce: court records in Katsina show a divorce rate of 40.7 percent for kin-based first marriages and 39.8 percent for nonkin-based first marriages (Pitten 1979, 153).)

The first marriage is the most important—the one around which brideprice and other negotiations have taken place. Once marriage has taken place, the emphasis is on fertility, not compatability. Thirty-five to forty percent of all marriages end in divorce, with the highest percentage of divorces being related to infertility (Pitten 1979; Saunders 1978).

A man has not only moral but legal responsibility for the support of his family. The remedy for nonsupport for a woman is divorce, which is granted by an Islamic court and generally is not difficult to get. Because a man has the obligation to support his family, any income a wife may earn is regarded as exclusively hers to dispose of as she wishes. Hence, the legal foundation for some financial independence exists for women within Islamic law.

Hausa marriage is a contract and remains valid only so long as both parties feel its stipulations are being observed. Since remarriage is likely, women have little incentive to stay in a bad marriage if there are no children or in a marriage where they do not get along with their co-wives. Second marriages may be initiated by the parties concerned, but like first marriages, nearly always require the approval of the senior male kin of the family. Without it, the marriage is not considered valid and the wife is not eligible for the property protections provided by Islam. Bridewealth (*sadaki*) must be paid by the groom's family to the bride's family. If, at any point, marriage negotiations break down, further bridewealth will not be accepted. When courting a girl and her family, a prospective groom gives the bride-to-be gifts of cloth, cosmetics, and jewelry; a sum of money is paid to the bride's family when marriage arrangements are finalized; and a formal payment (brideprice) is made to legalize the marriage under Islamic law (Schildkrout 1980, 78).

Young women experience great pressure to marry and have children. For their part, however, these women (or girls, since most are married by age twelve) often lack the inner resources to make choices, or even to think of choices outside the context of marriage and motherhood. Educated girls and young women do think of careers but only in addition to, not instead of, marriage and families. Parents are eager to marry their daughters early for prestige, to form an alliance or cement a family tie, or to assure that the girl does not become "spoiled." In a society where virtually no young women remain single for any length of time (unless they enter prostitution), the social advantages of an early marriage outweigh the possibilities of anything else imaginable a daughter might do.

At the University, as noted, most girls are married and most young men are not. The students feel secure with this situation and do not consciously want to change it. "Love" and "romance" are Western concepts and have little real meaning in this culture. In a survey of 686 university students, only twenty percent thought it desirable that they have the option of making their own decisions in marriage. The other eighty percent felt they would prefer a parentally arranged marriage, though a large percentage (fifty-two percent) wanted some input in the final choice. In Hausa marriages status considerations are very important, and young people do not want the responsibility for negotiating these alliances; students felt that family interests should be taken into account and were comfortable letting someone who understood all the ramifications of an "alliance" conduct the negotiations and make the final selection.

Since a woman's time after marriage is spent almost exclusively inside the walls of her compound, she expends an inordinate amount of time and energy organizing her room (or rooms, in the case of wealthier women). If her family can at all afford it, she will have a four-poster bed piled high with mattresses, covered with a satin spread adorned by many pillows. This bed is the central decorative piece in the room and she neither sleeps nor sits on it. In addition to the bed she is likely to have a carpet, and increasingly, a television. Her *kayan daki,* consisting of cups and saucers painted silver or gold and brought from Saudi Arabia and large brass and/or enamel bowls, is piled high around the walls. Delicate, breakable items, such as figurines and Arabian cups and saucers, are displayed in glass cabinets. A woman spends much time rearranging the decor of her room or rooms and much visiting time is spent discussing the acquisition of the various items. Gifts of cloth from her husband, relatives, and friends are also conspicuously on display, and much conversation concerns their origins and price. A woman establishes her worth and value by this display of her possessions. The room's furnishings, together with the *kayan daki* and other gifts, constitute the bride's dowry. The dowry remains her property until she bequeaths it to her daughters or otherwise disposes of it (Schildkrout 1978, 119).

Any income of a disposable nature that a woman might earn is likely to be spent on ceremonial exchanges with friends and relatives. Her ties, obligations, and social standing are manifested in her attendance at an unending series of marriage ceremonies, naming ceremonies, and funerals. The houses to which she is invited for such purposes and the houses she frequents establish her social position.

Hausa weddings bear little resemblance to their Western counterparts. The event Westerners would probably identify as the wedding ceremony is the saying of prayers in the mosque, which finalizes the agreements between the two families in regard to marriage. Neither the bride nor the groom is expected to be present at this time. The wedding ceremony itself is generally held at the home of the parents of the bride, although it sometimes occurs at the home of the prospective husband. Women and men are separated. At some point the groom's guardian or *wakili* blesses the union. Other than this, nothing resembling a Western ceremony occurs—there are no vows, speeches, or toasts. The bride receives her guests and gifts, often, bolts of cloth, and her sisters and other female relatives and friends cook vast pots of food to feed the many visitors. Small cakes or kola nuts (*goro*) are given to the departing guests who later pass them out among family and friends in their own neighborhoods; this is the bride's announcement that she is indeed now married. These ceremonious gift exchanges establish the female version of the elaborate clientage relationships that express status, equality, or the obligation of reciprocity (*kara*) among males.

Once prayers have been said in the mosque, the marriage is considered properly sanctioned. The contract, although not often written, is binding. The man is obligated to provide food, clothing, shelter, and sexual satisfaction (defined as producing children). If he is polygamous he must give equal time to each wife in order that each may be assured of equal opportunity to bear children; infertility in either spouse is grounds for divorce (Saunders 1978). In exchange for these obligations on the part of the husband, the wife is bound to provide household services, to display proper wifely deference in all matters, and to be sexually faithful. Marriage for her is a time-consuming, labor-intensive responsibility; a wife is considered "good" if she is modest, obedient, and shows evidence of domestic skills. A husband is considered "good" if he is prosperous and a generous provider.

Husbands and wives often achieve harmony at a high price—the near total subjugation of wives to husbands. A wife who makes no trouble for a husband or his other wives or his relatives, who is modest and quiet, and who earns her own spending money is likely to have a peaceful marriage. There may in fact be nothing on which husband and wife actually agree other than the importance of "peace," but disagreements are seldom spoken. Generally, spouses are distant from each other's emotional lives and, in fact, they may seldom cross each other's paths outside the bedroom.

After marriage, a woman's children belong to her husband. Should she be divorced, either for cause or simply because a man desires another wife (and already has four), her only insurance is her family.[5] Generally families readily absorb divorced women, but when this presents a strain, great pressure is brought to bear to arrange another marriage for her. While married, a woman automatically has membership in her husband's family, but unless she produces sons, she will have no permanent place.

Tense domestic relations are always blamed by men on women, who are seen as being "quarrelsome" (any woman who asserts independence will be so labeled) and inherently unstable and immature. Women are always treated as dependents subject to the discipline of their husbands.

While thirty-five to forty percent of women will be divorced at some point in their lives, most will not be out of marriage for more than a few months to a year. Schildkrout and Callaway found virtually no women unmarried between ages sixteen and thirty-five for a period longer than two years during the time of their research (1976–1978 and 1981–1983 respectively).[6] While ten to twelve percent of the adult women may be divorced and therefore between marriages in Kano City at any given time, very few divorced women fail to remarry. In Kano, less than ten percent of the 264 women over sixteen surveyed by Callaway and her students were unmarried. Divorce for men does not often result in single status, since most men have more than one wife.

Divorced or widowed women generally return home for a short time and then remarry (Schildkrout 1986). If a woman resists marriage for any length of time, and if she engages in successful economic activity and begins to become economically independent, she will be labeled a prostitute. Otherwise, she is expected to remarry and to continue bearing children (Interview #7, January 27, 1982).

The two sexes display differing perceptions of women who want to remain single. Women usually call a single woman or a woman who is not married *bazawara,* which translates as simply divorced or widowed, but men, unless speaking of women in their own families, usually use the word *karuwa,* which translates loosely as prostitute. It is often said that the Hausa word for a single woman "is prostitute in English." Men deny a legitimate nonmarried

If a Muslim Hausa woman sits outside her house selling cooked food it can be inferred that she is unmarried, as a result either of divorce or the death of her spouse, and moreover, that she expects to stay that way. Divorced or widowed women who intend to remarry observe some of the rules of seclusion and would not sell food outside their houses. Women who are not in seclusion have, for the most part, higher incomes than those who observe purdah.

state to women considered to be of marriageable age. A man will characterize his sister or kin as *bazawara,* but by using the term *karuwa* to describe any other unmarried woman, he provides a symbolic denial of the existence of women legitimately free of male attachments or supervision. *Jawarci* (nonmarriage) is a state recognized by women, but denied by men. *Jawarci* implies nothing about a woman's economic or sexual situation, but simply means, to women, that a woman is not living with or being supported by a husband. On the other hand, *karuwa,* which implies both sexual and economic independence, is the term that generally would be used by men to describe such a woman (Interviews #16, October 25, 1982; #22, February 25, 1983; #34, April 17, 1983; all in Kano).

In a study of *karuwai* (prostitutes), Renee Pitten discovered that virtually all such women in one Hausa city had been married at least once (Pitten 1979). Many had entered *karuwanci* to escape marriage. Most were either divorced or had left a marriage because they did not have children. Many had had multiple marriages while teenagers and were seeking any alternative to further marriages. The young age of these women was striking. One-third of the over 400 *karuwai* studied by Pitten were under age nineteen, and seventy-five percent of them were under age thirty. After age thirty, most would reenter marriage.

The extreme separation of men from women is largely related to two factors: the total proscription of sexual activity outside marriage, and the fact that most Hausa men can conceive of no reason other than sexual activity for men and women not married or related to each other to meet. Women are never free from suspicion and are viewed as being inherently crafty and promiscuous; any woman seen with a man other than her husband is assumed to be involved with him sexually. Contact between unrelated men and women of reproductive age is always viewed as being sexual and is thus also antithetical to ritual purity, which dictates the terms of association between the sexes on many occasions. For example, once having completed their ablutions in preparation for prayers, men may not touch women, who are polluting; because they are impure, women are not allowed in the central area of the mosque; sexual activity of any kind is prohibited during fasting. It is the will of the Prophet that men and women be protected against their natural and overwhelming sexual impulses; the practice of near total separation is the means to piety. Only children and postmenopausal women live in other than totally segregated social spheres.

Thus, men and women live in two separate worlds, normally do not share their thoughts or their lives, and function fairly autonomously and independently of each other in their different spheres. Even husbands and wives do not normally socialize together or with each other; in order to show respect in the home, they do not eat together, seldom interact, and avoid addressing each other by name. A controversial series of articles in a northern Nigerian newspaper in 1981 asserted that the high rate of prostitution among the Hausa was a consequence of the "unnatural" state of Hausa marriage and its lack of social intimacy (*New Nigerian,* November 8, 15, 22, 1981).

While women do not normally experience intimacy with their husbands, they do have intimacy with other wives, relatives, and friends with whom they are in daily contact. There is a certain element of security and certainty about their lives while they are in a marriage; Muslim women students at the University express fear of the insecurity and uncertainty they feel must necessarily characterize any form of "women's liberation."

In spite of the fact that Hausa society is a totally married society, there is considerable complexity in marital living arrangements. A survey of 180 women in 100 households in two wards of Kano City indicated that at any particular point in time, between twenty-five and thirty-five percent of adult women (above age sixteen) are not living with their husbands (see table 1).

For a few women, an unusual variation in the form of Hausa marriage can be arranged—*auren silkiti* or noncoresidential marriage (M.G. Smith 1955). Before the marriage ceremony takes place, it may be agreed that husband and wife will live in separate residences. Most often this type of marriage is arranged by a wealthy family with a "difficult" daughter (that is, one who is out of marriage and is objecting to suggested unions) (Interview #11, Kano, March 9, 1982; #17, Kano, October 28, 1982). *Auren silkiti* gives her marital status, but her separate residence eliminates her problems of living with co-wives or being "troublesome" to her husband. Brideprice in these cases is usually rather high. *Auren silkiti* may also evolve as the marriage matures, particularly if the husband is well off. A man may build another, usually more modern, residence is a newer part of the city, and an older wife may elect to remain in the "old" home where she is comfortable and well established. Most *auren silkiti* involve women over childbearing age who are regarded as past the "danger" of sexually attracting other men. Men's and women's worlds converge at so few points that with the loss of the woman's reproductive functions and lessening of sexual interest, there is little to keep many couples

TABLE 1
Women in the Survey in Kurawa and Gwagwarwa

	Kurawa	Gwagwarwa
A. Married women living with husbands	63%	58%
B. Married women living away from husbands	4%	3%
C. Nonmarried women	12%	10%
D. Old women*	16%	14%
E. Not known	5%	15%
	100%	100%
	(N = 80)	(N = 100)

Source: Adamu, Hannatu 1982, p. 37.

*"Old women" refers to unattached postmenopausal women living in the households of their children or other relatives.

together. This is especially so for the husband, who has other wives and interests outside the home. *Auren silkiti* is often also initiated by a wife who desires to escape her co-wives and who has developed her trade and wants to devote full time to it (Interview #47, Kano, July 11, 1983). It is estimated that three to four percent of women in Kano over age fifty live in *auren silkiti* (Interview #16, Kano, October 25, 1982). These women are considered properly married and are often on good terms with their husbands, who drop in and visit from time to time. Wives who have achieved *auren silkiti* are likely to be independent in character, women who in any other culture would have successful careers or businesses. They appear satisfied with their lives and maintain that it would have been impossible to create their current success by trying to change the system or by having rebelled when they were younger (Interviews #3, November 5, 1981; #10, February 2, 1982; #47, July 11, 1983; all in Kano). Content to have lived traditional lives, they now enjoy some degree of independence as their "just reward." Discarding purdah and breaking with tradition and family completely are exceedingly rare, and *auren silkiti,* for those who can afford it, offers an acceptable alternative.

In Kano, informants could think of only one woman who had conspicuously asserted herself—achieving *auren silkiti* and more. Her circumstances make her experience exceptional in nearly every way. A member of a family of very high traditional status, her position in the society was not typical and afforded her protections and privileges denied most women. She was married at an early age to an educated man whose career took him abroad, and all her children were born outside Nigeria. After the birth of her last child, the man took a second wife and informed his first wife that she was to return to Kano and live in *kulle.* She did return to Kano, but she refused to live in seclusion. Her family arranged for a divorce and for remarriage to a wealthy Kano merchant willing to provide *auren silkiti.* In her separate residence, she rented rooms to two non-Hausa women to start a beauty salon, opened a commercial shop to sell cloth, and began investing her profits in other ventures. She quickly became "notorious" and ran into difficulties even within *auren silkiti.* Her merchant husband demanded that she come to live in his house or be divorced by him. She complied, but could not get along with his first wife and was subsequently divorced by *talaq* (divorce unilaterally pronounced by her husband). Eventually she accumulated enough cash to build her own cement block house in Kano City. (After the walls were up the town council had the house razed on the grounds that no house built by a woman could be safe.) In spite of setbacks created by social reaction to her independence, she has persevered and become quite a wealthy woman in her own right. She has sent her daughter to school in England and insists that she not return to Kano or *kulle.* "In Kano, every woman is a slave. There is no such thing as freedom for women. I will not have my daughter living as I have lived" (Interview #28, Kano, March 24, 1983). Now in her fifties, she is well-known among men as "a very difficult woman" and among women as an "independent and modern" woman. Women point out, however, that it is only her social position that made it possible for her to be so "rebellious." This is not an option for women of lesser status for whom the social costs would be too high.

The woman cited here has encouraged her daughter to marry outside her culture, which she has done. She recognizes that her life style would make it very difficult for her daughter to live in Kano. Other women who might try to follow her example would have even more difficulty in regard to daughters and their marriage prospects. A girl's marriage chances are injured by contacts outside her home, as it is believed inevitable that she will succumb to sexual temptation; a mother who independently conducts business and brings nonfamily members inside her compound or business premises inevitably compromises her daughters. Hence, women assume a double burden should they elect a nonconventional life style. They injure not only their own reputations, but also those of their families. Most women cannot assume this burden and do not. Until recently, any woman who worked for a salary, whether married or not, was considered, if not *karuwa,* at least too worldly, *ta taba duniya,* "she has tasted the world." "Girls should be married off before their eyes are opened" (Interview #37, Kano, May 14, 1983).

ON DIVORCE

Islam does recognize that marriages may not always work out. Divorce is common among the Hausa and rather easily obtained. Divorce by women is sanctioned not only on grounds of nonsupport but also on grounds of long absences and nonfulfillment of the marriage contract (for instance, in choice of residence or agreement not to marry a second wife). There are three forms of divorce: divorce unilaterally pronounced by the husband (*talaq*), separation sought by the wife through a court (*kuhl*), and mutual dissolution granted by a court or arbiter. While both men and women have a right to divorce, obtaining one is not equally easy and the terms are inherently unequal. A man, but not a woman, may pronounce the *talaq.* If *talaq* has been pronounced three times ("I divorce you, I divorce you, I divorce you") in front of two witnesses, a woman is considered divorced no matter what her feelings or how blameless she may be. To divorce a woman without cause (in order to take what otherwise would be a fifth wife, for instance) is considered to be reprehensible, but only reprehensible. In such an event, a woman does not have recourse to a court of law for redress. Divorce by repudiation (*talaq*) is binding, even if it was done in jest (as for instance when under the influence of a spirit or drug) or in a fit of anger. Once *talaq* has been pronounced, the marriage is dissolved irrevocably, and the couple cannot be reconciled unless the woman has first married and then been divorced by another man. This stipulation was meant to discourage men from lightly pronouncing *talaq,* as pride is involved when a woman must first be married to another before being allowed to remarry a previous husband (Charnay 1971, 62).

Upon divorce, a woman keeps whatever she has accumulated, including any gifts given to her by her husband. After divorce, she waits as though in mourning (*idda*) before making any social contacts, and during this time her estranged husband is still responsible for her support and (except in the case of *talaq*) is urged to try to arrange a reconciliation. "If you fear a breach between a man and his wife, send for an arbiter from his family and an arbiter from her family. If both want to be reconciled, God will adjust things between them" (*Qur'an* 4:35). If there is no reconciliation, a husband's responsibility for his wife, financial or otherwise, terminates at the expiration of the *idda.*

Should a woman be divorced or become widowed, she may keep only an infant child (and is entitled to support for it), but upon weaning, the child may be claimed by the father or the nearest agnatic relative (Hinchcliffe 1975, 460). There are some branches of Islamic law that permit a woman to keep sons until puberty and daughters until puberty or marriage (461), but that is not generally the case in Kano. During the mother's period of custody, the father or the nearest male agnatic relative remains the guardian of the child and can arrange marriages or make any other important decision concerning the child without consultation with the mother. Should the mother remarry, she generally loses custody immediately (Interview #37, Kano, December 14, 1981).

Notwithstanding the great emphasis on sexual purity, there is little stigma associated with divorce. It is essential that a woman be a virgin at her first marriage, but after that, so long as she has not engaged in known sexual activity outside of marriage, she can contract subsequent marriages without stigma.

In Nigeria, where Muslim leaders assert that there is no such thing as reform in Islam, there is no discussion of eliminating *talaq.* Other Islamic countries, however—including Algeria, Egypt, Iran, Iraq, Malaysia, Morocco, Pakistan, and Somalia—have decreed that *talaq* is not a legal form of divorce (Coulson and Hinchcliffe 1978, 44). Curiously, Nigerian women do not appear especially interested in reforms of *talaq;* rather, data suggest that it often is provoked by discontented wives (Pitten 1979; Saunders 1978).

With the exception of the Fulani practice of first-child avoidance, the close relationship between women and young children is loving, warm, and respectful. This woman, from an aristocratic Fulani family, was eventually divorced and separated from her three children, who stayed with their father.

For a woman who desires a divorce in order to seek a more agreeable marriage, *talaq* is quick, simple, and final; recent research suggests that much *talaq* occurs after the wife has already left an unhappy situation (Interview #42, Kano, July 10, 1983). If for some reason a woman does go to court, she rarely fails to win a divorce. Pitten studied 329 divorce cases in Katsina area court brought by women between 1971 and 1972 and found that divorces were granted in all but five instances (Pitten 1979). Men generally do not contest divorce—any man who did so would be severely ridiculed, as any wife is thought to be dispensible and easily replaced by one more agreeable and obedient. A wife seeking a divorce is by definition "difficult," and a man choosing to stay with a difficult wife is considered weak and an object of pity. If he cannot "control" his wife, it is better to appear not to want her (Interviews #23, February 25, 1983; #29, March 28, 1983; #37, May 14, 1983; in Kano).

When a woman is divorced at her instigation or not, she simply leaves, taking with her all her personal belongings (which graphically gives rise to the expression "she has packed out"). A woman in fact may "pack out" in order to provoke her husband into a divorce.

Although women who seek divorce generally get it, many women remain in unsatisfactory marriages because of a desire to retain their children, the difficulty of supporting themselves outside of marriage, and the enormous family pressure to remain married. Although a divorced woman usually will be welcomed initially even into a poor family (especially by her mother), fathers, brothers, and male in-laws often discourage divorce and encourage almost instant remarriage in order to avoid responsibility for her support. The petty trading in which most women are involved rarely is sufficient to provide an independent existence; as we have seen, women do not go out to work in the wage sector. In any case, a once-married but currently single woman is a source of constant discussion.

Divorce is viewed as a temporary status. A woman is not expected to become independent unless she enters prostitution.[7] Because a divorced woman does not have custody of children (except in unusual instances) and is not a virgin, her brideprice will be modest; thus, she is a good candidate for someone's second (or third or fourth) wife. She is expected to enter into such a situation as soon as possible and resume childbearing.

The widespread practice of polygamy in Hausaland greatly increases the chances for a second marriage. In fact, both men and women note that any change in Nigerian law affecting polygamy would displace many women—although a surprising number of women, particularly educated women, favor phasing out polygamy and assert that they would choose monogamous marriages if they had the option. Seventy percent of the 114 university women surveyed in Kano during 1981–1983 held this view, as did over fifty percent of the 180 women interviewed for this study in three wards of Kano City. Women are considerably more ambivalent concerning the custody of children than they are concerning polygamy. Once sons marry or daughters reach adulthood, they generally reestablish relationships with their biological mothers. Because so many children in this society are not raised by their birth parents due to the practices of first-child avoidance (*kunya*) and fostering, there is little to indicate that children suffer psychological damage due to divorce. If women were given physical custody of children, it would be a disadvantage in their efforts to remarry following a divorce as men do not normally accept stepchildren. Some divorced women do manage to keep one child until the time of remarriage, when the child then automatically goes to live with its father or the father's kin.

AMBIVALENCE TOWARD REFORM

In Kano traditional values predominate; this is true particularly concerning the status of women. Early marriage is expected, high fertility is respected, submission to male dominance in domestic and political life is demanded, and polygamy and seclusion are the norm.

Marriage and family law, as well as religion and culture, establish the subordinate position of women, who overwhelmingly accept their circumstances as divinely ordained and do not challenge their implications. Socialization is impressively effective in this regard. Women know they have respect as wives and mothers and little respect in any other role. They are not ready to de-emphasize these uniquely secure roles for an alien Western notion of women's liberation.

While men control the public domain and assert their control over women, women retain a high degree of autonomy in their day-to-day living, which modifies the general impact of male dominance and helps to explain the acquiescence of women to it.

Within her own world, the society of women, the Hausa woman finds status and a role that provide meaning for her life. In Islam as practiced in Nigeria, women form a society within a society and in a very fundamental sense have more in common with each other than with their own husbands. It is with other women that they share a common lot and the joys and agonies of daily life. We may speculate that this kind of experience may more effectively produce women secure in their abilities and independent in their social personalities than does women's typically isolated and individual domestic experience in Western societies. Whatever the psychology of seclusion, it is clear that by and large Hausa Muslim women do not wish for wholesale changes in the status quo (Callaway 1984). Socialization into traditional values continues, and there is nothing to suggest that young Hausa girls of the current generation are particularly disaffected from the culture or their proposed role in it. Conversely, it is obvious that any change in the secluded domestic unit would presuppose or precipitate truly radical changes in other institutions and in broad cultural patterns in general.

Men view women with a curious dichotomy of perception. On the one hand, women are seen as being less capable than men—the notion of male/female equality is so incomprehensible that it always draws laughter. Yet, in spite of their inferiority, women are also viewed as being dangerous. They are not to be trusted, they cannot be relied upon to be faithful, and they will lead men astray if not destroy them, if they are not kept in their proper place.

Both men and women believe that the subordination of women is sanctioned by the *Qur'an* and inherently just. Most men believe, in addition, that women are impressionable and lacking in judgment and therefore must be both protected and controlled. They fear that women's involvement in employment or public affairs will strain or dissolve family ties; they are opposed to education or any extradomestic experience that might offer women economic and political independence or the sense that choices are open to them (see table 2). Husbands fear that women permitted to work with men will run off with the first more desirable (i.e., more wealthy) man they meet. "She'll see someone else," "get loose," "run off," "won't come back," were comments frequently made in response to the subject of wives working outside the home. Almost every family has stories of some woman somewhere in the extended family who has "run off" or "packed out."

It is within this context that the efforts of young radical politicians to introduce reforms affecting women and their life options must be evaluated. Virtually no popular support for any fundamental change in the status of women appears to exist. Fathers and guardians continue to arrange child marriages even though, at the behest of the government, girls are beginning to go to school; men continue to expect that their wives will live in seclusion. While sometimes appearing to advocate a more "secular" (worldly) society based on notions of a socialist state and equality between the sexes, these radical politicians nevertheless proclaim their devotion to the teachings of Islam and conspicuously attend Friday mosque.

The anger of some educated Nigerian women often finds its way into daily newspapers. This assessment of women's lives in Nigeria, offered by the president of the first women's national organization and a leading Yoruba politician, was quoted by *The Daily Times:*

> Women are worse than slaves in Nigeria—slaves could run away. . . . Husbands regard wives as perpetual and life-long slaves. The more help men need, the more wives they marry. A child goes to live with her husband when she is barely old enough to start a life of slavery. She suffers in quietness. Women cook, sweep, hoe and serve their masters. If they show reluctance to do their bidding, if they are tired or indisposed, they will be abused. . . . Women have to remain silent at all times. We should realize that our men are jealous and are used to being called masters and lords; so that it is not easy for a master to take the position of an equal (*Daily Times,* November 23, 1981).

TABLE 2
Men's Attitudes toward Educated Women

Category A 100 male secondary students (Anka 1982)
Category B 100 men with some education (Dan'tsohu Muhammad 1980)
Category C 100 uneducated men (Yusuf Garbo Adamu 1981)

Category	Agree	Disagree	Neutral
Question: Women should be educated beyond primary school			
A	74	11	14
B	49	32	19
C	15	68	17
Question: Education changes a woman's choices [Educated women should work]			
A	60	34	6
B	43	44	13
C	24	60	16
Question: All women should live in *kulle (tsari)* [whether educated or not educated]			
A	41	30	29
B	75	12	18
C	85	10	5
Question: The behavior of educated women is inappropriate			
A	45	50	5
B	65	15	20
C	68	30	2
Question: Women should stop the idea of claiming equality with their husbands			
A	68	22	10
B	80	10	10
C	100	0	0
Question: Women should not copy Western culture			
A	88	10	2
B	94	3	3
C	100	0	0

By contrast, uneducated women, though not unaware of their own suffering, appear resigned to it; they look for change only within the confines of the roles assigned them by Islam. These sentiments are typical:

> I am thirty-nine years old. That is very old for our people. My life has been long and strenuous. Thirteen births have worn me out. Six died

> and seven are living. That's about normal around here. Personally, I would have been more than willing to agree if my master wanted to have another wife, as this would mean that the two of us could share all the daily work. . . . I would have desired to be relieved of some of my work, but as long as he has made up his mind there is nothing I can do to change it (Interview #34, Kano, April 17, 1983).

Many wealthier families do, however, have daughters now in school, and these daughters are beginning to think in terms of careers and incomes earned outside the home. As they marry and move with their professional husbands to other parts of Nigeria or beyond, news of what they observe of women's lives and choices will travel home. Thus, while the face of reform is not yet visible, its basis may already have been laid.

It may be that the solidarity of Hausa women will work to bring about fundamental changes in the life prospects of their young daughters without overtly challenging the social mores currently governing relationships between men and women. The two great obstacles they face as they seek to navigate the difficult straits of change, Islam on the one hand and the perception of women's liberation as alien and un-Islamic on the other, may be overcome by the strength and cohesion of the protected world of women.

3

Hausa Women
A World of Their Own

RESEARCH on women in other male-dominated societies suggests that there are some societies in which women are so suppressed in a world dominated by men that they constitute a distinct, self-attuned social entity. A female model of society that is so "muted," i.e., not obvious to the casual observer, may actually function to counterbalance the more undesirable effects of the dominant male culture (Ardener 1975, vii–xxiii). The existence of a female sphere of life with female values presents the real challenge to the Islamic definition of female "place" and suggests that the seeds of change in the status and position of women are inherent in the structure of the society itself. It may be inferred from Ardener's muted group construct that within women's experience of apparently total subordination, the seeds of real independence exist in a value system that is generally potent yet does not rely upon male sanction or approval. Behind the walls secluding them, Hausa women have developed a kind of independence or at least a distinct sphere of activity in at least two respects: in regard to economic activity and in regard to their continued allegiance to Bori.

The unceasing economic activity of women and the continued strength of the cult of Bori indicate that women do maintain a value system that contradicts the Islamic value system and its dictates of almost total subservience to men. A closer look at *kulle* and at women's activities within it suggests how fundamental change might come about.

KULLE

Kulle literally means "confinement" or "imprisonment." It imposes severe limitations on interactions between men and women outside specifically defined categories of contact.

In most Islamic societies married women live in seclusion as they do in the northern states of Nigeria. It is not clear how the emphasis in Islam on separation of men from women and the division of homes into male and female physical space came about, but it is assumed that Islam accentuated preexisting social divisions (Dengler 1978). Because the *Qur'an* admonishes women not to reveal their "charms" to men who are not their husbands, Muslims believe Muhammad endorsed the practice of secluding women: "Tell believing women to avert their glances and guard their private parts and not to display their charms except what [normally] appears of them. They should draw their coverings over their bosoms and not show their charms except to their husbands" (*Qur'an* 24:30–31).

There is evidence that both veiling and purdah predated Islam and by the time of the Prophet had become symbols of male status and prestige. Veiling dates back to the first century A.D. (Beck and Keddie 1978, 25). In cities, the wearing of the veil differentiated free women from slave women, and over time the veil thus became a mark of honor, respect, and high status (Hussein 1953, 442). Seclusion of women had become established by A.D. 150 (Levy 1965, 127).

As an institution, wife seclusion is most prevalent in poorer countries and seems to be particularly accommodated by societies characterized by a fairly rigid social structure based on highly differentiated, hierarchically ordered ascriptive roles. In Hausa society, hierarchical relationships establish patterns of social distance and psychological subservience between social classes within the society and between men and women. Placing women in their "proper" place is an essential component of the sense of order. The social world is sharply segregated between men's and women's spheres, and deep-seated religious beliefs regarding basic human nature sanction this segregation. Anything overtly threatening to it is seen as a violation of the entire normative construct of Islam.

Kulle basically involves public recognition of dominance and dependency between males and females. While *kulle* is defended on religious grounds, it helps establish status and is a symbol of honor and family pride. Two variations of purdah or wife seclusion are fairly universal in the Islamic world: physical segregation and/or symbolic segregation achieved by covering the female head, face, and/or body in public. The degree to which these two manifestations of seclusion are enforced depends on the underlying value system concerning the separation of the sexes.

Hausa society recognizes three variations of *kulle. Kullen dinga* involves complete seclusion—a wife never goes out. Today this is largely restricted to the wives of the *mallams* and emirs: under no circumstances do these women leave the walls of the women's quarters of their compounds. Relatives and friends are received in their quarters and, in the case of illness, physicians or traditional healers are brought in. Their children are born at home with the help of midwives. If a child is sick and cannot be treated at home, a relative or servant will take him or her to the hospital.

In Kano, two educated women are among the four official wives of the reigning emir. One of them had been a teacher before marrying into the Kano royal family and after the marriage had accompanied her husband on his assignments as Nigerian ambassador to several countries. Once he succeeded to the emirship in 1963, however, she came back to Kano and has not since been out of her quarters at the emir's palace. In the palace, the four wives may not leave their own quarters even to go about within the grounds. The emir's two educated wives live in adjoining quarters; theoretically they cannot even visit each other, but in fact they do occasionally enter each other's rooms through secluded passageways.

A less severe form of purdah and the most commonly practiced in Kano is *kullen tsari.* In *kullen tsari* a wife may go out occasionally, with permission and accompanied by others, to attend ceremonies and seek medical care. The most "modern" form of seclusion, an option limited in practice to the wives of a few educated elite families, is *kullen zuci* (purdah of the heart). In *kullen zuci* the emphasis is not on physical seclusion, but on good judgment, modesty, and proper behavior. Women in *kullen zuci* freely go out to visit and are often seen driving their own cars to the homes of relatives and sometimes to school; occasionally they are seen shopping in the modern stores just outside the walled city. The women living in *kullen zuci* are among the very few well-educated Hausa women in the city; this fact testifies to the relationship between class and kind of *kulle* observed. Virtually no uneducated or nonelite women enjoy the more lenient *kullen zuci.*

The nearly universal observance of *kullen tsari* by both rural and urban Hausa families is a rather recent development. Older women in urban and rural areas recall its widespread introduction in their lifetime. Previously, poorer men could not afford to keep their wives in seclusion, and its practice was characteristic only of upper-class families, especially in the city. Over the past fifty years, however, Hausa women have come to believe that *kulle* is characteristic of Muslim women everywhere and that it was practiced and endorsed by the Prophet Muhammad. The leader of the Fulani Islamic jihad, Usman don Fodio, favored total seclusion, citing as his source on the subject the *Al Madkhal* of Ibn al-Hajj (Pitten 1979, 238); *mallams* in Kano today cite several Qur'anic verses in addition to the *Al Madkhal* to support their endorsement of *kulle.* It is further asserted that the Prophet's daughter, Aisha, narrated a *hadith* stating that she and other women should cover their faces when accompanying the Prophet (The Grand Kadi of Kwara State in a public lecture, June 1983, at Bayero University, Kano). Sura (chapter) 59 is also quoted: "tell thy wives and daughters and women of the believers to draw on their dressing gowns, that it is more proper that they be known and not affronted" (*Qur'an* 59:2). This Sura is also taken to imply that women who go out in public not properly covered from head to foot and not on sanctioned errands may indeed legitimately be affronted and insulted. Many educated women whose husbands have agreed to *kullen zuci* decline to go out often due to extremely rude and hostile treatment from men who claim they are not behaving as proper Muslim women and may be insulted with impunity.

Sura 33:33 asked the Prophet's wives to "stay quietly in your houses and not make a dazzling display like that of former times of ignorance." Some moderates, such as the Egyptian scholar Mohammed Al-Ghazali, stress that according to the teachings of the Prophet, veiling is commendable and desirable, but voluntary rather than compulsory (*wajib*); it is not one of the five requirements of a practising Muslim. Northern Nigerian radicals, such as Haroun Adamu (a one time political editor of the *Daily Times* newspaper until 1983 and the managing director of the Kano State Government-supported *Triumph* newspaper until the military coup d'état in December of 1983), stress that these injunctions advising seclusion and veiling for women were directed only at the Prophet's wives because of their very privileged position and are not binding on all women generally (Modibbo 1982, 10). Muslim students at the University argue that the *Qur'an* did not call on men to seclude their wives, but rather called on wives themselves to behave in a manner befitting their status—i.e., to observe *kullen zuci.* Others argue that the affairs of an Islamic community should be shouldered by men and women equally and no one should be excluded or prohibited from participation; it follows that women should not be kept in seclusion. In support of their view they cite the following: "And their Lord answered their prayers, I waste not the work of any worker among you, male or female" (*Qur'an* 3:95; Modibbo 1982, 18). Therefore, they contend, the practice of seclusion and the prohibition from performing social, economic, and political activities in public are not prescribed by the *Qur'an* and *hadith* expressly; what is prohibited is dressing, talking, or behaving in ways that lead others to impure thoughts.

The most obvious observation about *kulle* in the urban areas is that it excludes women from paid employment outside the home. Thus, because daughters of upper-class families are beginning to acquire education and are the only ones living in *kullen zuci,* those who can most afford to live in seclusion financially are the only ones sometimes discarding it. As some women become more educated and a few enter the professions (medicine, teaching), *kulle* in the city is likely to become more and more a feature of lower- and lower-middle-class families. These families value the status features of *kulle* more than the financial benefits of extended participation in the work force. No matter how poor the family today, families as corporate entities do not want women working outside the home, and individual men appear quite shocked by the suggestion that the economic status of the family might be enhanced by it.

Kullen tsari is widely practiced in Nigerian Hausaland in general, not just in urban Kano. The gradual spread of wife-seclusion during the past fifty years to the rural areas in Kano State, where it is now nearly universally observed, is intriguing. In these areas the physical conditions of the land and the rapid expansion of commercial agriculture do not facilitate strict seclusion, and economic necessity would seem to dictate that men abandon their strict control of women and allow them into wage labor and productive agriculture. But, in rural Hausaland, virtually all married women of childbearing age are in seclusion. It is clear that this is a relatively recent phenomenon, as poor women remember when their mothers and grandmothers were not secluded.

In the villages, until the beginning of the twentieth century, only the wives of the *mallams* were secluded. Today the seclusion of wives is nearly universal in Nigerian Hausaland, although this is not the case elsewhere. This is in contrast to Hausa women in the neighboring country of Niger and to Islamic women who live in the neighboring state of Bornu, and it is generally not true of other Islamic cultures in West Africa (Haswell 1963, 25; Hill 1972, 24; Nicolas 1965, 287). Learned Hausa men speculate that the dramatic increase in the prevalence of *kulle* in Nigeria is directly related to the elimination of slavery. As farming and wood gathering had been the chores of slave women, newly free women withdrew from them, and newly free men made their own status evident by keeping their wives in seclusion (Interview #41, Kano, July 2, 1983). M.G. Smith also observes that traditionally free women did not farm because only slave women performed farm labor. Also, Smith and Hill both point out that because of the high water table of northern Nigeria, wells could be dug inside the compounds, making it unnecessary for women to go out to fetch water; and since the donkey flourished as a beast of burden, women did not have to play this role as they do in so many other peasant societies. Today, small children gather firewood and pile it on donkeys for distribution to women in their compounds (M.G. Smith 1955, 22–24; Hill 1972, 24).

Early writers establish that the prohibition against "free women" working in the fields is longstanding. For the past eight decades, commentators on the scene in Nigerian Hausaland have noted it with interest. In 1889 Staudinger stated, without elaboration, that farming was men's, not women's work in Hausaland. In 1896 it was reported: "Farm work is not becoming for a wife you know: she is free, you may not put her to hoe grass as a slave" (Robinson 1896, 6). Krusius observed in 1915 that, unlike their Muslim sisters in the north, Maguzawa women (a small minority of non-Muslim Hausa) worked very hard on the farms (Krusius 1915, 298–99). Meek asserts that as of 1920, "among the Muslim peoples generally only slave women . . . are engaged in farming operations" (Meek 1925, 233), and M. G. Smith reports that by 1865 in Zaria free women did no farming (M. G. Smith 1960, 92, fn. 1). Polly Hill made the same observation a few years later and commented that Hausa society was unique in the strictness and prevalence of rural wife seclusion, particularly since "the poverty of some households is much exacerbated by the refusal of husbands to permit their wives to farm" (Hill 1972, 85).

All observers of the scene in Nigerian Hausaland comment that in rural Hausa communities, unlike elsewhere in Nigeria or in Africa, Islam is a major constraint on the economic roles of women since at a minimum *kulle* means that women are excluded from direct farm operations (M. G. Smith 1955; Abell 1967; Hill 1972; Raza and Famoriyo 1980). Unlike women in the cocoa growing areas of Ghana and Nigeria, or the yam areas of Nigeria where women do much of the farming and harvesting and hence control a large proportion of the cash market, or in the Gambia where men are dependent on women's rice farming to sustain them, Hausa women in Nigeria simply do not farm.

The religious and cultural constraints on women's working in agriculture have endured in spite of major economic and technical changes that otherwise would dictate participation. Although many scholars have noted women's work on farms throughout Africa, in this part of the continent, even in the nineteenth century, free women did not farm. M. G. Smith believes that in the Hausa states the practice of *kulle* is seen as a mark of improved economic status rather than of adherence to religious injunction (M. G. Smith 1955, 24). Thus, the large-scale and pervasive practice of slavery in Hausaland and the association of farming with slave-women's work partly explains the reluctance of men to have their women involved in farming. Islamic injunctions concerning modesty and seclusion reinforced the inclination not to have free women visible and in the open.

It is often claimed that women "prefer" seclusion because it gives them the freedom to pursue their own trading and an exemption from hard manual work on the farm. But this issue has yet to be systematically investigated. Women in seclusion are overwhelmingly illiterate and therefore do not write about themselves; thus their perceptions and opinions concerning their status must be both ascertained and interpreted by persons outside the system itself. Random discussions seem to suggest that if the choice is *kulle* or farming, women will choose *kulle,* as no one desires the drudgery of farm work. If, however, the question is whether or not women would like more freedom to pursue their economic interests outside the home, the answers are more equivocal. Usually, women simply reply, "Well, it is not possible."

Despite seclusion, Hausa women believe they are better off than nonsecluded peasant women elsewhere who work the farm, carry firewood, and fetch water, as well as complete their domestic chores. Nonsecluded rural women in other cultures often have so many responsibilities that they are unable to engage in activities generating income for themselves. Nonseclusion and the freedom to come and go is no advantage if the chores women are then expected to perform are exhausting and nonproductive of income.

One would hypothesize about most societies that with the changes set in motion by the mechanization of agricultural production and the replacement of subsistence agriculture by "agribusiness"—both of which are rapidly occuring in Hausaland—old forms of social organization in the rural areas would begin to break down. But, rural *kulle* appears to be gaining ground in the Hausa areas, becoming more deeply entrenched and generally aspired to and accepted. The ability to keep a wife (or wives) in seclusion is a mark both of rising social status and devout religious practice.

In 1975–76, two researchers investigated farming practices in three villages in Zaria. They discovered that in each, most of the women surveyed were in *kulle* and none was involved in farming. However, the majority of the 200 women surveyed did have income-generating work (food processing and preparation—sixty-four percent, trading—ten percent, spinning and capmaking—eleven percent, weaving and mat-making—three percent). Few ever left their compounds to perform the chores left to women in other rural African societies—fetching water or firewood, or going to market. Monthly incomes were small, about naira 7 (or $10.00), but women were determined against all odds to generate some income of their own. (For additional analysis of this data see Raza and Famoriyo 1980, 933–49.) By the end of the 1970s, it is estimated, women contributed less than one percent of the total farm labor in Kano State (Baba 1980, 1006). Children and the elderly also provided virtually no direct farm labor. This exacerbated an acute labor shortage, as adult males constitute only 22.11 percent of the adult population (District Tax Assessment records, Kano State, 1982).

A survey conducted in 1980 revealed that 95.5 percent of 2000 men interviewed on the Kano River Project believed that women should have an insignificant to nonexistent role in agricultural development (Baba 1980). The Kano River Project is part of the Kano Agricultural Development Project, a $500 million plan of "integrated rural development" involving mapping and building of roads, siting and digging of wells and bore holes, damming of rivers and development of irrigation systems, and introduction of new crops and new forms of agriculture. Financed jointly by the World Bank and state and federal agencies, it is pledged to change the economic structure of agriculture in the state and will affect approximately one million farmers and their families. A component of this massive project is targeted to reach women, but the extent and purpose of such "reaching" remains vague.

In a survey conducted in 1978 as the project was being introduced, 94.4 percent of 515 male respondents reported that their wives lived in *kullen tsari* or strict seclusion. Eighty-seven percent of the men said that women should remain in *kulle* and that labor should be imported from elsewhere as needed. The farmers indicated that they would rely on nonfamily labor for additional help. Of the 515 respondents, 430 reported that irrigation created a demand for extra labor, but only one person identified female members of the family as potential sources of labor. Ninety percent, or 463 of the respondents, said they themselves would hire labor from outside before considering hiring women (Baba 1980, 1006).

Project reports for the years 1978–1983 are striking because of the nearly complete absence of reference to women. While token concern is shown for the integration of women into the project, as evidenced by the assigning of home economists to each of its four zones in Kano State, this effort is tangential to the real purpose of the project, which is to increase agricultural production. The early efforts of the home economists to reach women were frustrated by the fact that women could not come out, even to attend classes conducted by female professionals. Perhaps this was due to the fact that at first the home economists were Christian rather than Muslim women. Since 1982, the project has employed graduates of the Home Economics Program in the College of Agriculture at the Ahmadu Bello University in Zaria, and they have been more effective in reaching the women with their programs in nutrition, health care and pre- and postnatal care. But, there is no indication yet that this massive project has altered or is altering traditional women's labor. Since women have no role to play in agricultural production per se, they are very peripheral to the project. Ten years of intense activity and dramatic change in the countryside has not altered this fact.

Although not involved in farming, rural women are very much involved in production for profit, albeit on a very small scale. The villages in the rural areas are characterized by what Polly Hill has called "honeycomb" markets. Since women cannot go out, they obviously cannot gather in a central market place as they do almost everywhere else in Africa. Instead, they turn their homes into individual markets, or "cells," to use Hill's term, that are in continuous session and in which women engage in the cooking and sewing for trade and sale that characterize women's activity all over West Africa. This tradition is deeply ingrained, predating Islam, and endures in spite of Islamic injunctions that men should support women and that women should remain

A woman washing lettuce with the help of her five-year-old daughter. Salad is sold as a garnish on cooked rice. When ready, the rice is taken out of the house and sold by an older daughter. Since this woman is in seclusion, she must rely on her children for daily purchases of raw ingredients and for selling the prepared food. Were the daughters to go to school, this whole operation would be jeopardized.

quiet and nurture their families. So long as the activity can be carried on in seclusion, there is no objection from husbands or religious leaders. So much a part of the culture is it, that men generally ignore this activity or pretend it doesn't exist; but it consumes most of a woman's time, and women go to extraordinary lengths to assist each other in these very, very small-scale economic efforts. In the rural areas, women own sheep, goats, and chickens that are cared for by small children and that provide a foundation for their food retailing businesses.

The households in the honeycomb market are linked by children who shop on behalf of their mothers and help determine what the prices will be on any given day; the women are highly competitive with each other. The demand for cooked and processed food is great. Women buy snacks for themselves and their children as well as cooked food for men, and men too buy snacks and meals throughout the day. Hill notes that there has not been much change in rural Hausaland in the past ninety years. Over eighty years ago, Baba of Karo's mother produced millet balls, bean cakes, groundnut (or peanut) cakes, and groundnut oil for selling, as her descendants do to this day (M. Smith 1954, 54; Hill 1972, 269).[1]

Because of the tradition of house trade, wives of the poorest farmers often find themselves better off than their husbands. Since the advent of Islam, some women have simply abandoned husbands who could not provide for them. In the village of Batagarawa, Hill discovered that in fact many women also engaged in house trade on behalf of their husbands by selling the produce of their farms (grain, groundnuts, and cowpeas). Others made bean cakes or similar snacks and sold salt vegetables (pepper, locust beans) and thus compensated for lack of support from poor male farmers.

An interesting observation made by Polly Hill in this regard is that, in terms of independent incomes, a wife's economic standing is more related to her father's position than to her husband's. Richer fathers give more dowry and other gifts to their daughters,[2] which starts them in business, and any income they earn is theirs alone and generally not shared with a husband (Hill 1972, 334).

Perhaps the fact that men live so much apart from women explains why they do not connect women's economic productivity with economic independence and hence do not appear threatened by it; however, they do appear very much threatened by the notion of women's breaching their seclusion in the course of developing their incomes.

In the villages, as in the city, each wife has a defined space of her own—generally a separate hut (*daki*). Men in the villages, as in the city, have no such defined space exclusively theirs. The owner of the compound shares his room at its entrance with young boys and any unmarried men who might be staying there. He rotates his sleeping mat among the huts of his wives, spending one or two nights with each, depending on how many wives he has. In principle, the wives rotate cooking responsibilities, but in practice all generally pitch in and help, both in cooking for the household and cooking for sale outside the household in order to earn small sums of money.

There is little pressure to limit the practice of *kulle* among Hausa women. Social pressure, custom, and religious belief all combine to discourage any such aspiration. In Kano, girls tell of horrifying stories, told them by the *mallams* in Qur'anic schools, of punishments women will receive if they do not practice *kulle.* They are told it would please Allah if they did not go out at all from the day they entered their husbands' houses to the ends of their lives. Such devotion to "the will of Allah," they are told, will be richly rewarded when it really counts, in the afterlife. They are warned that if they do insist on going out after being married, they will face heavy punishment in the hereafter and bring punishment and shame on their parents and close relations as well. Eternal hunger, thirst, and damnation await them. One girl was told her tongue would be wound around her neck 70,000 times, her eyes would be gouged out with fire, and her brain would be boiled and poured over her body. On the other hand, so long as they practice *kulle,* in heaven they will live "a wonderful life full of good things, and will be given a beautiful horse which they can ride anyplace and view all the things not seen in this lifetime" (Interviews #42 and #43, Kano, July 10, 1983).

In spite of these stories and threats, it is clear that as girls gain access to education, the chances lessen of their living in the strict seclusion their mothers have known. There appears to be a direct correlation between levels of education and expectations concerning *kulle.* Fifty university graduates, fifty secondary school graduates, fifty primary school graduates, and fifty women with no *boko* (Western education) were surveyed to gain an impression of the relationship between seclusion and education. The results were quite dramatic.

While no overt disagreements are noticeable between mothers and daughters concerning *kulle,* it is clear that uneducated women believe it to be a religious obligation that will be rewarded in heaven. Educated women are beginning to question both its religious legitimacy and its psychological implications and consequences. At a conference on women and the family in April 1983, Muslim women remarked, *Aure ba bauta bane,* "marriage is not slavery." Women students repeatedly asserted, "Marriage should not be prison," "Purdah retards development," "Women should not be locked up

TABLE 3
"Are you in *kulle (tsari)*"?
(All respondents were married.)

Educational Level	Yes	%	No	%
No *boko* (none)	50	100	0	0
Primary school	36	72	14	28
Secondary school	28	56	22	44
University	4	8	46	92

Source: Modibbo 1982, Table 5

and made nonproductive," and "*Kulle* is inhuman and not necessary." Others pointed out that when they went to Mecca on hajj, they saw men and women from other Muslim countries mingling together in all the holy places: they asked, why is it wrong in Nigeria? (Women in Nigeria 1983).

The educational level of husbands is more indicative of whether wives will live in *kulle* than is the educational level of the wives themselves. There are many examples of educated women and girls marrying older, wealthy but uneducated men and finding themselves living in strictest *kullen tsari.* Their classmates express sympathy for their plight. There are also cases of educated men not able to persuade their uneducated wives to go either to school or into the outside world.

Although the kind of *kulle* practiced is more highly correlated with the educational level of men, attitudinal change is more highly correlated with the educational level of women. University students predict that with rising levels of education for girls, attitudes will change and so, eventually, will practice. Women university students firmly believe, along with secondary school students, that their options will be much greater than their mothers' and that they will be expected to live only in *kullen zuci,* not *kullen tsari.*[3]

A time of significant discord concerning the institution and practice of purdah may be at hand. Initial response to the idea of change is predictably reactionary, as educated women are accused of becoming "Western" and *kulle* is defended on grounds of "traditional values." Fundamentalist religious leaders take a strong position on the status of women. Among those persons who stress the importance of religious or other values of a "traditional" nature that bind Muslims (and/or northern Nigerians) together, the status of women as symbolized by *kulle* is not to be taken lightly. While at least among educated women pressures for reform appear inevitable, any concerted effort toward wholesale change will meet formidable opposition.

Even though ideas about *kulle* are changing and educated women do not expect to live in strict seclusion, most of them also do not expect to work outside their homes. Traditionally, women cannot even begin their household trade until they have been married a year, and wives of wealthier men initially do not trade even then. Their lives are characterized by conspicuous leisure. Later in life they may begin to trade, but only as an avocation, an antidote to *maganin zaman banza,* "sitting about uselessly." The limited lives of women of high status is hard to imagine. They literally have nothing to do—even the most educated among the wives of the highest government and civil servants are not likely to entertain with their husbands or attend special events with them. The vice chancellor (president) of the University, whose own wife is a university graduate, never entertains in his home, and his wife does not accompany him when he is an official host at University events.

Spinning is a traditional occupation of older secluded women, but very few young women know how to do it. While cotton is still grown in northern Nigeria, its importance has diminished. Imported and machine-made cloth became a prestige item in the colonial period and continues to be an important part of the gifts exchanged at marriage.

Likewise, the wives of the state governor and other senior civil servants do not accompany their husbands on social occasions. These women complain of not being allowed to do anything. They have servants—cooks, gardeners, drivers, nursemaids, and housekeepers. Their primary activities are attending each other's naming ceremonies when children are born, condoling each other when deaths occur in the family, attending wedding parties, and taking naps.

Much of the defense of *kulle* has to do with men's perceptions that women are vulnerable, or rather, that their own pride or reputations are vulnerable and that women are the source of that vulnerability. By a convoluted logic, it is concluded that women must be sheltered or protected from forces "outside." Underlying belief about the seclusion of women are assumptions about the nature of men and women. Sexual impulses are seen as being overwhelmingly strong and difficult for an invididual to resist. Hence, seclusion is made to bear the burden of impulse control by mediating face-to-face contact between the sexes. Women are seen as both victims of sexual desire and the temptresses prompting such desire. Therefore, they must be protected both from themselves and from others; they must be segregated.

Women's behavior as sheltered persons is an important indicator of the status of their protectors. In a culture where male pride is very significant and very fragile, where great emphasis is put on identity and status, the seclusion of women is an important aspect of male control. A challenge to the subordination of women is a challenge to the whole structure of power and prestige in the society. Hence, "women's rights" are a very delicate political issue that is commanding more and more attention in the press and the media as well as in intellectual circles and in considerations pertaining to manifestos and programs of political parties. Educated women recognize that reform must come about through more liberal interpretations of Islamic doctrine rather than through direct challenges to it.

ECONOMIC ACTIVITY

Overview

As noted, women in purdah, while in theory wholly dependent on their husbands for food, shelter, and support, manage to be economically active. Historically, only wealthier men could keep their wives in seclusion, while poorer men were forced to rely on wives' labor outside the home to contribute to the support of the family. Today virtually all Hausa families, rural or urban, rich or poor, practice seclusion, and wives are secluded in Kano even where it is clear that husbands cannot support them adequately. This means that as a practical matter, wives must engage in some sort of remunerative activity at home in order to sustain the family and particularly, in order to ensure adequate dowries (or that part of it for which they are responsible, the *kayan daki*) for daughters.

Women in fact do work primarily in order to finance their daughters' marriages. The *kayan daki,* literally the "expense of the room" furnished by the bride's mother for her own use in her husband's house, probably will constitute the major portion of the dowry. Thus, while it is correct to emphasize that Hausa women do work, it would be misleading not to emphasize that they do not, technically, work to earn a living. At the same time however, it is also true that women's cash income may make subsistence possible in many poor families. Poor farmers who do not earn enough to support their families survive in part because their wives, from within seclusion, are engaged in income-producing activity. Theoretically men support women, but in the poorest families, particularly in the rural areas, the reverse is more likely the reality; many poor families are sustained by the economic activities of wives in seclusion.

As has been pointed out elsewhere, for women in seclusion children are essential in linking their private domain to economic activity in the public domain. Children give women access to the market and help to subvert the limitations of purdah in many ways, but most especially in the realm of trade and economic activity (Schildkrout 1978a, 1978b, 1979, 1981, 1982).

The economic roles of women have been described by a number of researchers, but no one has discovered a hierarchy of roles or work chores related to class and status for them as for men (see Barkow 1972; Bashir 1972; Hill 1977, 332–409; Schildkrout 1978a, 1978b, 1980, 1982; Jaggar 1976; Tahir 1976; M. G. Smith 1962). The traditional male occupational structure defines a man's status in the society as well as his economic or productive role. The aristocracy by birth (the *sarakuna*) hold offices (*sarauta*), while the scholars (*mallams*) and merchants (*attajirai*) are followed in order of status by craftsmen (*masa-sana'a*), small traders (*'yan kasuwa*), brokers (*dillalai*), farmers (*manoma*), blacksmiths (*makira*), hunters (*maharba*), musicians (*maroka*), and butchers (*mahauta*).

Unlike for women's work, membership in these occupational groups is largely ascriptive and determines marriage patterns, levels of education to be obtained, and future careers. Women's differential expertise is noted among women but does not translate into socioeconomic status because that is determined by the status and class of the men in their lives. Hausa society's emphasis on the "Islamic way of life," which stresses the importance of marriage for women and proper behavior within marriage, obscures the very interesting economic activities of women.

Variations in women's economic roles and factors that lead to economic choices are related to age, class, childbearing activity, and marital status. Because women's socioeconomic status is determined by their fathers' and husbands' standing, they do not think of the success of their work as affecting their own status. But some women are in fact known for their skills in sewing, cooking, or trading. Even these women, though, will acknowledge that they work for only one reason—to earn money to ensure their daughters a proper start in marriage by providing appropriate *kayan daki.* Women seem to be inordinately concerned with the establishment of worth and status among themselves through the conspicuous display of their *kayan daki* and dowry.

Although it provides some insurance in the case of dire emergency because *kayan daki* can be sold, this investment is essentially nonproductive. Women whose support is not needed for family essentials indulge their taste in wax cloth and gold jewelry, as well as investing in *kayan daki.* Since theoretically Muslim women do not engage in income-generating activity but are supported completely by their husbands, any income a woman earns is "invisible" and belongs to her. In the city it is generally not reinvested in income-generating ventures, and it rarely goes into acknowledged household support.

Survey of Three Wards and a Village

Data on the economic activities of women were collected in three wards of Kano City (Kurawa, Kofar Mazugal, and Gwagwarwa by Callaway and Schildkrout) and in the village of Malumfashi (by Bayero students). The three wards and the village were nearly 100 percent Muslim and shared beliefs regarding the status of women, particularly the emphasis on early marriage, high fertility, and seclusion.

The data indicated that for most of these Hausa women, economic activities are confined to the informal sector of the economy where the level of competition is intense and the level of remuneration low. In the urban setting there are, however, differences in the types of income-generating activities in which women engage that reflect status, albeit status determined by the standing of the woman's husband in the society. Differences between Kurawa and Kofar Mazugal reflect a long history of male occupational specialization associated with the two wards, and this male specialization is reflected in the organization of women's work (Schildkrout 1979, 1981).

Kurawa, located immediately behind the Kano Central Mosque and the emir's palace, traditionally was the home of the Genawa clan, a clan noted for its *mallams* and learned men. Today, most of the men here continue in slightly more intellectual or modern middle-class pursuits than the majority of the population. They are primarily civil servants working for state and local governments, teachers or Islamic judges, and *mallams.* Women live in *kulle* (*tsari*) and most engage in embroidery and small-scale trade in gold and cloth to earn incomes of their own. Most young girls are in Western or English-speaking school, *boko,* as well as the traditional Qur'anic school. All the girls were in school in 1978 when Schildkrout did her original research and were still in school in 1981 when Callaway began her work. Sending girls to school is a recent development, but the "learned men" here point out that the new emphasis on education for girls in fact reflects Islamic values. Usman dan Fodio, the leader of the Fulani jihad in this area of the world, stressed the importance of Qur'anic education for women in purdah. Today Shehu dan Fodio's concern for appropriate education for women provides a rationale for accepting Western education for women as not in conflict with the ideals of Islam. And, among educated and more elite families in Kano City, educated girls are becoming a mark of high status. But as Schildkrout has explained in detail elsewhere, because girls are now in school, women have less help in their income-generating work (1979, 1980, 1981, 1982). Girls are now available for only a very few hours a day to go shopping or to deliver materials and goods to customers. Women in Kurawa engage in work that is now almost leisure work, and although they fret about their small profits, they do not think in terms of alternative strategies (see table 4). Their main concern is the generation of appropriate dowry for their daughters, and increasingly a high level of education is seen as a substitute for extensive dowry.

Kofar Mazugal is one of the oldest wards in Kano City, and its Habe inhabitants predate the Fulani settlements in Kurawa by several centuries. It is the home of small traders, butchers, and other men of traditionally lower social standing and educational attainment. Trade continues to be the predominant form of male employment in Kofar Mazugal, although a few younger men are employed at low levels in government offices, and some are branching into construction and minor contracting. Women are almost ex-

TABLE 4
Occupations and Incomes of Secluded Women in Kurawa

Naira (N) = $1.42

Occupation	# of Women	% of Women	Average Monthly Income (N)
None	4	7.5	0
Sewing men's caps	9	16.98	5.80
Knitting, embroidery	4	7.50	5.00
Machine sewing	3	5.66	5.00
Hair plaiting	2	3.77	5.00
Selling cooked food (without children hawking)	5	9.43	11.25
Selling cooked food (with children hawking)	8	15.09	12.81
Trade in gold	10	18.86	6.80
Trade in cloth	8	15.09	5.50
TOTAL	53	99.88	6.35

Sources: Schildkrout survey taken in 1981; Callaway survey taken in 1982

clusively engaged in food preparation and sale; in this, they are highly dependent on female children to go to the market, purchase ingredients, and sell their products on the streets (*talla*). Schildkrout commented that girls did not go to school in Kofar Mazugal at the time of her original research in 1976–1978. Five years later in 1981, girls still were not in *boko* school and instead spent most of their time before marriage (at about age twelve) helping their mothers prepare food and then selling it on the street (Schildkrout 1984). Food preparation and selling generates more profit than does embroidery and sewing, and thus women's incomes in Kofar Mazugal are about three times higher than in Kurawa (see table 5).

Gwagwarwa Ward, newer than Kurawa and Kofar Mazugal, is located along the outer city walls. The majority of its inhabitants are drawn from rural areas within Kano State, but longstanding residents rent rooms to other Muslims from other parts of Nigeria or to Hausas from outside the state. Hence, male economic pursuits are more mixed within the ward, and fairly wealthy and very poor families often share quarters or live side by side. Women's economic activity is also more varied, and although most girls are in school, they also are expected to sell their mothers' goods. Women's incomes are appreciably higher than in Kurawa and Kofar Mazugal, perhaps reflecting the larger percentage of single men renters who buy all their food on the streets (see table 6).

A survey of 294 village women in Malumfashi (all of whose husbands were primarily farmers and secondarily, traders) revealed that eighty-nine percent, or 261, of the women reported engaging in income-earning activity *every*

TABLE 5
Occupations and Incomes of Secluded Women in Kofar Mazugal

Occupation	# of Women	% of Women	Average Monthly Income (N)
None	0	0	0
Sewing men's caps	6	17	5.80
Hair plaiting and sewing caps	2	6	9.50
Machine sewing	3	9	7.50
Pounding grain	2	6	7.50
Selling cooked food (without children hawking)	3	9	14.00
Selling cooked food (with children hawking)	19	54	25.66
TOTAL	35	101	17.74

Source: Schildkrout 1981, 92

TABLE 6
Occupations and Incomes of Secluded Women in Gwagwarwa

Naira (N) = $1.42

Occupation	# of Women	% of Women	Average Monthly Income (N)
Grain pounding	7	7.14	5.00
Cap-making	11	12.22	7.00
Hair plaiting	2	2.04	5.00
Food processing (pounding)	21	21.42	15.00
Selling cooked food (without children hawking)	17	17.24	12.00
Selling cooked food (with children hawking)	40	40.81	120.00
TOTAL	98	100.00	27.33

Source: Survey conducted by Rabi Mohammed, 1982

day: thirty-six percent cooked and sold food for a major meal, twelve percent cooked snacks, sixteen percent were involved in some other sort of food processing (i.e., pounding grain or yam, shelling peanuts, making bread, removing the hull from rice, or pounding for other women). Sixty-four percent were involved in some sort of food preparation, but monthly earnings were low (see table 7).

Whether in the city or in the countryside, the most common occupation for women is the preparation of food items for sale by young girls. The trade in ready-to-eat food (both main dishes and snacks) is an important component of both rural and urban household spending patterns. The profits, however, are variable, depending in large part on the extensiveness of regular patronage.

Analysis of the data collected by Hill in 1977 and by Callaway students in 1982 suggests that in rural areas there is little relationship between the scale of a woman's trade and the economic (not the social) standing of her husband. In the city this was not the case, as the work of Schildkrout indicates. Women in Kurawa married to men of higher status tended to engage in trade yielding smaller incomes, whereas women in the lower status ward (Kofar Mazugal) earned nearly three times more profits from their trade in cooked foods. In the villages, however, there was little difference in the types of wares handled by the wives of richer (higher-status) or poorer (lower-status) husbands, and the differential between incomes of the women was also less. In all cases, income earned by women was considered theirs and did not go

TABLE 7
Occupations and Incomes of Secluded Women in Malumfashi

Occupation	# of Women	% of Women	Average Monthly Income (N)
Preparing a main dish for immediate sale	107	36.39	10.00
Preparing snacks (bean cakes, *kake*)	36	12.24	5.00
Other food processing	47	15.98	5.00
Trading	30	10.20	4.00
Spinning, cap-making, embroidery	33	11.22	4.00
Weaving and mat-making	10	3.40	5.00
Other	2	.06	7.00
None	29	9.86	0
TOTAL	294	99.35	5.00

Source: Survey conducted by Najah Abdul-Azeez and Rabi Mohammed, June 1982

Note: It should be noted that the minimum wage in Nigeria in 1982, when this research was conducted, was naira 150.00 ($213.00) per month or naira 1800.00 per year.

into any acknowledged household account. It is interesting to note, however, that in the case of households of poorer men women felt they needed to earn more for *kayan daki;* whereas in wealthier households the bridewealth expected from marriage negotiations and gifts from suitors was higher, and a portion of this bridewealth could be used to assure appropriate dowry, thus taking some of the pressure off mothers to earn income for this purpose.

It is indicative of significant social change that education for girls is becoming acceptable as a form of dowry; wage-earning and professional men increasingly desire at least one educated woman as a wife who can "understand modern hygiene or appreciate television" and to signify high social standing. These men are willing to pay higher brideprices for educated girls. Hence, in a sense, education is becoming a component of *kayan daki* and is valued in the same way. (For a more extensive discussion of this development, see Schildkrout 1979, 1981, 1982.)

Daily Workings of the Invisible Economy

The food distribution network is indicative of the complexity of Hausa exchange patterns among women. Binta's case is not unusual. Binta is a seventy-

Unmarried women, young and old, are exempt from the confines of purdah and spend their days cooking food for sale. These two are sitting outside a compound wall making fried bean cakes, which are purchased and eaten for breakfast and as snacks.

five-year-old widow of twenty years. She lives alone in a room in Kurawa in her late husband's house. She receives food daily from a married son who lives nearby, from her late husband's two brothers' wives, and from a married daughter (Interview #17, Kano, October 28, 1982). She sends food to her youngest son and his wife and to an elderly woman, a relative of her late husband who lives in the compound across the street. What food she doesn't eat or redistribute, she sells in order to have a small income. She is not technically a producer, but rather a recipient and distributor. She is not economically self-sufficient, but she does not think of herself as living in a state of dependency either. She expects food to be sent to her, and it is accepted that she will in turn sell some of it in order to sustain herself in other essentials.

This rather involved pattern is repeated, with appropriate variations, between husbands and wives in most households. Customarily, husbands provide an allowance to wives for the usual purchase of food to be cooked by them for the household. However, while most men eat three meals a day, virtually no woman (or combination of wives) actually cooks three meals for the family. Instead, women spend most of the day preparing food for sale, and men purchase one or two meals elsewhere. Thus, men inadvertently subsidize women to buy ingredients for cooking as nascent entrepreneurs from within *kulle* (Schildkrout 1982, 63–64). In short, women divert the money from their husbands for household use into their own exclusive sphere of exchange and support each other through multiple mutual purchases. The street foods industry is visible everywhere in the city and on all the highways. Even in the villages, where food is sold within the cells of the honeycomb market instead of out in the open, it is quite obvious that there is a booming business in the exchange of food between households.

While the practice of wife seclusion is based on the premise that the household is a unit of consumption, not production, and that women are dependent consumers, women are in fact independent producers who generate income of their own by diverting cash provided by men for domestic consumption into domestic production. By eating often outside their own homes with other men, men support women's prepared food production efforts and underwrite their businesses. The separation between men's and women's incomes and accounts and the pattern of income flow between them presents yet another instance in which relationships between men and women are more complicated than they at first appear. "Thus, through their control over the daily operation of the domestic economy, women gain a measure of control over their own lives that is denied to them in the formal definition of sex-roles in Hausa society" (Callaway and Schildkrout 1985, 65).

In recent years Nigeria has faced increasing pressures due to dramatic increases in the cost of food. Certainly the growing dependence on imported food has contributed significantly to this problem, but it may also be that the women's street food industry and honeycomb markets of the villages inflate the cost of food subsistence. By purchasing and by paying for cooked food, men are in fact paying for the cost of the female labor necessary to produce it. Or, to put it another way, "by taking resources which their husbands give them for consumption and diverting them into a remunerated female sphere of production, women are in effect receiving payment for their domestic labor" (Schildkrout 1982, 64).

Elaborate patterns of gift giving, both in the city and in the countryside, further extend the network of women's exchange. Women give gifts, especially in time of need, and expect a return gift (usually with interest) in due time. Gift-giving relationships are usually formed early in life, at the time of marriage, and are an important source of informal credit. Traditionally, a woman does not engage in work for profit during the first year of marriage. During that time her relationships begin to take form, and at the end of the year a young girl will receive gifts from other women that will make it possible for her to go into business on her own (Interview #16, Kano, October 25, 1982).

The complicated gift-giving networks and small-scale trade in other commodities (often acquired through gift exchanges) are standard sources for supplementing women's meager household allowances and incomes. Gifts received from husbands, relatives, and friends often are exchanged for other goods or sold to generate income for special needs. While profits generally go into *kayan daki,* on occasion part of the *kayan daki* might be sold to generate new income for investment in a new line of business or expansion of existing enterprises. In this sense, the dowry system "constitutes an investment in savings, capital and insurance for women in a male-dominated society" (Schildkrout 1982, 64).

It should be emphasized, however, that there is little comparison between the wage sector and the hidden economy of women. The incomes of most women would not even support them at a subsistence level. The minimum monthly wage in Nigeria in 1982, when this research was conducted, was naira 150 ($213), while the average income of the women surveyed here was naira 14.28 ($20.27).

Women living in seclusion conduct their businesses as single-person enterprises; they do not form cooperatives or buying collectives, nor is it the rule for wives to help each other out. Hence, these businesses are very small-scale operations. Capital accumulation is almost impossible and in and of itself seldom a goal. The drive for self-gratification through work is not acknowledged, although it is plainly visible in the pride many women do take in their work. Most women do not yet see that their independent economic drive can be associated with "women's liberation"; they see their work as supportive of traditional obligations to provide daughters with proper *kayan daki;* since the birth rate is high, there is always another daughter to be properly married off. While men pay brideprice and contribute bridewealth, their families generally provide only a portion of this "fee," and then more commonly in families of higher status, where men are expected to marry at somewhat younger ages and generally to marry first cousins. After his first marriage, a man is on his own to generate the gifts and brideprice required for subsequent marriages. It is young girls who need adult support in the marriage system, and it is older women who must generate this support for them. A girl's social standing is determined by her father's position, yet individual women try to improve their daughters' social status by creating enough wealth for them to attract men of higher status, thus advancing the social standing of daughters through their own efforts.

Education and Economic Change for Women

In both rural and urban areas a girl's socialization into the world of work begins early. As noted, all girls are given child-care responsibilities early in life. From age five or six years girls receive gradually increasing responsibility; they engage in shopping, running errands, and delivering messages for their mothers; escort women on visits to other houses; sweep, help in the preparation of food, and in most homes, sell food on the streets. By nine or ten years they often are charged with the care of an infant. Girls learn early to be involved in these economic activities and that they are a part of a separate and private women's world. These activities do not involve men except as customers. Women's productive energies are centered in the household and as yet, in women's minds, are not translated into activity in the public domain; the goal is simply to ensure a good start in marriage for one's daughters. In this sense, education and work are not the obvious forerunners of emancipation for women in the short run, but they rather provide alternative means to a traditional end. "The limited profit that individual women amass is reinvested almost immediately in the very marriage system that defines their position in the first place" (Schildkrout 1982, 74). The means are shifting to reflect changes in the social reality of the outside world, but the immediate end remains the same—early marriage and significant *kayan daki* for girls.

As more and more girls go to school and as the level of their education rises, some girls may begin to enter the professions. The first Kano woman to enter a medical school (who was of Fulani descent and related to the "royal" family) began her internship in 1983. When more women undertake such careers, it is likely, given the value system of the society, that their income will continue to be seen as essentially their own. At the present time, the marriage ethic is so pervasive that it is not likely that women capable of earning independent incomes will think of this as an opportunity to live independent lives. "The expectations of adult female roles have not changed; school girls or those who have not attended school are all expected to marry, live in purdah, and bear children for their husbands" (Schildkrout 1979, 13). Perhaps, however, as more women are educated, they will begin to invest in productive enterprises, laying the foundation for economic self-sufficiency and providing alternatives to *karuwanci* (prostitution) should they desire to be unmarried.

This economic independence, should it become a reality, might begin to establish women in statuses of their own and thus create the foundations for social change that would affect the form of marriage relationships. Government policies that encourage education for women may prove more revolutionary in the context of Islam than overt challenges to the system proclaimed by radical, secular politicians.

Structural change may actually be occurring already as more and more children spend more and more time in school as a consequence of the introduction of universal primary education. As Schildkrout has described, women are highly dependent on children to carry cooked food, messages, and money back and forth between them and their customers as well as to help around the household. One explanation for the lower income of the more middle-class women in Kurawa and the higher income of the less well-situated women of Kofar Mazugal is the fact that greater numbers of children are in school in Kurawa and thus are not available to help their mothers in income-producing activities. Hence, the impact of girls' entering *boko* school is likely to be deeply felt by their mothers, who were dependent on them for transactions outside the home (Schildkrout 1978b, 1979, 1981, 1982). While women may suffer some deprivation of income due to the unavailability of children for work, it is also likely that this will force some women out into the visible economy in order to pursue their paid activities.

The determination to have an independent income is deep and longstanding, and married women are not likely to forgo it. One middle-aged widow in Kofar Mazugal was quite distressed that her adult sons would not permit her to work for a salary in a factory. She was articulate in explaining to the women around her the advantages of an assured wage income (Interview #8, Kano, January 28, 1982). At the present time there is a persistent belief among women in *kulle,* in both rural and urban settings, that a married woman must have a skill (*sana'a*) in order to establish herself as a respectable adult in the community. In Kano, the few women married to wealthy men who have not established a trade of their own are viewed as being selfish, lazy, and "useless" (Interview #16, Kano, October 25, 1982). The ethic that every adult should be in some way economically "useful" survives the adoption of *kulle* and seclusion for women. Educated girls are already insisting that they will live in *kullen zuci* instead of *kullen tsari.* Men do not expect their educated wives to work, although some modifications are being made in the way *kulle* is practiced by educated women. Among them, *kullen zuci* is becoming the norm rather than *kullen tsari.* Thus, education may be creating new expectations about both marriage and work that may require changes in the division of labor by age and sex and a consequent transformation of the family structure based on this division of labor. This will not occur by a direct challenge to Islam, and women will continue to play economic roles

When this picture was taken, this thirteen-year-old girl spent most of her time helping her mother sell cooked food. She was saving money to purchase the enamel bowls that made up most of her dowry, or *kayan daki,* for her imminent marriage.

and generate income while giving lip service to the myth of their total dependence on men.

Concluding Observations

At present (1985) there is often a self-limiting quality about women's economic activities. Women's perceptions of work are defined by their perceptions of domestic roles; their participation in the local labor market is conditioned by the peculiar demands of the female economy. Seclusion and physical separation of men from women has underscored clear economic separation. Seclusion gives food and shelter to women and permits them time to carry out their income-producing work. But it also means a low ceiling on returns and restriction of women to small-scale household trade. By engaging primarily in the exchange of cooked food, women are essentially "taking in each other's laundry"; nevertheless, it provides them with a floor, even if the ceiling is low. (For studies of rural women elsewhere and their work, see Hanger and Moris 1973; Haswell 1963; Hill 1978; Abdullah and Zeidenstein 1978.)

At the same time, Schildkrout has argued that by investing men's money for profit and by not cooking three meals a day for domestic consumption, women are freeing themselves from household routines in order to engage in paid activity (Schildkrout 1982). They are a part of a cash economy and contribute to the circulation of money while increasing it by their own productive labor. Thus, the ideal Islamic model of dependent, nonproductive women is already not an accurate depiction of reality, although this depiction has not been overtly challenged.

The study of Hausa women's money-making efforts points to several requirements characteristic of their work. It is, in every instance:

1. compatible with reproduction and care of children;
2. related to class (women married to wealthier men engage in the less labor-intensive efforts even if income generated is lower, or trade in high-cost goods purchased—or smuggled from—abroad);
3. independent of men's work;
4. considered an extension of domestic activities; and
5. concentrated in the least visible activities.

Urban/rural distinctions applicable elsewhere do not seem to apply to Hausa women. The obligations of men and women to each other, the sexual division of labor with men working outside and women working inside the home, the seclusion of women of childbearing age, the restriction of female enterprise to the home, and the role of children in working, selling, and carrying messages is the same in both urban and rural areas. In both settings there is an impressive cash orientation. Even in the poorest household, barter is not encouraged; even close kin exchange goods and services for money. Over a decade ago, Polly Hill noted that, "A woman who makes groundnut oil for sale is in business on her own account and there is nothing immodest about buying groundnuts from her husband at the market price, or buying oil from herself with her household money and selling to her sisters' and husband's families" (Hill 1972, 29).

The persistence of pre-Islamic West African values asserts itself in the ability of women to function as producers and traders within the domestic economy. This ability gives them some measure of control over their own lives, which is theoretically denied them within a life defined by Islamic values and injunctions. These values are deeply entrenched and survive dramatic structural change in the society.

At the same time, when women are primarily in the home, they are indeed a conservative force, for their world is mostly family and children. The household is subordinate to the society at large, and hence women confined to the household are subordinate. In Kano women work for incomes, but only from inside seclusion. They have no public role in production. And, their incomes are used to perpetuate the very marriage system which stresses their dependence on men for basic support.

RELIGION

In religion also, women preserve an amount of autonomy that belies their totally subordinate status. The pre-Islamic cult of the Bori, which thrived until the introduction of Islam into the Hausa states, remains a formidable presence and the particular province of women practitioners (Greenberg 1966). In Bori, spirits (*iskoki*) reveal themselves through human beings whom they have chosen or selected. Those chosen are summoned by appropriate drum rhythms as the spirits possess them; spectators can speak directly with the *iskoki* through the one possessed, and individuals can approach the spirits separately with their needs.

Women especially turn to Bori to ward off or discover causes of misfortune in their lives, to act against a foe, or to ensure success in some enterprise. Failure to bear desired children, fear of the arrival of a co-wife or jealousy toward a new one, severe, chronic or undiagnosed illness, or the anticipation or experience of the loss of a husband's regard are among the plights commonly brought to Bori. In return for cash, goods, or animals meant for sacrifice, the Bori priestess aids the supplicant with information, supernatural protection, or other required assistance.

After the Fulani jihad, the *mallams* became both spiritual and temporal advisors to the emir and were critical in determining what of traditional Hausa culture was acceptable to Islamic practice and what was not (Greenberg 1946, 64). The effectiveness of the Bori *iskoki* was not denied by the *mallams;* rather, they were identified with the (pagan) evil spirits condemned by Islamic doctrine. Bori was thus simultaneously condemned and lent added credibility in Hausa society (Greenberg 1946, 69–70). Today's *mallams* continue to assert that a sick person appealing to the *iskoki* might recover, but that Allah "does not like it that way" (Interview #16, Kano, October 25, 1982).

It is clear that belief in non-Islamic supernatural beings has survived the adoption of monotheistic religion.

Of the nearly 300 women in Kano interviewed by the author in the course of this study in the early 1980s, all claimed to be devout Muslims and all acknowledged the existence or continuing importance of Bori, though all claimed to believe Bori and Islam to be antithetical. None of the women suggested that they themselves participated in Bori, but all knew women who did. It was widely claimed that "most" women turn to Bori in times of crisis.

The women who practice Bori publicly, *'yan kwarya,* are both ridiculed and respected in Kano. The existence, hold, and power of Bori are acknowledged, but its legitimacy is denied, and its practitioners stand on the lower rungs of the social ladder; its presence might be described as "muted." While it is asserted that "true Muslims" would not practice or participate in Bori, it is also asserted that women in the highest reaches of the society do so. Because Bori was originally associated with the emir's palace, today's practitioners are said to have a personal interest in and understanding of local power relationships and hence to be effective in dealing with their manifestations. In early Bori, religious and political power were linked. Thus, it is not surprising that today's spiritual descendants of the pre-Islamic early Bori cult should preserve an interest in the trappings of local power. It was commonly believed by the women interviewed that Bori is practiced in the emir's palace; this perceived sanction by the most revered of traditional institutions gives it a special legitimacy outside the accepted norms of the society.

Perhaps more dramatically than any other readily acknowledged force, the practice of Bori represents a form of confrontation between the wholly male structure of Islamic society and a submerged traditional system that allowed a more active role for women. Bori has officially been banned by the emirs in the respective emirates, yet it is tacitly accepted as a nonlegitimate but flourishing activity, even within the walls of the emirs' palaces themselves. Women in the palace of the Emir of Kano claim that no Bori is practiced there, but admit that women in the palace will turn to Bori in times of crisis; since women in the palace cannot normally go out, any such appeal in fact would have to occur within its walls.

Bori is not seen exactly as a religion—it is viewed as separate and distinct from religion, yet it involves the interference of the spirits, of the supernatural, in the human world. It is essentially a spirit possession cult practiced by those who have been dispossessed by Islam, by the spiritual descendants of women who are aware, at some level, that they have lost a place they formerly had in the upper echelons of traditional religion. Bori offers a means by which the socially deprived and politically powerless women of this society may expect amelioration of their grievances. In short, it offers women access to a source of power not available to them in the public social, political, or religious order.

The thriving existence of the Bori cult in a society that proclaims itself devoutly Islamic and its practice primarily by women who claim to accept devoutly the "Islamic way of life" highlight some of the muted, but nonetheless potent, forces at work in the world of Hausa women.

Ironically, then, one area in which women have maintained some modicum of influences in spite of the jihad is in the area of religion itself—albeit a kind of underground religion—Bori. Bori is now submerged, but it coexists as a kind of unofficial religion that predates Islam and provides an alternative source of help in times of trouble. Islam did not totally displace or replace Bori. Historically, "the *bokaye* (Bori priests and priestesses) came to share power with the *malamai* (Muslim teachers) and the *Sarki* (chief or Emir) came to occupy an uneasy position as leader of both groups" (M. G. Smith 1955, 197). Women were the guardians of Bori ceremonies, rights, and rituals and symbolized the fertility of the earth and the fortunes of the community. Belief in women's supernatural and extraordinary ritual powers lent them status and influence in other spheres, so that a symbiotic relationship existed between the status of Bori and the power and influence of women. With the adoption of Islam, Bori was relegated to a subordinate status; but both women and men continue to turn to it for assistance in times of stress or when special good fortune is needed. Nonetheless, as Islam became entrenched, so the public standing of the Bori priestesses diminished until, for all practical purposes, it disappeared. As Bori became a sub-rosa court of last resort, its priestesses came to be drawn not from royal lineages, but from among nonconformist women, often referred to as *karuwai,* or "free women" (Hill 1972, 279).

4

Politics in Kano

Bringing Women into the Polity

POLITICS IN KANO: BACKGROUND

Women in Kano voted for the first time in 1979. But appropriate roles for women, both public and private, have long been a theme in modern Kano politics. For more than thirty years, three interrelated factors have defined Kano politics and the place of women in it: Islamic concern with the nature of politics, the leadership of Mallam Aminu Kano, and the particular nature of radical politics in Kano.

In spite of five military coups d'état, two civilian republics, and a civil war, politics in Nigeria has remained remarkably consistent over the twenty-four-year period since the country gained its independence from the British in 1960. Five prominent political leaders, who participated in the first pre-independence elections in 1952 and 1954, continued to serve as leaders of their parties in the 1960 and 1964 independence and postindependence elections. Three of them continued to lead their parties in the elections of 1979 and 1983 when the country made a second attempt at civilian rule. These three leaders, Nnamdi Azikiwe, Obafemi Awolowo, and Aminu Kano, each led one of Nigeria's five major political parties in 1960 and each led one of the five parties in 1979 and six parties in 1983 recognized by the Federal Electoral Commission. Thus Nigeria has had remarkable stability of political leadership in spite of considerable instability in the political history of the country.

For over three decades, politics in Kano were dominated by one personality—Mallam Aminu Kano. More than any other Nigerian politician, he is associated with concern for the rights of women. A brief review of Kano politics and the career of Aminu Kano will provide a context for evaluating politics as a road of emancipation for women.

After thirteen years of military rule, Nigeria returned to civilian government and free elections in 1979. The presidential election fell to the National Party of Nigeria (NPN), an expanded version of the old Northern People's Congress (NPC), which itself had first been elected to national power in 1960. Like its predecessor, the NPN built upon a base of northern traditional elites and modernist members of an emerging class composed of administrators, military officers, members of the professions, and businessmen. By expanding upon its northern base and appealing to these elements across Nigeria, the NPN had managed to transform itself from a regional into a truly national party representing the interests of an emerging bourgeoisie. Two original leaders of the old NPC, the Sardauna of Sokoto, Sir Ahmadu Bello, and the former prime minister, Sir Tafawa Balewa, were killed in the first military coup of 1966, but the core leadership of the reformulated party, now the NPN, remained predominantly with northern elites (Diamond 1982, 631–34).

Three of the remaining four parties participating in the 1979 election were the creation of political leaders of the 1950s and 1960s; though the party names were new, their positions were familiar. Dr. Nnamdi Azikiwe, the first president of Nigeria[1] and the leading politician, continued to lead an eastern-based party representing the commercial and ethnic interests of the people. Chief Obafemi Awolowo, the founder of the Yoruba-based Action Group in the 1950s and the leader of the opposition in the First Republic, continued to head a party based in the three states comprising the former Western Region of Nigeria; like the Action Group, it advocated a liberal/socialist ideology. The divisiveness of politics in the old Action Group areas was healed when Awolowo was proclaimed "father of the Yoruba" and his Unity Party of Nigeria (UPN) became virtually the only party in Yorubaland.

In the far north, Mallam Aminu Kano rebuilt the old Northern Elements Progressive Union (NEPU) as the People's Redemption Party (PRP) and continued to represent the radical sentiments of northern common people and to challenge the established authority of the northern elite. In the 1950s and 1960s, NEPU had been an exclusively northern party in alliance with a southern party (NCNC). In its emergence as the PRP, it aspired to a national base, looking for support among the more radical sectors of the Nigerian electorate. But, despite its efforts and like the NEPU two decades before it, the PRP remained essentially Kano-based (although it did win the governorship, but not the legislative elections, in Kaduna State, which surrounds Kano to the north and the south). The party boasted only negligible leadership and electoral strength outside Kano and Kaduna states. In 1979 and again in 1983, Mallam Aminu Kano's PRP, resisting the national pattern in which the regional parties continued to dominate the states under their control, won both the local and national elections in Kano State.[2]

Over the course of the past twenty-five years, the dynamics of politics in Kano have continued to reflect the same alignment of forces that emerged from the 1960s. The leadership of Mallam Aminu Kano continued to be credited by the common people with setting the tone and substance of opposition and radical politics until his sudden death in the spring of 1983. Despite his death, his party went on to win the elections that summer in Kano State (although it should be noted that all election results in 1983 were questionable) (Diamond 1984, 910–12).

The origins of political parties in northern Nigeria centered around Kano, the largest city in the largest traditional state of the north and the city increasingly recognized in the twentieth century as a seat of Islamic learning. Politics in Kano differed qualitatively and substantively from politics elsewhere in the country. The themes were often religious and class-based, rather than ethnic or inter-ethnic. It was in Kano that the largest nonlocalized northern political society was formed in 1946–the Northern Elements Progressive Association (NEPA). The word "progressive" came to be synonymous with radical politics in northern Nigeria from this point on.

From 1946 on, an impressive connection endured between the leaders of the radical position in northern politics and membership in a family of *alkali* (judges in Islamic courts) and *mallams* and imams (scholars who study Islamic law). Radical politicians routinely employed Qur'anic justifications for their concerns and actions; Sa'adu Zungar, the most learned Qur'anic scholar of his time in the north, and Aminu Kano, a Qur'anic scholar and son of the scribe to the chief *alkali* judge of the Sharia Court in Kano, were the most prominent leaders of the NEPA (Whitaker 1970, 329–31). Perhaps part of the explanation of this phenomenon is to be found in the fact that prior to the 1950s, very little "Western" education was available in the north and the only learned men were Islamic scholars and teachers. In 1947, only 251 northern students were enrolled in Nigerian secondary schools—only 2.5 percent of the total. In 1951, out of a total of approximately sixteen million people in northern Nigeria, there was only one university graduate—Dr. A.R.B. Dikko, a member of a Fulani family in Zaria who converted to Christianity and was educated in England by the Christian Missionary Society (Coleman 1960, 132–40). The only other northerners with postsecondary training were four men (including Mallam Abubakar Tafawa Balewa, the future prime minister) sent to London in 1945 for a two-year course of professional teacher training and a second group of four sent in 1946, which included Mallam Aminu Kano (Sklar 1983, 90–91).

NEPA membership consisted primarily of a small number of educated young men working in the public service in the north. They were either discharged or transferred from their positions by the colonial government shortly after the founding of NEPA, which collapsed as a result. After the NEPA's demise, a less overtly political organization was formed in Kano in December 1949—the forerunner of the NPC, the Jam'iyyar Mutanen Arewa (Northern Peoples Cultural Society). Both Mallam Sa'adu Zungar and Mallam Aminu Kano spoke at the organizational meeting of this "cultural society." Aminu Kano raised what was to become a continuing concern of his political career, the eligibility of women for membership in the organization. This became the most contentious piece of business of the organizational meeting and continued to be a major and controversial matter in northern politics. At this same meeting, Sa'adu Zungar, who was the Government's official advisor on Islamic law, was called upon to express a ruling consistent with such law. Zungar ruled in favor of membership for women, citing arguments used by Shehu Usman dan Fodio when he permitted women into his classes during the period of the jihad (Sklar 1983, 93).

In August 1950, a group of eight radical youths formed the first official and publicly recognized political party in the north in Kano—the Jam'iyyar Neman Sawaba (Northern Elements Progressive Union or NEPU). Aminu Kano was not a member of the founding group, as he had just returned from his teacher-training course in London and was serving as the chief education officer in Sokoto Province, where he was acting headmaster of the Sokoto Teacher Training College. He resigned his position three months later and assumed the leadership of NEPU, which he held until the military coup of 1966. While NEPU originally was organized as a political wing or vanguard of the Jam'iyyar Mutanen Arewa, under Aminu Kano's leadership it soon staked out its position as the party of the "dispossessed," the *talakawa* (commoner class), and as the advocate of the rights of women. The traditional leaders and the emirs of the north promptly branded these positions as "dangerously radical." The moderate leaders of the NPC agreed that the radicals must be eliminated if it was to survive as the dominant organization in the north in the approaching era of party politics and democratic elections. At the second annual convention of the NPC, held in Jos in December 1950, a resolution was passed barring NEPU members from continuing in the NPC. At this point the NEPU Kano delegation walked out of the convention and broke with the NPC, a division in public leadership in Kano that endures to the present day. In October 1951, the NPC announced that it too was now an official political party (Sklar 1983, 96). This division of political loyalties set the context of northern Nigerian politics from 1951 through the elections of 1983.

Thus, from 1950 through 1983 there were essentially two political parties in Kano, the NPC-NPN and NEPU-PRP (although during the periods of military rule, parties were officially banned). NEPU-PRP advocated immediate adoption of a system of direct democracy with universal adult suffrage, including the enfranchisement of women, to replace the old, traditional class-based and hierarchical structures upon which the British had tried to build and which the NPC had protected, preserved, and expanded upon. Throughout this period, the leader and spokesperson of the party was Mallam Aminu Kano.

It is most relevant to note at this point that from the beginning of his political career, Aminu Kano was widely regarded as a religious as well as a political leader, and hence in Kano he was universally referred to as "Mallam." Mallam's family, part of a clan (the Genawa) known for the Islamic juristic learning of its men, enjoyed substantial status in Kano. His mother, who herself had a Qur'anic education (a most unusual accomplishment for a woman), taught him the beginning of the *Qur'an* and initiated his study of Arabic (Feinstein 1973, 35). Aminu Kano felt strongly about his mother and the limitations defined for her life by Hausa society. It was to her memory that he dedicated his lifelong effort to improve the status of women, stressing education and their full participation in the polity (Interview #46, Kano, April 14, 1982).

Mallam Aminu Kano was trained as a scholar, schooled in Islamic law, and educated by the British, both in Nigeria and in London (1946–1948). While a schoolboy in Nigeria at the Kano Middle School, Kaduna College, and the Katsina (teachers) Training College, Aminu Kano was well-known for his deep commitment to Islamic teachings, his politically caustic poetry, and his reading and writing of satirical plays containing thinly veiled ridicule of the pompous postures of traditional emirate rulers. Upon his return from London in 1948, he entered the administrative service, where he worked until 1950, when he resigned in order to devote himself full time to politics.

Aminu Kano was modernist and progressive in his practice of Islam. An early and lifelong advocate of female education and the full political emancipation of women, he had written all of his term papers while in London on "The Problem of Girls' Education in Kano." In 1956 he published articles on the status of women in Nigeria in the *Nigerian Citizen:* "It is impossible to promote the status of women and men (I now like to say women and men) in this twentieth century while maintaining this medieval form of government" (quoted by Paden 1973, 288, and Sklar 1983, 101). For his running mate in the 1983 presidential elections, he chose the first Nigerian woman nominated for high national office, Mrs. Bola Ogunbo, a sixty-nine-year-old successful businesswoman from Bendel State (*Sunday Times,* September 4, 1983). (She remained on the PRP ticket after Aminu Kano's death in the spring of 1983, but the revamped ticket, no longer bearing Aminu Kano's name, failed to win a single state in the presidential election.)

Other than the three years he served as a federal commissioner in the military regime of 1967–1975, Aminu Kano remained a rebel in Kano society who provided spiritual and political leadership to the dispossessed, the poor, and the radicals of northern politics. He never accumulated personal wealth, living all his life among the common people of Kano City. At his death, his compound immediately became a place of prayer.

Another significant aspect of Kano politics is the importance of class. Like all the Fulani-dominated emirates, Kano is a genuine class society. The transition from feudal government to colonial administration involved no transfer of privilege or prestige from the traditional ruling class to the depressed class of commoners (see Whitaker 1970). Government service was dominated by the sons of noble families and by members of families bound to them in customary service or dependent upon them as "faithful retainers." The introduction of democratic forms of representation did not alter the fact that high traditional elite class standing was normally an unstated but understood prerequisite for nomination to a political position by the dominant party (the NPC).

While class divisions in the society are clearly recognizable, class loyalty is considerably less clear cut. The ambiguous position of traders and merchants is indicative. After about 1958 an increasingly large class of wealthy merchants (*attijirai*)—an occupation traditionally barred from high status—was allied politically to the noble or nobility-related politicians. Their role and influence in the NPC became greater as politics at the national level became increasingly concerned with control of the country's wealth and the distribution of its resources. Their eventual ascendency in the NPC is perhaps best indicated by the defeat of Aminu Kano in the 1956 parliamentary elections by Ahmadu Dantata, a son of the richest merchant family in Kano (Whitaker 1970, 333). However the merchants remained *talakawa* (commoner class) despite their wealth; and partly as a result they maintained populist social attitudes, continuing to identify with the needs of the common people and, in accordance with Islamic prescriptions, remaining relatively generous concerning the needs of their neighborhoods. Their influence and position in the NPC (and later in the NPN) was sufficient to countervail the NEPU (and PRP) appeal to *talakawa* values. The *attijirai* also have been notoriously reactionary in regard to both women's education and enfranchisement. Their close affiliation with the NPC/NPN and ties to the *talakawa* have not benefited women's progress in either domain.

For many commoners, grateful acknowledgement of *attijirai* generosity requires political loyalty to their allies. Thus, it has become a paradox of the northern social scene that class consciousness actually mitigates the intensity of the modern class struggle. In Kano, the affluent business community and the traditional nobility and their retainers are tied together in opposition to radical populist movements as represented by the NEPU and PRP, but large segments of the *talakawa,* to whom the latter appeal, remain loyal to the traditional elite through continued traditional ties and obligations.

It it a well-known axiom that mass political parties often draw their leaders from above the class of the rank and file of the party (Michels 1962, 85–114). In the 1950–1966 era NEPU had no real organization in the rural areas of Kano State and thus represented more of a "movement" than a political party, to use Hodgkin's terminology (Hodgkin 1956, 141–45; 1961, 50–56). As did many other early African political parties (the CPP in Ghana, the PDG in Guinea, the PDCI in Ivory Coast), NEPU depended upon the charisma of its leader, a man of high traditional class standing, to attract commoners to its banner. Other than the leader and his personal lieutenants, the party had no organization. In other words, in spite of its rhetoric, the party did not present a vehicle for social mobility. The sources of both its support and its leadership were peculiarly problematic in Kano due in part to the nature of Islamic political beliefs and in part to the class configuration of Hausa-Fulani society. *Mallams,* who would normally be expected to follow the leadership of Aminu Kano, often held back because of pressure brought by the parents of their students; the parents themselves were often pressured by emissaries of the emir, to whom they owed fealty, to withdraw their children from the schools of *mallams* associated with NEPU. Since the *mallams* were dependent on contributions from their students or their students' families for their livelihood, their alternatives, thus, were to disassociate themselves from NEPU or forgo their means of livelihood. As a consequence, NEPU was deprived of its most effective leadership base in the rural areas. While Mallam (Aminu Kano) was clearly personally popular, his party had difficulty organizing and winning elections. Both its leadership, aside from Mallam himself, and its supporters lacked concrete identification, a perceived place in the society over the long run. And, in spite of Mallam's longstanding advocacy of female emancipation, his followership lacked any enthusiasm for the issue.

ISLAM AND POLITICS IN KANO

The themes of northern politics as developed by Aminu Kano and others were often both religious and class-based. The north was striking for its lack of ethnic politics; the Fulani conquest and domination of the Hausa was never an overt theme in the political relationship between them. In contradistinction to southerners, who tended to identify themselves on the basis of ethnicity first and then nationality and perhaps religion, the primary source of identity for all non-Christian northern politicians was first as Muslims and then as northerners. They saw themselves as members of an Islamic world governed by universal Islamic teachings. The rhetoric of Aminu Kano was characterized by Islamic themes—especially justice and equality—rather than ethnic or tribal themes. "We believe that there is no other form of equality than Islam, pure Islam. Equality in Arabic means dignity" (Aminu Kano quoted in Paden 1973, 288).

Explicitly religious concepts of political authority and community have been important in Kano from the time of Muhammad Rumfa (acknowledged as the first Muslim emir) onward. This legitimation of the emirate structure in terms of Islamic religious doctrines dates from the time when Hausa emirs converted to Islam (late fifteenth century) and was reinforced by the jihad of the early nineteenth century. The first written treatise on Islamic government was addressed to Emir Muhammad Rumfa in the late fifteenth century by Muhammad b. 'Abd al-Maghili of Tlemsen, a learned man associated with a trans-Sudanic caravan. This work, *Risalat al-Maluk,* was translated by T. H. Baldwin as *The Obligations of Princes: An Essay on Muslim Kingship* (1932). The essay, commissioned by Rumfa, exhorts the emir to follow sacred law, confirming its precepts and principles. "Verily, kingly power is a vice-regency from God and stewardship from God's apostle" (*Obligations,* 3–4, quoted in Paden 1973, 214–15, and discussed by Hiskett 1963, 15). Al-Maghili's treatise establishes the interrelationship between legal, political, and religious systems in Islamic government and provides an ideological foundation for perceptions of legitimate government in Kano.

At the beginning of the nineteenth century, Abdullahi dan Fodio, one of the leaders of the Fulani jihad and the brother of Shehu Usman dan Fodio, composed a four-volume work, quoting liberally from al-Maghili, on the nature of legitimate Islamic government (dan Fodio 1961).

Muslims contend that Islam advocates a political system characterized by two features: a) that the state be judged in terms of its provisions for social welfare, popular participation, justice, and human rights; b) that Sharia laws be fully implemented within the established constitutional framework. That there might be a conflict between secular notions of justice and human rights and those of Sharia law is not considered a legitimate observation. Islamic scholars emphasize that the purpose of the Islamic state, as opposed to the secular state, is not simply to provide for political administration under Islamic concepts of the rights and obligations of the people; rather, the purpose of the Islamic state is "to seek qualities of purity, beauty, goodness, virtue and prosperity which God wants to flourish—exploitation, injustice, disorder in the sight of God are to be suppressed and prevented" (Mawdudi

1976, 9). At Bayero University in Kano in 1983, 637 of 686 students believed an Islamic state was inherently superior to a secular state.[3] In an Islamic state, they too believe, "truth, honesty, and justice flourish over material considerations" (Mawdudi 1976, 9).

As the NPC, and to a lesser extent the NPN, also identified themselves with Islam, religious themes retained their powerful underlying place in the politics of northern Nigeria. Both the NPC (and NPN when addressing an exclusively northern audience) and the NEPU/PRP claimed to represent the consensus of the society, the Islamic *umma,* and asserted that not to accept this consensus was in fact heretical and un-Islamic. In addition to 'Abd al-Maghili, Nigerian *mallams* adhere to the teachings of Al-Gazali, an Islamic scholar of the twelfth century who postulated that for all practical purposes the caliphate (the Islamic state) contains only the sultan (or caliph) and the ulema (*mallams* or scholars). The people may disobey or rebel against the caliph when such action is sanctioned by the ulema. In normal circumstances, however, no Muslim should draw the sword against a fellow Muslim, and disruption of public peace is viewed as a serious act (Binder 1955). The words of the Prophet are quoted: "The hand of God is upon the Community, and he who sets himself apart from it will be set apart in Hell-fire. He who departs from the community by a handspan ceases to be a Muslim" (quoted by Jalingo 1980, 23). Only Allah is sovereign, but rulers on earth deserve support as long as they are faithful to the ways of Allah (Jalingo, 8). Muslims believe there should be maximum popular participation in the election of leaders, who can only be deposed for oppression and corruption. Obedience to a ruler on earth who does not himself "obey" Allah is not required (Gibb 1962, 151–65). Thus, while the established northern governments (both pre- and postindependence), dominated by the descendents of the Fulani jihad leaders, characterized themselves as appropriately representative of the community (*umma*), the radical politicians in opposition stressed the corrupt, oppressive, and therefore unholy nature of the traditional Fulani government (Jalingo 1980, 8–12).

Islamic teachings do inspire Muslim reformers, and the history of Islam is replete with religious reformations and jihads (holy wars). Much of the history of Islam is, as a matter of fact, a history of continuing struggles between radical and conservative authoritative interpretations of doctrine (Hodgkin 1980, 1972). While never a focus of specific struggles, various reforms have addressed, in passing, the inequalities experienced by women in Islamic societies.

In its attack on the NPC and the power of the traditional leaders in that party and its government, NEPU argued that present-day Fulani rulers had betrayed the Islamic ideals set down by dan Fodio at the time of the jihad and attempted to place the stamp of Islamic approval on its own political program. The radicals in that party and later in the PRP stressed the implication of Islamic concepts of government, especially the values of justice and egalitarianism. Their speeches and poetry habitually employed religious allusions and justifications; during the 1960s, NEPU was well-known for its apocalyptic language and parables depicting its eventual deliverance of the masses from oppression and the eternal damnation of its opponents. In the later 1970s and early 1980s, the PRP increasingly emphasized Islamic themes of equality and justice, casting itself as the party opposing class privileges and class-based domination.

In this way, a consistent theme of NEPU/PRP politics was an ideological attack on the entire emirate structure, including the political position (or nonposition) of women. Reiterating and expanding upon the Islamic concepts of "freedom," "jihad," and "justice," Aminu Kano made the position of women an early and basic concern of the party. While in the 1950s and 1960s he and his colleague, Isa Wali, were virtually alone in addressing this issue, by the late 1970s and 1980s this subject had become part of the PRP's party platform. The PRP remained, however, the only Nigerian party to address the issue.

In its 1979 platform the PRP pledged to "introduce legislation to abolish child marriages; to give protection to all women married under all laws; and to ensure that both male and female children have equal rights in education and opportunities" (People's Redemption Party 1979b, 24). By contrast, the NPN party platform of 1979 did not mention women (National Party of Nigeria 1979). In 1983, the NPN party platform asserted only that "the NPN regards the woman as the 'Mother of the Nation' and as the teacher of the child. The Party is therefore committed to the moral, mental, educational and social upliftment of our womenfolk" (NPN 1983).

Aminu Kano saw himself as helping people to define Muslim responsibilities in times of great social change and used the *Qur'an* to define orientations toward authority (the sovereignty of God vis-à-vis temporal authority) and community (what it means to be a Muslim) (Paden 1973, 299). In a speech at Bayero University in December 1982, he quoted the *Qur'an* to the effect that "And their business is [conducted] through consultation among themselves," and argued that "According to this principle, the right of every Muslim is that he should have a direct say in the affairs of the state or a representative chosen by him or her" (Convocation Address, Bayero University, Kano, December 4, 1982). The *Qur'an* is regarded as the basis of Islamic life and provides the paradigm of values, historical interpretations, and orientations toward authority and community to be followed by all Muslims. Its teachings are made clear both through revelation and through interpretation by Islamic scholars. Thus, the connection between a radical leadership position in modern politics and membership in a family of *alkali, mallams,* and imams, is not surprising: such religious leaders are the only recognized interpreters of Islamic law and its moral and spiritual values. The *alkali* (judges) are concerned with the exposition of the Sharia and the doctrines derived from the *Qur'an,* and as such, can present the only legitimate criticisms of the Islamic state. These interpretations also may be given by *tafsir mallams* (*mallams* who have mastered the *Qur'an*), who are generally recognized by the community as legitimate interpreters. Since part of the nature of reform is reinterpretation of the basic framework of society, Islamic scholars engaged in reevaluating the nature of government are often trained as *tafsir mallams.* Aminu Kano, Sa'adu Zungar, and Isa Wali, three early leaders of the NEPU, were all trained and recognized as *tafsir mallams.* Aminu Kano regularly gave *tafsir* readings during Friday afternoon prayers in Kano and during the fasting period of Ramadan. *Tafsir* readings do not make specific references to the contemporary political scene except under the most exceptional circumstances, but rather underscore certain principles of belief and action. *Tafsir* interpretations by Aminu Kano stressed the centrality of justice in Islam and its interpretation primarily in terms of equality. The NEPU and PRP ideological aspiration was a "radical" democracy in which principles of Islamic justice applied and in which the *talakawa* and their interests would be fairly represented. Aminu Kano was a "patrician radical" whose ideological and religious convictions led him to identify with the *talakawa;* his high ascriptive status was very important in mobilizing political support in a highly status-conscious society. His original attractiveness to young, self-proclaimed "radicals" in northern universities in the 1970s and 1980s was a function of his identification with the *talakawa* in spite of his traditional social standing.[4]

Of course, the manipulation of Islamic ideas and symbols was not confined to Aminu Kano's parties; both northern political camps engaged in it. A spokesperson for the NPC explained the relationship of his party to Islam this way: "Many people have been saying that religion is different from justice. . . . It is a well-known fact that religion and justice are the same. . . . We have been working with the *Holy Qur'an* which gives justice. . . . The constitution of authority and other important bodies have come from the *Qur'an* and what the *Qur'an* has brought is called religion and what is called religion is also called justice. It is God who ordained that there can be chiefs and rulers, that they should be respected and he has commanded them that whatever they do and say is the justice of Allah. . . ." (Paden 1973, 329, quoting Alhaji Junaidu, Waziri of Sokoto, Debates, Northern House of Chiefs, 1965).

Specifically Islamic organization and inter-Islamic divisions are also important in understanding the nuances of politics of Kano and the related intricacies of political support, as well as the historical irrelevance of women. Kano Muslims are Sufi; in Kano, two Sufi brotherhoods (Qadiriyya and Tijaniyya) are dominant. For most of the Islamic period in Kano, dating from the fifteenth century and reinforced by the Fulani jihad of the early nineteenth century, the dominant Islamic brotherhood was Qadiriyya. The Fulani jihad was a Qadiriyya effort and established Sokoto as the center of Qadiriyya in the central Sudan. During World War I, Emir Abbas of Kano converted to Tijaniyya, centered in Senegal under the leadership of Sheik Ibrahim Niass.[5] This fact symbolically represented the negation of Kano religious dependence on Sokoto (Whitaker 1970, 113; Paden 1973, 116). It is relevant to note that Tijaniyya is particularly popular in Kano also because its leaders resist Western education and believe that only through Arabic literacy and religious education can goodness be found. Thus, it is associated in particular with hostility to Western education, the English language, association with the West, and conservatism in regard to women, which in part explains the lack of non-Islamic education in Kano.

In the 1950s, "reformed" Tijaniyya had become the dominant brotherhood in Kano, its position enhanced by the public and official endorsement of the emir, Muhammad Sanusi. His demise in 1963 was engineered by the Sardauna of Sokoto, a member of the Sokoto royal hierarchy, premier of Northern Nigeria from 1952–1966, and president of the NPC. The Sardauna (Sir Ahmadu Bello) had become increasingly concerned with the political ambitions of the emir of Kano (Whitaker 1970, 279–82). Emir Sanusi's predecessors had also converted to Tijaniyya, and although Tijaniyya membership grew rapidly, this was regarded as a personal, not a public matter. In contrast, Sanusi had used his office to increase the status and authority of the brotherhood. Kano became a base for Tijaniyya growth in Nigeria, and this had political repercussions vis-à-vis Kaduna and Sokoto—the seat of northern government and the traditional religious center of the north respectively. Its leader, Ibrahim Niass, visited Kano in 1962, and Emir Sanusi subsequently married one of his daughters, thus emphasizing Kano's religious connections to Senegal rather than to Sokoto. Shortly after this event, the emir was investigated by the Northern Regional Government for "mal-administration" and subsequently deposed. In Kano, the endorsement of Tijaniyya by the royal family complicated the political situation since most of the NEPU followers were also by this time Tijaniyya. Hence, the emir was closely identified with the majority of common people in terms of religious affiliation, somewhat muting attacks on him and the traditional nobility by NEPU. Political alliances between the Kano Fulani ruling family and the *mallam* classes thus are complicated and add an unpredictable element to city politics because electoral support for NEPU and the PRP had an important religious as well as a class component.

The perception of Kano as the center of both radical politics and the Tijaniyya brotherhood in Nigeria was accented by the establishment of Abdallahi Bayero College (renamed Bayero University)[6] in Kano as a branch of Ahmadu Bello University (located in Zaria). The close ties of this university to the Fulani ruling class (both religious and political) was seen as an endorsement of Islamic learning at the university level in Nigeria. The leadership and student body of this university has been notably more conservative in terms of national concerns than those at other federal universities, but more radical in terms of the connection between religion and politics associated with Islam. The themes that "all civilization can be found in the knowledge of Islam" and that "Islam is a total way of life" are consistently repeated at university functions.

Islamic education has been a concern of political and religious leaders alike in Kano for the past several decades. The Northern Muslim Congress was established in Kano in 1950 for the purpose of upgrading and expanding Islamic schools and was strongly encouraged by Reformed Tijani *mallams* who advocated instruction in Arabic (rather than English, the language of Christianity) in all schools in Kano. Mallam Aminu Kano, the emir of Kano, and large merchant families all established schools that tried to graft Western education onto an existing Islamic one. Although English in fact did become the language of instruction in Kano, student leaders and faculty members in the Faculty of Arts and Islamic Studies at Bayero University strongly encourage the study of Arabic and the University requires it in certain curricula, such as law. Arabic is described as "the language of the Prophet" and hence, of true Islam. In sum, while class divides, Islam unites political actors in Kano. Women emerging from subordination and seclusion through education and politics must navigate these difficult straits.

The Islamic genesis of political themes, constantly reiterated in the language of politics, gives Kano politics a very distinct cast. This close association with Islamic themes on the part of both major political parties is relevant to the efforts after 1979 to develop public policies affecting women and to involve them in the political process. Clearly all such efforts must be justifiable by Islamic principles. With this background, the political involvement of women in Kano politics may better be placed in context.

WOMEN AND POLITICS: THE FIRST REPUBLIC

Islam recognizes basic human rights, including life, justice, minimum standard of living, and the equality of human beings regardless of race, color, or nationality (but not sex) (Mawdudi 1976, 36–37). Although they have never been invoked by women, human rights in Islam also include the right to protest government tyranny, the right to equality before the law, and the right to participate in the affairs of state: "God has promised to appoint those of you who believe and do good deeds as his representatives on earth" (*Qur'an* 24:55).

Beginning in the 1950s and for the next thirty years, NEPU/PRP rhetoric was phrased in terms of Islamic reform. Campaign themes centered around notions of equality, knowledge, literacy, political reform, and "modernization" (meaning Islamic reform, not development in the Western sense). (It is relevant to note that the emphasis was always reform rather than "revolution"; although Marxist themes were used in later years, the Marxist analogy was taken only so far. Radicals in Kano politics built upon the principles of the Islamic jihad, not Marxian revolution until recently [1983].) Equality was a notion extended to include women, but only insofar as Qur'anic interpretations allowed; NEPU's advocacy of education and political emancipation for women did not imply support for Western feminist concepts, and both men and women clearly understood this.

Aside from Mallam Aminu Kano, the public spokesperson most identified with concern for the status of women during the 1950s and 1960s was Mallam's colleague, Isa Wali, himself a respected student of Islamic law. In the summer of 1956, Isa Wali wrote a series of articles in the *Nigerian Citizen* that set the tone of debate on women's place in the polity for years to come:

> As for public life, there is nothing in Islam which prevents a woman from following any pursuit she desires. There is no distinct prohibition against her taking part in public leadership, as Aisha, the Prophet's widow, demonstrated. . . .
>
> When discussing the rights and scope given to women by Islam, I touched on some leading Moslem women, such as Aisha and 'The Mothers of the Believers,' the wives of the Companions of the Prophet, and their successors, who played a full and active part in public life, education and leadership in Moslem history. . . . Aisha . . . as a widow . . . turned her energies and talents more and more into political channels, until, for a time at least, she came to dominate the political situation with great spirit and energy (Isa Wali, quoted by Paden 1973, 290).

In a society in which deeply ingrained patterns of female subordination generally are believed to find sanction primarily in religious rather than secular prescriptions, any attempt at redefinition must also proceed on religious grounds. Both Aminu Kano and Isa Wali repeatedly challenged the near total exclusion of women from the public world by emphasizing that no Qur'anic text denied full political participation for women.

But, fundamental notions of social place are challenged in addressing this area of deeply ingrained social mores. "Being sensitive to some inner awareness of motivations attributable to socially submerged groups, it is difficult for men in dominant positions to avoid feelings of possible retribution from exploited segments of their own society. . . . The greater the political dominance of men over women, the greater the fear of women, and consequently the greater the need to maintain barriers securing the social status of men. Generally, the greater the exploitation of subordinate groups, the greater the social need to maintain external symbols of status differentiation" (Del Vecchio Good 1978, pp. 470–71). However, even as these and other reformers succeeded in introducing female equality as an accepted ideal in religious life, the daily lives of women moved, if anything, further from emancipation. Radical politics and progressive religious ideas continued to do battle with conservative and retrogressive notions of "right" concerning women's proper place. While exhortations for education and political emancipation of women were increasingly voiced, more and more women were moving more deeply into total seclusion in both rural and urban areas. This fact of life for Hausa Muslim women in Kano was reflected in developments at the national level in Nigeria.

Under Nigeria's first constitution after independence in 1960, women were not specifically granted the right to vote. The regional governments in the east and west immediately enacted legislation extending the franchise to women, but the NPC resisted it strongly. Addressing the National Assembly on March 25, 1965, Waziri Ibrahim stated: "We in the North are perfectly happy: our women are happy about their condition and I appeal to other members of the Republic to please leave us in peace. There is not a single Northern woman who has told anybody that she is unhappy. We know what is right for women and our men know what is right for themselves" (quoted in the *Sunday Times,* May 27, 1979). The premier of the north, then the president of the NPC, wrote in his autobiography, "Female suffrage is inimical to the customs and feelings of the great part of the men of this region" (Bello 1962, 223). NEPU, which advocated the female franchise, was never elected to power. Extending the franchise to women was labeled incompatible with the customs and feelings of the greater part of the population, and the low level of education among women in the north was cited by the regional government as an additional reason to hold back the vote from them. "The education of women must reach a far greater strength, and the number of properly educated women must be increased to many times the present number before the vote would be used to full advantage" (Bello 1962, 233). In the

First Republic representation was based on population, but in the north only half the population was allowed to vote.

Nevertheless, all political parties in Kano had "women's wings" affiliated with them during this time. The wings were organized by the parties and closely watched by them; membership was recruited by the men; financial support came from the party itself; the leadership and the central committee of the wings in both the NPC/NPN and NEPU/PRP were appointed by the party leadership. Women sometimes were permitted a representative on the party's executive committee.

Participation in the women's wings came to have a derogatory connotation. The women's wing of the NPC, in particular, existed primarily to provide "entertainment" at political rallies. It was popularly believed during this period that "only prostitutes are involved in politics" and, in fact, the head of the women's wing for this party was a rather well-known *karuwa,* meaning that she was a woman of questionable reputation in proper society (Interview #37, Kano, May 14, 1983). She herself asserts that she was "put in charge of the women" because she showed respect to the men and followed their orders well (Interview #33, Kano, May 8, 1983). Thus, the NPC, an antifeminist party, was able to involve women in politics by choosing well; proper deferential behavior exhibited by women not acknowledged by proper society was rewarded by appropriate responsibilities in the party.

There is little doubt that most of the women "involved" in party politics through providing entertainment (chanting, singing, and dancing at rallies) during the 1960–1966 period were from the ranks of the *karuwai.* As chapter one indicated, prior to the establishment of Islam as the dominant religion of this area, Hausa societies maintained traditional women's titles such as *magajiya* ("speaks for women") and *alkaliya* ("women's judge"). Where those titles continue to exist in Katsina and Daura they are empty and honorary, indicating no substantive functions. In Kano they have ceased to exist altogether. Thus, it is conjectured that women of strong character and personality who might in an earlier day have found a place for their energies and abilities often enter *karuwanci* in order to be independent of male control of their lives (Pitten 1979). The large number of women in *karuwanci* in Hausaland is seen as an impressive indicator of significant female struggle to achieve independence from male social and spatial control. However, the political significance of this large component of female deviance has not been exploited;[7] no effort to appeal directly to women as voters could be made.

In the absence of any substantive female role in the public sector, it was perhaps natural that political parties would turn to the only women not in seclusion for political support—the *karuwai.* Their chief function—in the NPC, virtually their sole function—was to turn out for demonstrations and rallies for the purpose of attracting voters and entertaining the crowds and the politicians themselves. The presidents and active members of the women's wings of both parties were all associated with the *karuwai;* this was so partly because husbands, even politicians, would not allow their own wives to be involved in anything so public as a political rally. For their part, the *karuwai* received many benefits from their association with the parties: most particularly, they got to travel at party expense, and since their function was to mingle among the crowds and provide amusement, they could presumably also conduct their own business.

Because women could not vote prior to 1979, women's wings of the party obviously were irrelevant to a (nonexistent) women's vote; they were simply an attraction to the male voting population that came to the rallies to listen to the oratory and watch the entertainment.

Of the political parties active in Kano, only the NEPU and its successor, the PRP, had genuine concerns about the role and social position of women and advocated public policies, especially education, for their welfare. But as we have seen, this advocacy was couched in the language of Islamic justice, not feminist revolution. In 1959 Aminu Kano supported the right of women to vote, and in 1979 his party, the PRP, promised to promote women in politics and to extend educational opportunities to them. Aminu Kano sponsored a school for women that operated in his home from 1952–1983; providing courses in handicrafts, machine sewing, Hausa, and basic English literacy, it offered little to encourage women to organize other women for political activism other than in support of Mallam himself.

The enfranchisement of women in 1976 so that they might vote in the 1979 elections opened up old controversies about women's participation in politics. NEPU and PRP leaders emphasized that seclusion did not necessarily mean that women should be excluded altogether from the political process. Isa Wali and Mallam Aminu Kano asserted that Nigerian women had suffered because of misinterpretations of the *Qur'an.* It was they, for example, who first made the point that four wives were sanctioned by the Prophet only if all of them were treated equally and that since this is beyond human capability, the *Qur'an* actually is not endorsing polygamy (Interview #46, April 14, 1982). Others among the "radicals" were careful to declare that the feminist movement per se was foreign and made it clear that reform was called for only according to Islamic teachings. Women's education was justified because of women's role in the family as the teachers of children and had nothing to do with abstract political rights or the capacities and ambitions of individual women. Any change in the position of women would have to be legitimated by the needs of the society and not by the rights of women, as such.

This point of view was ably illustrated in a widely distributed article written by Alhaji Shehu Galadanci, a member of an important Fulani family in Kano and at that time the vice chancellor of the University of Sokoto. Writing in 1971 during the period of military rule, Galadanci set the framework for expanding the education system to include girls and women. Like Aminu Kano, he stressed that seeking knowledge is commendable and obligatory for all Muslims and should not be limited to men only. "The *Qur'an* exalts those who have knowledge (not just men). Chapter 58, v. 11 states 'God will exalt those who believe among you, and those who have knowledge, to high ranks'" (Galadanci 1971, 6). "Women have heavy responsibilities as wives and associates of men, and secondly as mothers and trainers of younger Muslim generations" (9). Galadanci cited three examples that established Islamic sanction for the education of women: (1) that the Prophet had two educated wives, one of whom recorded 1,210 *hadiths* "direct from the mouth of the Prophet" and the other of whom was the custodian of the authentic Qur'anic manuscript; (2) in Nigeria, dan Fodio allowed women to attend his lectures and preachings; and (3) the two daughters of dan Fodio accomplished a high standard of Islamic education. As further evidence he cited dan Fodio's daughter, Khadijah, who wrote verse in Fulani concerning Maliki law and also an Arabic grammar "which is still used as a reference" (10). According to Galadanci, it is the Europeans who were responsible for the disappearance of learning among women in the North African Islamic world.

Galadanci also set forth the arguments that were to find their way into the PRP platform ten years later. He argued that in a good marriage, a husband and wife should have "compatibility and harmony in a standard of general knowledge and intelligence" and thus the same educational opportunities should be afforded both sexes. Girls in the north should be educated, but a great deal of emphasis msut be placed on teaching the "Islamic ways of life to girls so that they can provide a congenial Islamic environment at home and moral training for children" (Galadanci 1971, 9). This leading educator never advocated knowledge for women so that they might discover their own intellectual interests, but so they would be better Muslims, wives, and mothers in the Islamic way.

THE DEBATE ON THE SHARIA IN NIGERIA

In Kano, Islamic law has increasingly become a fundamental symbol of Muslim identity. The Native Courts Proclamation of 1906 authorized British colonial officers to establish Islamic courts, which in essence meant that the British recognized the authority of the emirs and the Islamic legal system as it had come to function after the jihad under the overall direction of Sokoto. This system remained substantively unchanged until the northern Nigerian legal reforms of 1959, which assigned four categories of law (criminal, land, subversion, and taxation) to the regional government and incorporated them into a civil law code that was, theoretically, legislated and secular. The Islamic legal code (Sharia) continued to apply to a fifth category of law; family law continued to be essentially religiously based on a part of the Islamic legal system left under the authority of the emirs. In the early 1960s, the emir of Kano played a leading role in defining the nature of Sharia family law and its application throughout the states of northern Nigeria. In the process he worked closely with a panel of Pakistani and Sudanese jurists, greatly increasing the sense of identity of northern Nigerian Muslims with the Islamic communities throughout the world. This strong sense of Islamic identity and its foundation in the preservation of Islamic family law culminated in contentious debates concerning the adoption of the 1979 Nigerian Constitution.

These debates occurred during the course of the Nigerian Constituent Assembly, which met in 1979 to ratify a draft constitution developed the previous year by a Constitutional Drafting Committee (CDC) appointed by the military government (Callaway and Schildkrout 1985). The Assembly nearly floundered over the issue of the creation in Nigeria of a Federal Sharia Court of Appeal that would review cases of Islamic law heard at the state level. The Constitutional Drafting Committee had included a provision for such a court in the constitutional draft. In the end a compromise was reached wherein the federal court of appeal would include judges versed in Islamic law, who would, when the occasion arose, form a subunit of the court in order to hear such cases. This compromise was reached, however, over the strong objection of the Muslim members of the Assembly, who walked out of the debates once the vote was taken. While these members eventually returned in order to vote on the final version of the constitution, their walkout severely threatened the success of the Assembly and highlighted the enormous tension generated between the Muslim and non-Muslim members over the issue of the proper role of Islamic law in a secular state (*Proceedings*).

It should be noted that in Nigeria, Muslims are not an absolute majority of the population (although they are a simple majority or the largest single religious community), but rather represent Nigeria's largest minority (Nigeria is approximately thirty-eight percent Islamic). Ten of Nigeria's nineteen states have Muslim majorities and thus would be governed by the Sharia.

During the course of the debates, several important issues were raised, including the proper relationship between sacred and secular law in general, the position of Islamic law in a secular state in particular, and the separation of Islamic "personal law" out of the general body of Islamic law.

While it was stressed in the debates that Islam is a "total way of life" and the Sharia sacred in its totality and not subject to change in order to suit changing social conditions, the Muslim members compromised in this instance, as they had with the British, in order to make a separate Islamic court system more palatable to non-Muslims. They argued that the Sharia courts would deal only with Islamic personal law, except where the parties concerned voluntarily submitted other issues to these courts, as provided under the provisions regarding "customary" law in the new constitution. Islamic law includes criminal law, law of contracts and property, land tenure and succession, and law of evidence and procedure. Islamic personal law was defined as:

a. "marriage, divorce, family relationships or the guardianship of an infant" (Section 242);

b. "any question of Islamic personal law" (Sec. 243);

c. "any question of Islamic personal law regarding an infant, prodigal or person of unsound mind" (Sec. 241(4)).

The final version of the constitution as promulgated into law established a Sharia Court of Appeal in each of Nigeria's ten Islamic states (*Constitution,* Sec. 240 (1)). The grand kadi (chief justice) of such courts and the number of *kadis* in each state are prescribed by the state houses of assembly (*Constitution,* Sec. 240(2)) and must have considerable experience or be distinguished as scholars of Islamic law (Sec. 241 (3)).

The Constitution makes it clear that marriage laws are under the jurisdiction of the states. Thus, for Islamic women, matters that most deeply affect them—marriage, divorce, child custody—are not under the protection of the Nigerian Constitution but rather, under the sole jurisdiction of the states; in states with Muslim majorities, they are relegated to the Sharia courts. The appeal from these courts is not to higher secular courts, but to a subcommittee of the federal appeal court composed of Muslim men "learned in Islamic law."

Debate on this matter was most acrimonious and feelings on both sides ran high. However, concern for women's rights per se was not an issue, even though it was women who were most affected by the protections for Islamic personal law finally adopted in the Constitution. It is significant that although there were three women in the Constituent Assembly, none of them took part in the debates. Objections to the protection of the Sharia in the Constitution were based on arguments concerning the wisdom of establishing what was in effect a dual system of justice in a large part of the country. Serious reservations also were expressed about elevating Islam above other religions practiced in Nigeria by giving it a special place in the Constitution through the provision of the Federal Sharia Court of Appeal.

Advocates of the Sharia court pointed out, however, that in the ten Islamic states in the northern part of the country there were in fact already ten Sharia courts of appeal. If no Federal Sharia Court of Appeal were permitted, millions of Nigerians then would have no appeal beyond the state level (*Proceedings,* 2012–19).

Non-Muslims argued that they had nothing against the Sharia, but that they did not want a parallel court system enshrined in the Constitution; they argued that states could set up any court system they deemed appropriate under the Constitution. "Any State can set up any court of Sharia, if they wish to call it Sharia or native law and custom or any other name" (Mr. Garba-Matta in *Proceedings,* 2224).

It was also pointed out during the debates that the Sharia has been abolished in many Muslim countries with Muslim majority populations: for example, Egypt, which is 91.5 percent Muslim, abolished Sharia in 1956, and Turkey, which is 98.8 percent Muslim, abolished Sharia in 1924 (J.O.J. Okezie in *Proceedings,* 2038). Nonetheless, the Assembly voted a federal Sharia appeal procedure into the new Nigerian Constitution: "The President in exercising his power to appoint the Justices of the Supreme Court and the Federal Court of Appeal, shall include in his appointees persons learned in Islamic law and these persons shall sit and determine appeals relating to Islamic law" (*Constitution,* Sec. 150 (5)(ii); Sec. 180 (2)). The disadvantages to women of the Sharia was not among the concerns expressed by opponents of this measure, although it was also pointed out that only a Muslim judge could determine these matters and that the judge "must not only be male, he must also be of mature age" (*Proceedings,* 2020). The provision was passed on April 6, 1978. On April 8, the pro-Sharia "hardliners" walked out of the Assembly, thus threatening the whole proceedings. They contended that during the debates Islamic law had been denigrated.

It is pertinent to note that only that part of Sharia law most affecting women, personal law, was emphasized by the proponents of the Sharia in the debates and in the press. Although Islam is a "total way of life," and criminal, contract, and commercial law as well as family and social law are covered by the Sharia, as remarked by a Muslim member of the Assembly, "Moslems want only a few matters concerning Moslem Personal Law to come under this provision . . . marriage, divorce, will or succession, guardianship of infants, endowments and gifts" (Alhaji Garba Ja Abdulkadir in *Proceedings,* 2020). The subsequent assumption on the part of non-Muslim members that because these matters were few they were also trivial was instrumental in gaining passage for the Sharia provision, but also deeply offended the Muslim members. The reference to the nonimportant nature of the issue was made in a speech by Justice Udo Udoma, the chairman of the Assembly. Justice Udoma had said:

> There is nothing very important about it. After all it is about a right of succession of an average man and woman who is [*sic*] a Moslem: it is a right of marriage and dissolution of marriage which is open to the average Moslem, woman or man. The question of all these is to my mind, very, very minor. And I can assure you that I would be the last person to sit down and allow the reputation of Nigeria to be jeopardised because of what I consider a very minor question. . . . Let us not make ourselves a laughing stock because if people outside, beyond the boundaries of this country, were to hear that a galaxy of intelligent people who had gathered here were not able to decide reasonably, something dealing with this sort of matter I have been discussing, I think it would be a disgrace to Nigeria (Udo Udoma in *Proceedings,* 2047).

The chairman of the Assembly had been urging that the debate on the Sharia be concluded and the amended versions of the draft constitution dealing with the Sharia court of appeal be approved. In announcing the walkout, Alhaji Kam Salem stated explicitly that "we do not agree that any constitutional issue affecting the lives of millions of the citizens of any country can be said to be very, very minor. We also disagree that matters affecting the family or succession can be said to be of no importance" (Alhaji Kam Salem in *Proceedings,* 2077).

Thus, in order to insert provisions protecting Sharia law into the Constitution, the Muslims were willing to minimize the importance of the matters concerned, but when non-Muslims accepted this assertion at face value, it was clear that in fact Muslim men regarded these matters as of vital concern. In fact, by providing for the federal Sharia appeals procedure, the Nigerian Constitution enshrined an obvious conflict between law relating to women in the Sharia and the "Fundamental Human Rights" provisions found elsewhere in the Constitution. Section 11 (i) (a) states that "every citizen shall have equality of rights, obligations, and opportunities before the law." Yet, the provisions in the Sharia that render a woman's testimony equal to half that of a man or decree that her property rights are less than those of men, render a woman less than equal before the law. Section 11 (1) (b) of the Constitution states that "the sanctity of the human person shall be recognized and human dignity shall be maintained and enhanced," and (d) that "human exploitation in any form whatsoever shall be prevented." A clause in the draft constitution (Sec. 11 (2)) stated that "the provisions of paragraph (a) above shall not invalidate Islamic law." This clause was dropped from the Constitution while the Muslim members were absent from the Assembly, but in point of fact the protections provided for Islamic personal law preserve this contradiction in regard to the application of the "fundamental human rights" clauses to women who live under Islamic law.

It is not absolutely clear from the debates on the Sharia courts whether the concession that the courts deal only with personal law was a means of easing the compromise, or whether in fact family law was what Muslim men were most vitally and more or less exclusively concerned to protect.

In Hausaland, customary forms of behavior are accepted as Islamic injunctions, even where varying interpretations of Islamic law are possible. The position of Hausa women, which is more restricted even than it would be in most official Islamic states, is accepted by both men and women as being sanctioned by Islam. The legal system clearly is not a means through which to reform women's position since Hausa Muslim women are essentially under the jurisdiction of conservative Muslim judges. As noted above, some Muslim scholars are more liberal than others. According to the Grand Kadi of Kano State, however, legislation must be held within the limits prescribed by the law of the Sharia. "No legislation can alter or modify an injunction of God and his Prophet. The responsibility for determing the real intent of the Sharia must rest with people with specialized knowledge of the Sharia, with men learned in Islamic law" (Interview #15, Kano, June 21, 1982).

It is conceded that secular courts have great scope on questions not covered by the Sharia. Where the Sharia has jurisdiction, however, it is the sole earthly authority, for the judges are answerable only to God. "Judges are appointed by the Government, but once they occupy the bench, they administer justice according to the law of God" (Mawdudi 1976, 10, 19; 1960, ch. 6, sec. IV–VI).

In order to foster national integration in pluralistic countries such as Nigeria, uniform legal codes are applied throughout the society. The Nigerian Constitution is generally perceived as both democratic and secular, but the special position of Sharia law means that in actuality, Muslim men receive favored treatment and Muslim women are disadvantaged, Islamic laws of contract, criminal law and evidence are clearly superseded by Nigerian constitutional law, but there has been no outcry in the Islamic areas; these areas of law, too, are part of the immutable Sharia and the "Islamic way of life." It is only personal law that causes such passionate concern, although nothing in Islamic teaching suggests that it is more sacred than other parts of Sharia. We may speculate that a more fundamental and threatening anxiety is touched upon when personal law becomes an issue. In sum, Islam is a force for legal conservatism, particularly in the realm of family relationships and the consequent position of women.

It took a military decree in 1976 to extend the franchise to women in the northern states. The ban on politics was lifted by the military government on September 23, 1978. By the 1979 election campaign in preparation for the return to civilian rule, it was recognized that women would need to vote in the north to assure that the northern-based NPN would have the population base to assure its victory. Thus, the franchise was extended to all adults, male and female, in the 1979 Constitution. By then, both parties agreed on the importance of education for girls and on the necessity of women's right to vote. The traditional leaders of the old north, particularly the Sultan of Sokoto, as well as all the political parties, then urged women to register and vote, as this could be supported in Islamic law. Women in fact did register, and indeed more women than men voted in the 1979 elections in Kano State (Federal Electoral Commission, 1979, Kano State Returns).

Thus, Aminu Kano's program for reform for women was basically adopted. It is important to repeat that it was essentially defensible within an understanding of Islamic teachings. The rhetoric and continuing impact of Mallam Aminu Kano kept notions of Islamic justice and equality at the center of political debates. The dominant northern party, the NPC/NPN, was represented as having corrupted Islam; as part of Islamic reform, Aminu Kano advocated the extension of education for girls and the greater involvement of women in public affairs. By the time of the Second Republic, education had been extended to and for girls, and his party, the PRP, was able to implement programs for women and to appoint women to public positions as a means of demonstrating its commitment to greater involvement of women in public affairs.

5

Paths of Emergence

Parity in Politics

THE SECOND REPUBLIC: THE PRP COMES TO POWER

From 1966 to 1979 Nigeria experienced a succession of military regimes. It was the final military government of 1976 that took the first two dramatic actions affecting women in Kano in fundamental ways: implementation of Universal Primary Education (UPE) in 1976, and initiation of the process resulting in the promulgation of the 1979 Constitution, which enfranchised all adult Nigerian women.

In the 1979 elections, the People's Redemption Party (PRP) won the elections in Kano State, whereupon it began rewarding its supporters with contracts for state projects, such as wells, roads, and schools. Overnight a new social class of young contractors and businessmen dependent on government financial support for their ventures was created, adding a new social element to the party's base. Older, more established businessmen and the large class of Hausa merchants continued to be loyal to the government in power at the national level, the National Party of Nigeria (NPN).

The PRP drew its support from nascent middle-class groups and entrepreneurs—craftsmen, shopkeepers, tailors, butchers, and small traders. The Marxist ideology of the young PRP radicals, offering notions of a secular state and a class-based revolution, held little appeal for these men intent upon advancing within the system. Thus, the vision of the young radicals came to represent simply the language of protest rather than the real aspirations of the rank and file. Substantial businessmen were not interested in either radical or opposition politics and supported the NPN, the party of the federal government, which could offer them lucrative contracts and protection against competition from both southern Nigerians and foreigners. NEPU/PRP had couched its campaign in terms of Islamic reform. NPC/NPN also appealed to religion where appropriate, but its political style was essentially pragmatic and flexible, and it looked both to tradition and to the growing commercial class for help. The NPN successfully played upon the fear of southern domination, the belief in the superiority of northern traditional institutions, and the "responsible" nature of its membership. These themes overrode real class interest and division and certainly any concern about recently enfranchised women. The NPN was the party of the traditional ruling class, the members of the federal civil service, the business elite, laborers employed by firms dependent on government largesse, and those among the poor who lived on alms from the rich. Increasingly, also, it was becoming a party of a new bourgeoisie with national interests.

In northern Nigeria, unlike most other African countries and southern Nigeria, the transfer of power had not been to an indigenous political class of "new young men" long anticipating and preparing for it—i.e., in Nigeria, the southerners—but to the descendants of the precolonial Hausa/Fulani traditional ruling oligarchy and its strong allies, rich Hausa merchants and businessmen. This provided a somewhat unique aspect to Nigerian politics because a true elite class, which came to power in Lagos at the departure of the British, did exist in the north; and this class has been in power at the federal level, whether the government has been military or civilian, for the past twenty-five years. By 1979 this northern-based elite was again making alliances with an emerging southern business-oriented class, whose orientation was pragmatic rather than ideological. In contrast, the PRP was a regional party based on a populist appeal to the masses; once in power at the state level, it became an essentially middle-class party increasingly led by young university graduates under the influence of Mallam Aminu Kano. The PRP billed itself as the party of the nonaristocratic elements, although many of its intellectuals (theoreticians) were in fact members of aristocratic families. In the main, however, the mass of PRP membership represented a petty bourgeois populism that found the traditional northern aristocracy oppressive. The revolutionary ideology of the party intellectuals, on the other hand, increasingly drew inspiration from Marxist concepts rather than from Islamic political beliefs. They aspired to create a national class consciousness to overthrow the northern "oligarchy." Thus, against the NPN conception of society as an ongoing organic entity forging national links with all "responsible" segments of society, the PRP increasingly projected a picture of the conflict of irreconcilable interests (PRP 1979a, 4–10).

In the 1979 elections, Mallam Aminu Kano was defeated in the presidential race, one of the five elections held that year. However, PRP candidates for state offices in Kano won. Thus, the governor of Kano State was a member of the PRP, but Aminu Kano himself held no office in the state. Shortly after the election, there was a subtle but noticeable change in radical rhetoric, most notable in the speeches of the governor. He and other members of his government, endorsed by newspaper columns written by young intellectuals at Bayero and Ahmadu Bello Universities, further developed the themes of "antagonism of interests" and the "class struggle" between the ruling class and the *talakawa* (those without official position in this hierarchical society). Political parties were cast as expressions of diametrically opposed class interests. Added to this were assertions about the schemes of "international capitalism" and United States inspired "imperialism" designed to exploit the Nigerian working class and peasants with the help and endorsement of the NPN. Mallam himself increasingly invoked the specter of Western domination to account for both moral decline at the national level and the ruin of the Nigerian economy. Resentment was kindled toward the civilian government in Lagos both on traditional grounds and on new grounds of callous indifference to the needs of the people.

In this discourse there was also much concern about the place and role of women. Education for women continued to be urged, but increasingly, concerns were raised about alien notions of women's liberation, and the superiority of Islam's treatment of women in contrast to that of other religions, particularly Christianity, was adduced. Further, in the new Marxist vocabulary, the old NEPU concern with Islamic justice and its meaning for the place of women was muted. Instead, women were urged to join the revolution against capitalist oppression.

> The historical growth of capitalism while allowing for limited liberation of some women noticeably tended to force more women under the yoke of capitalism. In this light the role of the presently existing women in high offices and women's organizations is no positive contribution to development but a camouflage to enhance the perpetuation of capitalism, via women (Alache Ode-Ahmed in *The Triumph,* October 17, 1982).

> Therefore, if this revolution which women in Nigeria have now begun in earnest is to be successful and meaningful, it has then to focus its attention in seeking ways and means by which in collaboration with the other oppressed classes in the country, the Nigerian state can be pressurized into taking over more and more responsibility for the provision of the society's basic material wants on an equitable basis (Richard Umaru, *The Standard,* May 6, 1983).

Other writers stressed that Islam offered equality of rights, responsibilities, and status to women as witnessed by the *Qur'an.* Whether or not equality before Allah translated to social equality on earth for men and women was not a question for debate, as no discrimination in the creation or treatment of women in Islam was detected; in fact, the divine nature of women's roles in the family was noted.[1]

> Now, Woman has always been man's dependent, if not his slave: the two sexes have never shared the world in equality. And today woman is heavily handicapped though her situation is beginning to change. . . . Thanks to the pervasive influence of non-Islamic culture . . . woman is seen strictly as a sex machine. . . . In Islam, a woman is not a sex object; she is a human being carrying responsibilities and destined to perform defined fundamental roles in life (Ibraheem Sulaiman, *The New Nigerian*, April 24, 1983).

> Thus so long as you will stick to the European and customary notion of human relationship, I am afraid, your lives will inevitably lead to misery and regrets. You have no alternative therefore, but to live according to the principles of Islam, and see yourselves not as objects of amusement and satisfaction of some ephemeral pleasure, but as servants of Allah carrying heavy responsibilities and destined to fulfill basic roles in life. . . . Marriage is a fundamental duty in Islam, because, according to our Prophet, it enhances the practice of Religion and imposes restraint and discipline on people. . . . Through marriage a woman gets the moral and social security that are so vital to her (*The New Nigerian*, May 1, 1983).

Except in its proclamation of devotion to Islam and Islamic culture, the content of the PRP program made few concessions to traditional culture and values. Islamic ideals of social equality were again represented as forming the essence of the party's ideological commitment. PRP ideology, like the old NEPU oratory, stressed popular participation in the widest possible sense and the widest possible access to social roles and rewards. Islamic themes were combined with secular concerns and labeled "socialism." This conception of socialism is what is understood by the ordinary people and to some extent by Mallam Aminu Kano himself; the relevance of socialism in this society in the classic, industrial sense is questionable. The stress of the party's message was on "equal opportunities for all men and women" in the name of Islam and of socialism.

Articles in the student newspaper (*The Bayero Beacon*) at Bayero University in Kano stressed the Marxist interpretation of history during the period of the Second Republic. They cast Nigerian politics as a continuing struggle between opposed classes, leading to recurring crises that in turn would produce a revolutionary movement against Nigeria's repressive social order. Like the jihad, the revolutionary and radical government in Kano, joining with the "progressives" in other states in Nigeria and following Islamic principles, would overthrow the corrupt forces represented by the NPC and reincarnated by its successor, the NPN. Ultimately, the oppressed (including women) would be victorious (see *Bayero Beacon,* April 1982, June 1982, October 1983).

In this context the PRP demanded restructuring of Nigerian society to allow more political and economic opportunity for the "oppressed" and the development of a socialist economy that would benefit all the people. In order for "all the people" to benefit, they advocated education for both women and men. Therefore, the pressing need for rising levels of education was consistently stressed, and fathers and husbands were urged to send girls to school in compliance with the law establishing Universal Primary Education and the principles of Islam.

> The fact is, Islam did not forbid women from acquiring education. In fact, it even encourages and enjoins women to go to any level to acquire education as their males counterparts [*sic*]. We should encourage parents to be more vigilant in sending their female children to schools. . . . Moreover every effort should be made to see to it that none of the girls enroled [*sic*] are allowed to be withdrawn for marriage (Maryam U. Aji, *The Triumph,* November 14, 1982).

In fact, the PRP began to suggest that although education for girls was now voluntary, it would soon become compulsory and fathers would be fined for not obeying the law. In addition to increasing literacy and raising the general level of education, the PRP proposed the gradual nationalization of state assets and the freeing of the economy from domination by the forces of multinational capitalism in order to eliminate poverty in Nigeria. At this point, women as well as men would be emancipated and all would live according to the principles of justice.

THE SECOND REPUBLIC: WOMEN PARTICIPATE

In spite of the PRP's rhetorical emphasis on issues quite removed from the immediate concerns of women, there is evidence that women voting for the first time recognized it as the party promoting their interests; its platform, unlike the NPN's, specifically promised programs benefiting women, and the long legacy of Mallam Aminu Kano and his concern for women was frequently cited. Voting patterns in two of Kano's 132 wards, Kurawa and Kofar Mazugal, apparently reflect women's recognition of the PRP as the party of their interests. In Kano, certain wards today, as in the past, are associated with occupational categories that in themselves carry connotations of social standing in Hausa society. Administrative and middle-rank civil servants generally live in the predominantly Fulani wards, such as Kurawa; traders, merchants, and craftsmen live in the predominantly Hausa wards, such as Kofar Mazugal.

It was from wards like Kofar Muzugal that NEPU drew its votes during 1950–1965 and in which the PRP won overwhelmingly in 1979 and 1983. In Kofar Mazugal, the Hausa *talakawa* formed the bedrock of PRP support, and women and men clearly voted alike. Kurawa, on the other hand, had been a NPC stronghold in a NEPU city, and the NPN expected to win easily in 1979 and 1983. Thus, its slim margin of victory lent credence to the PRP assertion that it was women, voting for the first time, who created their overwhelming victory in Kano. As women apparently distinguished their interests from men's and supported the PRP, providing a wide-ranging and cross-cutting voting bloc, it would seem that electoral politics in Kano has come to be marked by a "gender gap" (see tables 8 and 9).

It might be accurate to assert in general terms and in reference to the national scene that "What can be said for sure . . . is that the average Nigerian voter in the 1979 elections may have behaved 'rationally' only with respect to maximizing ethnic, regional, religious, and personality-leadership parochialisms, but irrationally with respect to maximizing his potential or actual political pay-offs" (Tajudeen 1982). This apparently was not true, however, in the case of women.

Once in office, the PRP demonstrated a powerful desire to remain there and a pragmatic approach to doing so, much to the displeasure of Mallam Aminu Kano. Eventually, in 1981, the party split over this issue. Its two segments, one led by the governor (Abubakar Rimi) and one by Aminu Kano, each expelled the members of the other; the Federal Electoral Commission recognized that branch of the party headed by Mallam Aminu Kano as the "real" PRP, thus enabling it to wage the 1983 election campaigns under the PRP banner. (For a deeper analysis of this split, see Diamond 1982, 645–47).

Established in power in Kano, members of the Rimi faction of the PRP evidently were more intent on securing their reelection than on inciting a revolution. Hence, the party began to tread softly, particularly in regard to women. It continued to stress education, but it conspicuously sought endorsement from Muslim leaders for its efforts and increasingly exhorted women to observe proper Islamic behavior. Any revolutionary action or scheme henceforth looked simultaneously to the requirements of society and the hopes of

TABLE 8
Voting Patterns in Kofar Mazugal and Kurawa, 1979

Kofar Mazugal		Kurawa	
Party	Vote by party	Party	Vote by party
NPN	4,020	NPN	13,001
PRP	18,551	PRP	14,491
GNPP	136	GNPP	451
UPN	0	UPN	247
NPP	0	NPP	47
TOTAL	22,707		28,237

Voters Registered

	Kofar Mazugal	Kurawa
Men	26,350	17,160
Women	23,650	17,840

NPN—National Party of Nigeria
PRP—People's Redemption Party
GNPP—Greater Nigerian People's Party
UPN—Unity Party of Nigeria
NPP—Nigerian People's Party

Source: Federal Electoral Commission Register of Voters, General Election 1979

TABLE 9
"Does it make any difference to women which party is in power?"

Respondents	Yes	No	No opinion
Female university students (N = 114)	73	28	1
Girls secondary students (N = 144)	80	30	10
Urban women (N = 188)	90	62	15
Rural women (N = 138)	63	41	20
Male university students (N = 572)	241	315	12
Urban men (N = 97)	30	40	8
Rural men (N = 57)	15	25	5

(Does not account for missing cases)

Sources: These data collected as follows: Female university students—Barbara Callaway in 1982–1983; girls secondary school students—Indo Aisha Yuyuda in 1982; urban women—Barbara Callaway and Bilkisu Mohammad in 1982–1983; rural women—Bilkisu Ismail and Bilkisu Mohammad in 1982; male university students—Barbara Callaway in 1982–1983; urban men—Mohammed Jabo in 1982; rural men—Sani Mohammed Kura in 1981.

the incumbents to return to office. The young PRP leaders' attacks on the "traditional system" and its treatment of women (among other things) were in reality primarily attacks on the incumbent holders of traditional offices from which they had been excluded.

This issue was partly played out in the split between the governor and Mallam (the governor favoring expedient alliances with other parties in Nigeria for purposes of national opposition and Mallam insisting on PRP "purity"). Nevertheless, the situation posed an intriguing question on a more theoretical level—how can authority legitimate itself and carry on its routine business while transforming or destroying the social bases on which its legitimacy rests? In the case of women's rights, the party had no intention of trying it. The essence of its social policy toward women remained conservative: the issue was not women's rights, but merely the promotion of Islamic teachings. Women were to be educated so they could better understand how to be good Muslim wives and mothers, not so they could advance their own interests.

> The purpose of this piece is to inform you briefly what status Islam accords you in society with a view to stressing the need for you to strive to maintain and enhance that status; to warn you about the dangerous trend in the present day society that has been confused by both customary and western ideas, with regards to women's role in Society; and finally to urge you to strive to achieve real fulfillment as a wife as desired by our Creator (Ibraheem Sulaiman, *Sunday New Nigerian,* April 17, 1983).

Some women, once educated, might be appointed to office or become teachers, and so long as they did not overtly challenge Islam itself, they were likely to be encouraged; this might in fact bring about significant progress in the daily reality of women's lives. Women's votes were sought for the defeat of the traditional order; but as in Algeria, once they had made this contribution to the political process, they were to resume their proper place in the home and certainly were not expected to attack the patriarchal aspects of that order.

In 1979, seeking to gain the women's vote, both parties resurrected the mechanism of "women's wings." Once again, the parties turned to "free women" (*karuwai*) for membership and leadership of the wings; this time however, the leaders of the *karuwai* were designated "Magajiya," thus reviving the traditional title attached to women's legitimate leadership of women and signifying the new respectability of women's participation in politics.

The main challenge of the PRP women's wing was to recruit the women's vote; entertainment was de-emphasized, and women voters were reached through radio and television rather than mass rallies. The party itself decided which women's issues (education and participation) should be raised and endorsed, and pledged itself to action on them. While it did not encourage discussion about women's inherent inequality in the structure and nature of Islam, it did repeatedly assert that "development cannot occur until women are educated and equal to men" (PRP 1979b, 4). Among the five parties officially participating in the 1979 elections, only the PRP offered a specific platform plank of this nature.

The PRP also endorsed those sections of the 1979 Constitution that would guarantee equal rights to all Nigerians, specifically, "The right to life, the right to dignity of the human person, right to liberty, right to a fair hearing, right of privacy, freedom of thought, conscience, or religion, freedom of speech and of the press, right to peaceful assembly, and association, freedom of movement, freedom from discrimination, and the right of property" (*Constitution,* ch. IV). Many of these rights, if literally extended to women in Kano, would have been revolutionary. The PRP asserted its full support of these provisions of the Constitution, and both student and more general surveys indicated that women were aware of the party's position.

The new Constitution also barred "discrimination on grounds of belonging to a particular community, ethnic group, place of origin, sex, religion or political opinion" (Sec. 39(1)(b)) and provided that every citizen was entitled to move freely throughout Nigeria (Sec. 38), thus leaving open the question whether or not the seclusion of women was unconstitutional. There does not appear to be any case brought in a Nigerian court based on either the discrimination provisions or the freedom of movement provisions; in order to illustrate how discrimination may occasion relief, Nigerian law schools cite cases from American constitutional law. Radical women students at Ahmadu Bello University in Zaria indicated their belief that seclusion was, in fact, unconstitutional and expressed hope that in the near future women "would not fear to raise such questions as part of a political platform" (Women in Nigeria 1983).

> Also advocated was the need to improve women's legal status by enforcing equal rights of both sexes guaranteed by the Nigerian constitution. This includes rights to inherit land, to gain custody over children in the case of divorce and to have equal rights in marriage. . . . Discussions at the conference highlighted various aspects of women's oppression in the family. The practice of forced and early marriage was condemned, as it causes permanent physical damage and sometimes death to the young girls involved. This is a threat to life as guaranteed by the constitution (Bilkisu Yusuf, *The Triumph,* May 29, 1983).

Cases brought by women on these or other antidiscrimination grounds would surely open a new chapter in Nigerian legal history.

Finally, the Constitution directed the government to eradicate illiteracy, promote science and technology, and when practicable, provide compulsory and universal free primary, secondary, university, and adult education (Sec. 17). This position has since been endorsed by all political parties; the PRP established an Agency of Mass Education to eradicate illiteracy and ordered all illiterate government employees to attend literacy classes.

While the PRP built upon a long history of perceived concern for women, particularly their education and full enfranchisement as citizens, it continued to try to defuse the issue from a women's issue into one prompted by religious concerns. Like the NEPU before it, the PRP tried to defend its long advocation of extending political participation to women on the grounds that all "believers" should participate as equals in the state and that Islam required women to be educated in order to understand their duties as wives and mothers. Further, with regard to "women in the rural areas, the basic aspects of house-keeping, hygiene, being good housewives and mothers should be the goal of the journalist" (Antonia Ashiedu, *New Nigerian,* June 15, 1981, writing on the responsibility of female journalists to communicate with rural women).

The women's wing of the party was not expected to venture beyond these matters, and in 1979 it was not unlike its counterpart in 1960 in being beholden to the male party leadership. It is undoubtedly true that any women's organization created by an essentially male political party as an intrinsic part of its own structure and dependent on that structure for its survival, is not likely to support women who would develop or push an agenda of their own. As noted at the WIN conference:

> None of the women's organizations as they currently exist on the Nigerian scene is committed to the task of raising women's level of consciousness by working towards establishing their political and economic independence, granting them equality, and improving their condition both at work and within the home. . . . It is this lopsided system and the gap that an organization like WIN is determined to fill (Bilkisu Yusuf, *Triumph,* May 29, 1983).

Indeed, as in the First Republic, the primary activities of the women's wing consisted almost entirely of generating support for the party's candidates. But in the 1983 elections, the party nominated a female candidate, Mrs. Kande Balarabe of Dawakin Tofa, for a seat representing Bagwai constituency, and she won her seat; once again, it appeared that a women's vote could be crucial in elections. It should be noted, however, that Hajiya Kande Balarabe is a woman out of culture. Born and raised in Sierra Leone where her father was in business, she attended Freetown Girls Secondary School and Hartford Secondary School for Girls before proceeding to the Royal School of Nursing in London. In 1977 she returned to Kano and began her career as a staff nurse and midwife at the Murtala Mohammad Hospital. In 1981 she joined the PRP because it was "the only one, out of the six political parties in the country, that has persistently worked for the welfare of Nigerian women" (*New Nigerian,* November 13, 1982). Before the election Kande Balarabe served as the secretary to the women's wing of the party and after the election became the deputy national president. During the election she appeared on many radio and television talk shows, drawing much enthusiasm from women and amusement from men with her vivacious and lively exhortations to women to become involved in politics, to "participate in whatever the men are doing . . . these things that make the men seem so strong" (*New Nigerian,* November 14, 1982).

In general, the leaders of the women's wings of both parties gained experience in the political arena as well as an appreciation for the power inherent in the women's vote. Moreover, outside of Kano State where women do not live in strict seclusion, there was evidence that northern women were indeed becoming mobilized on issues of concern to them. In Bornu State (northwest of Kano), a woman, Hajiya Hassana Hassan, contested for the NPN nomination of governor, asserting that the party was not meeting the needs of women (*Nigerian Standard,* October 2, 1982).[2]

The *Nigerian Standard* reported in March 1983, that 50,000 women in Jos, the capital of Plateau State, "went berserk and took to the streets" protesting the failure of the state government to pay teachers' salaries and make grants to schools for a period of four months (*Nigerian Standard,* March 9, 1983). According to the *Standard,* the NPN leadership in the state was "bewildered by the action of the women" and "many of them who could not tolerate what was happening quickly ran into their cars and vanished" (March 11, 1983). The action of the women was roundly condemned, and the speaker of the House of Assembly labeled it a serious problem which, if left unchecked by the legislature, "would bring disaster to the State and the country at large" (*Nigerian Standard,* March 11, 1983). The student leader of the Nigerian People's Party (NPP) in Plateau State was equally condemnatory, accusing the women of an "act of thuggery" that was "also a display of their (women) [*sic*] disrespect for the rule of law and the game of politics." Further, according to the newspaper, "the student leader made it clear that the issue of non-payment of salaries to workers is a nation-wide phenomenon and not peculiar to Plateau State. . . . In Benue State . . . government workers were not paid their salaries since the last eight months, yet . . . women there did not lose their head or take to the streets molesting pedestrians and motorists as did the hired free women and other people of low virtue who misbehaved in Jos last Tuesday" (*Nigerian Standard,* March 12, 1983).

Perhaps such action did not occur in Kano because the Kano State government seems to have had a better record in meeting state salaries than most state governments in Nigeria during 1979–1983. In any case, remarkably, in its four years in power the PRP in large measure did carry through its campaign promises to women. Girls' schools were built, women's centers were established that offered adult literacy classes at night open only to women, and women were appointed to public office.

In all this, there was no public outcry against the government's efforts, but there was enormous private pressure on individual women appointed to public positions. The PRP government appointed three women commissioners (home affairs, trade and industry, health), one woman permanent secretary (education), and one woman to each of the ten parastatal boards. These were significant and important beginnings. The high visibility of the female commissioners and the permanent secretary was a double-edged sword, however. First, their appointment set an example that was certainly noted and commented upon, and as a consequence many girls for the first time began to contemplate a public life. Data from a survey of girls in an urban secondary school clearly illustrate this. Of 144 respondents, 25 (seventeen percent) indicated they would aspire to serve as commissioners, and 18 (twelve percent) could visualize themselves as politicians in the future (see table 10). At the same time, however, the lack of experience of those appointed meant that the women in fact had difficulty mastering their responsibilities, and thus for all practical purposes the titles were honorary. Two of the commissioners had not yet reached the age of thirty and had no employment history; the permanent secretary had no experience in the domain of her ministry. The government's difficulty in finding qualified women for these appointments underscored how severely limited women's opportunities had been in the preceding decades and centuries.

The new commissioner of home affairs was a twenty-five-year-old university graduate student and teaching assistant; the appointment was symbolic in a very significant way, for she was a member of a family well-known for its principled nonconformity.[3] Poised and articulate in public, the commissioner nevertheless was too inexperienced to handle her responsibilities with professional maturity. In a society that venerates age, her youth as well as her sex were great handicaps. She was subjected to unremitting moral pressure and eventually was made to resign by her husband (who then assumed a place in the cabinet himself).

TABLE 10
Career Aspiration: Dala Government Girls Secondary School, Kano

"In the future, what do you want to be?" (Mark only two choices.)

N = 144*

Choice	Number	Percent (of 144)
Teacher	41	28
Nurse	5	3
Doctor	10	7
Commissioner**	25	17
Politician	18	12
Engineer	3	2
Scientist	1	.06
Astronaut	20	13
Lecturer***	2	1
Civil servant	5	3
Journalist (radio, T.V., or newspaper)	7	4
Wife and mother	140	97

Source: Questionnaire administered by Indo Aisha Yuyuda, 1982.

*Eleven of the 144 respondents marked only one choice, therefore totals do not equal 188.

**In this context, a commissioner is a political appointee who heads a branch of the state government.

***A lecturer is a university professor.

The permanent secretary of education was a woman of mature age; but until her appointment, she had worked only as a pharmacist and she lacked the bureaucratic experience to administer a large and dramatically growing school system.

A young woman who had been educated abroad was appointed commissioner for trade and industry. She functioned only as a figurehead, while day-to-day responsibility was assumed by the permanent secretary, and, since this ministry oversaw large-scale contracts, by the governor himself. However, the close stewardship of this ministry by the governor led to widespread (though baseless) public speculation that the commissioner was the governor's "girlfriend"; given the culture and its popular perception of male-female relationships as necessarily sexual in nature, this misconception of the situation was virtually inevitable. Unless and until the nature of private relationships between men and women changes, it is difficult to envision more favorable public perceptions of young women in politics.

The appointment of these four women to political positions in the PRP government thus indicates a very real problem. The party and the government wanted to make a dramatic statement concerning the new roles that women could be expected to play in a "radical" and "modernizing" regime. But the society was such that there literally were *no* qualified women available for appointment. With a literacy rate (in English) for women over twenty-one of less than one percent in a society where ninety-eight percent of adult women live in near total seclusion, the difficulty of finding women with skills or experience is enormous. Whether or not this can happen gradually over time as more and more women are educated and a few of them enter professions, or whether it can only come as the result of a genuine social revolution, is not clear. In this specific instance, for the PRP government, the time was too short: the military coup of late 1983 preempted all efforts to sustain these developments. In any case, Mallam Aminu Kano's unexpected death in April 1983 brought an ironic end to this story of attempted progressive reform. Sabo Bakin Zuwo, succeeding to the de facto leadership of the party and then becoming governor of Kano State, proceeded to choose primarily illiterate men to fill high government positions, remarking that "my government will go down in history as the government for the illiterates by the illiterates."[4]

Even though women played only tangential roles in the PRP government, it was the first time Hausa women were organized for the purpose of attracting female voters and the first time that they were visible in any sort of institutionalized public role. From these experiences they at least learned something about organizational concepts and rudimentary principles of operating in the public sphere. The PRP did succeed in politicizing women to some extent and did bring women into the public domain: it offered educated women an outlet for their views, and by opening its leadership positions to women and bringing them into the government it was beginning to create a more socially heterogeneous environment for the traditionally isolated and class-bound northern Hausa Muslim woman.

However, the circumscribed male conception of the nature of women's political roles is illustrated by the fact that even in a party headed by Aminu Kano, the women's wing was simply an adjunct to the men's party. Further, women were invited to address only those issues defined as of particular concern to women, viz., the right to an education and to a vote. Issues such as family planning or changes in the marriage laws and divorce rights were not addressed. In fact, women were not encouraged to confront any issues on their own. In terms of the party organization, the women's wings were neither reformist nor revolutionary vis-à-vis women. It did not attempt to appeal to the revolutionary potential of women as a suppressed group in a changing society.

As the recent political history of Kano makes all too evident, a nascent ideology of sexual egalitarianism like what the PRP offered may integrate women into politics, but may achieve little more. Women's absorption does not necessarily either challenge the male agenda and control of the party and government or generate a female agenda. To the contrary, in the short run, cooptation of the women's issue clearly constrained the development of a woman's agenda decided by women. It remains to be seen whether, if a clash of interests should become manifest, Hausa women would display the will and ability to sustain a challenge. Newspaper columns in 1983 suggested that both men and women were interested in the question of whether or not women could (or should) form a political pressure group.

A small group of radical women began to challenge the status quo prior to the 1983 election, but other than coverage in the press they had no visible following. The president of the Nigerian International Women [*sic*] Society stated that "the formation of women's wings in political parties in this country is one of the methods used by men to perpetually dominate the political affairs of the nation" (*New Nigerian*, January 27, 1983). She appealed to women to carefully study the manifestos of all registered parties in order to choose parties concerned with equality for women and regretted that women's wings were "being used to foster men's political ambitions" (*Ibid.*). WIN noted that "unfortunately at the moment the best that can be hoped is that a few women may be appointed for symbolic and electoral reasons" and acknowledged that such appointments "do not always reflect a desire on the part of the administration to see women play a truly full role in society" (*New Nigerian*, August 28, 1983). Writing in *The Sketch*, Mrs. Ibironke Adefope urged women to organize as women:

> like our counterparts in other countries because the time is definitely now for women to be heard. . . . We should not continue to allow male members of the National Assembly to determine our fate because they will continue to vote on issues concerning women without a fighting change [*sic*] from the female voters. If we do not have women in high places where it really matters there is absolutely no way we can fight for causes. (*The Sketch*, February 5, 1983)

The 1983 coup precluded further development of this dialogue.

REFLECTIONS ON WOMEN AND POLITICS

In spite of all the stress on Islamic concepts of equality and economic socialism, the male/female dichotomy is sharp, and nothing that directly challenges the authority of men over women is likely to be tolerated: neither men, nor women—who fear loss of what standing and security they now possess—are friendly to it. Although a majority of the population and a majority of the voters, women are not in reality yet a political majority. The potential is great, but whether or not this potential will be seized is problematic. In other Islamic societies women have not become policy makers, and this society is likely to become more and more consciously Islamic by reaffirming, supporting, and legitimizing actions determined to be in support of Islam. Even when a "radical" ideology appears to be widely adopted and supports women's political participation, the nature of that participation is limited. Islamic women do not yet have a political position on change in regard to their religion and do not believe they can introduce such change. The vote is not particularly powerful when power rests and is exercised largely outside the formal political process. All legislation directly applicable to women must respect Islamic teachings and fall within the directions of the *Qur'an.*

Liberation or emancipation for Muslim women in Kano will not be the same as for Western women—it begins not with the struggle for voting rights, but with the belief that public recognition of women's existence and interests separate from men's is legitimate within the Islamic tradition. Reforms that can be justified by appeal to Islamic teachings may well be accepted; women, at least, seem eager for reform under these conditions.

At the same time, a cautionary note must be sounded. There is some evidence that radical rhetoric together with an appeal to fundamental Islam can lead to disastrous developments, as witnessed by events in Kano at the end of 1980. In Sufism, a Mahdi appears at times of profound historical crisis to conduct a jihad.[5] He brings a brief period of justice and equality during which tyranny and oppression cease while the end of the world is approaching. In this context, a fanatical and heretical religious movement arose in Kano during the latter part of 1980, led by a self-proclaimed Mahdi (the Maitatsine), Mohammad Marwa. Economic hard times and corrupt civilian government were both viewed by the Maitatsine as "unjust" and were widely and loudly decried by a wide spectrum of people in Kano. Large numbers of unattached and largely unschooled young men were attracted to the leadership of Marwa, who proclaimed himself the "black Mahdi" sent to purify Islam and rescue it from nonblack and Arab domination. Women explicitly were warned to keep off the streets. Within weeks the Maitatsine had literally taken over a part of Kano City. Women who ventured out in areas where the Maitatsine had ousted the inhabitants and established his followers were kidnapped and used to prepare food in his headquarters. Such were the disturbances caused by this movement in Kano that eventually the Nigerian army had to be called in to disband it; nearly 10,000 adherents were killed in pitched battles between the fundamentalists and the army and police. (For a review and summary of the Maitatsine crisis, see "Maitatsine Revisited," *The Guardian,* January 4, 1985.) Although Marwa was killed in these confrontations, outbreaks of the movement were continuing until 1985. The strength and appeal of the Maitatsine incident is indicative of deep levels of social discontent and reactionary responses to confusing social change. In this situation, women are very vulnerable.

The decision of the federal military government to enfranchise all Nigerian women was crucial in breaking the deadlock on an issue that had been debated by politicians, religious leaders, and in the press in Kano for nearly twenty years. But the Nigerian Constitution's protection of Islamic beliefs and the Hausa culture's promotion of them ensure that women will remain disadvantaged for a long time to come; sexual equality in such matters as inheritance, divorce, free choice in marriage, and the right to keep children after divorce is foreign to the current Islamic vocabulary.

Further, because these issues are defined as religious rather than political, changes in them are unlikely to come through the legal system. The reaction of Muslims to the equal rights provisions in the 1979 Constitution is instructive; as chapter four recorded, they launched an intense campaign to enhance the Sharia and protect it from the interference of the state. Any attempt directly to confront the subordination of women as enshrined by the Sharia or the *Qur'an* will be vigorously attacked and is likely doomed to failure.

Rather, it will be legislation in areas that do not immediately involve traditional Islamic belief that will mark significant change for women; education is one such possibility. Islamic leaders now agree that learning was advocated for women from the time of the Prophet through the time of Usman dan Fodio. Hence, education is the real threat to continued female subordination. Secondary school and university student survey data give credence to the expectation of change introduced through education (see table 11). We will look more closely at the effort to extend educational opportunities to women in the next two chapters.[6]

Again, however, women's participation in education and in political and economic activities depends on changes in the popular perception of what is endorsed by Islamic principles and on changes in resulting social values. Girls are often pulled from school soon before or upon puberty, secluded closely, and married to men who are older and with whom they are barely acquainted. At this point, childhood ends abruptly and career dreams cease. When this happens, the girl's peers express great sympathy, and the girl herself may express profound unhappiness and even signs of depression. Fortunately, since women live within a supportive female environment, such depression seldom leads to mental illness as it often does in other societies.

TABLE 11
"What will make life better for girls?"

	University Students		Secondary School
	Male	Female	Girls
Religion	120	15	21
Education	108	90	58
Good husbands	221	7	20
Better health	35	2	10
No answer	80	0	15
TOTALS	564	114	124

(Does not account for missing cases.)

Source: Survey conducted by Barbara Callaway and Indo Aisha Yuyuda, 1982–1983.

University males—N=572
University females—N=114
Secondary school girls—N=144

In addition to Islam, customary practices give implicit or explicit sanction to the status quo for women. Nothing protects women who do not fit the mold; they are assumed to be and are labeled prostitutes, and there is little they can do about it. In Kurawa, one young woman returned from school abroad where she had earned an advanced degree in an American university, provoked a divorce by *talaq* from a man she had never wanted to marry, refused to remarry, and entered a professional career. Because she is a member of an important aristocratic family she is somewhat protected, but, nonetheless, she is widely regarded as "difficult" and her conduct is publicly questioned, much to the distress of her family.

In assessing the prospects for female political emancipation in Kano, one needs to look at both the forces for change and the contradictions inherent in any such efforts. In times of "politics," adherence to conservative Islamic teachings and law and radical ideology coexisted. Government plans for "women's emancipation" coexisted with exhortations in the press, on the radio, and in the University emphasizing increasingly fundamentalist adherence to Islam. Also, the reality of the society that is to be transformed through politics, education, and radical party ideology is as far from the one projected in political debate as can be imagined. The socialist rhetoric of the young radicals is addressed to one of the most commercially active societies in all of Africa. Even the PRP politicians were openly accumulating private resources from public funds while in office to launch themselves as independent entrepreneurs. There is great urgency and conviction concerning the evils of capitalism and multinational exploitation expressed on the part of the young; they appear to believe that through rhetoric they can overcome the centuries of Hausa imperviousness to attempts by outside forces (both the Fulani and the British) to manipulate the traditional economic system and its mores. The traditional elite and commercial classes deem radical ideology itself one such outside and alien force. There is an intriguing contradiction of ideals here: radical, Marxist young men confront traditional, conservative, and elitist elements, and both claim to be within the Islamic tradition. Hence, it is realistic to predict that the ideological confrontation here is more likely to be between two different groups interpreting Islam, rather than between radicalism and conservatism per se or between social classes in the Marxian sense. Women are likely to be a key element in this struggle. It may well be that the mobilization of women in support of a movement of Islamic reform and the rising levels of education for women will ultimately undermine the old traditional order and result in the restructuring of relationships between men and women, albeit within the constraints imposed by Islam.

"In reality, Islam does not endorse our all embracing tyrannical shackles. In Kano, shrouded in senseless taboos and deprived of contact with the rest of the world, women tend to be inward looking. But things are changing and women are beginning to enjoy more liberty. Through literacy comes enlightenment" (Rabi'u 1981).

Female education and employment are indeed powerful instigators of change, but political activism on the part of women is constrained in Kano by Islam and the role of the family in defining women's lives. One caution appears particularly relevant. In Islamic societies, the replacement of the extended family by the nuclear family is not widespread. Therefore, family pressures have great importance in such matters as marriage, childbearing, and lifestyle. While most families aspire to greater material comfort and middle-class status, there is still little impetus for a wife to work outside of the home. Hence, the overwhelming majority of women are confined to the domestic sphere of life in spite of the role of rising political consciousness. Islam still requires that men support their families in all essential respects and women work to support the marriage system, not for personal gratification or public emancipation. The traditional culture rewards subservience in women and punishes women who take private or public initiatives. Thus, women are likely to remain "traditional," at least in the domestic setting.

Islam is no longer a barrier to girls' education, and perhaps in time it will not be a barrier to economic and political participation outside the home. Nevertheless, most men still consider the household and domestic activities menial and thus suitable only for women. Should women succeed in forging a more public role, they will be much advantaged over Western women in having both an extended family and a polygamous household to relieve some of the burden of the "double day." In other words, if the nuclear family does not become the norm, women's dual roles might be more manageable. But, dual roles will still be required.

At present, programs calling for societal transformation in line with women's needs (protections in divorce, support for children, opportunities to support themselves independently, etc.) engender reactions that make such transformation difficult. It is not likely that the political awakening of women will be allowed to overtly threaten mechanisms of male social control over them. The few women thus far given leadership opportunities have tended to reinforce sex-role norms, as the structure of sex stratification and male authority is largely unquestioned. Well aware of men's hostile reactions to the notion of sexual equality, women avoid provoking them. Thus, any direct movement towards equality is inhibited by conservative Islam on the one hand and on the other, the hostility of men (whom women fear to offend) toward women's liberation—the push and pull of women's narrow hopes.

There is some evidence of change, but it is not widespread. Two girls in the Kurawa survey succeeded in convincing their families to postpone their marriages until they had completed secondary school. In the case of two other girls forced into undesired marriages, mothers and daughters alike expressed their personal opposition, while acknowledging that nothing could be done (Interviews #56, December 26, 1984; #16, October 25, 1982; #17, October 28, 1982, all in Kano). A few women are entering careers, and a few husbands are genuinely supportive. And, as more and more young men gain experience outside the Islamic world, they may see and appreciate the benefits of wives' working and helping to support the household. Given the likelihood that Nigeria's already shaky economy will continue to deteriorate, this point may become increasingly salient.

It must be noted that although long a theme of radical politics, the commitment to improving the status of women has been limited to a small group of reform-minded politicians and intellectuals. The continuing preference for sons and the lack of experience having men and women associate with each other without sexual implications or expectations are inextricably mixed with Islamic beliefs. Hence, Islamic reform rather than political ideology is the key to the emancipation and increasing status of women.

Obviously, reforms affecting the status of women are more likely to succeed if they are urged by men of standing than by radical women. Women want and need the support of men if they are to be brought into the public arena. By the same token, men who are genuinely committed to equality and who are supportive of education and other opportunities for women, can be enormously effective in gaining the support of women for their parties, programs, and policies. There is female electoral support to be tapped—the gender gap can be very effective so long as it does not directly challenge Islam. That was why Mallam Aminu Kano was an effective spokesperson for women. The potential of women as a force for change by themselves is problematic and elusive. The introduction of choice into a world of duties is the essence of a "feminist" revolution here; this choice, however, is more dependent on a change in male attitudes and beliefs than female ones.

In daily life, the difficulties of social radicalism—of the appearance of disaffection from one's culture—are too great to attract many women or men. The promotion of women's education has become socially acceptable, and support for women living in *kullen zuci* and working outside the home is beginning to develop among the young educated elite. But notions of female autonomy, the possibility that a young woman might live outside of marriage, that birth control or family planning might be practiced, are still generally unacceptable.

Life in Kano City does not generate pressure for individual change or motivate women to seek alternatives. Confrontation with non-Muslims, both foreigners and southern Nigerians, has reinforced, not challenged, commitment to Islamic principles. While Kano increasingly has become the center of northern Nigerian economic, political, religious, educational, and cultural life, its women have become increasingly secluded and excluded.

Although secluded physically, increased exposure to radio and television, and political emancipation and voting rights, together with education may yet prove to be the beginning of the end for the particular kind of female powerlessness in the public sphere that has existed for the past several centuries in Hausaland. As noted in the first chapter, ruling-class women had public authority in the past. Women's present exclusive social world is in part a response to the loss of limited but nonetheless formal political authority in an earlier age. Women have withdrawn and disengaged from a male world. But women freely associate with each other, discuss new ideas, and form their own opinions without much male input. Ninety-eight percent of the women interviewed in the course of this study clearly supported change, although they objected to the words "women's liberation."

At present large families as well as early and arranged marriages limit choices and options for women. With education, some women will perceive their situation as disadvantaged and mobilize politically for individual rights—for the right to work, to have custody of children, to pursue education, to make choices in marriage. If these issues find a place in organized politics, women are likely to be a formidable voting bloc. As stated by Maryam Aji in *The Triumph* (January 9, 1983):

> Yet in spite of all the difficulties we have some few women from the North who actively participate in politics and are ready to be the subjects of victimization and all sorts of punishment in their effort to protect the interest of other northern women. . . . In spite of the relatively improved participation of the northern women in political affairs the way is still far off for women to play more effective role [*sic*] and in this regard women should take their initiative and assert their rights so that they can take their rightful place in the affairs of their localities.

The 1979 and 1983 elections yield some indication that women's votes are effective, that women do perceive a difference between parties in regard to their own interests (see table 9). And nowhere else in the Islamic world has there been such an emphasis on education for girls. Thus, it may be education endorsed by Islam, rather than a challenge to Islam per se, that is likely to "emancipate" women. But, education as endorsed by Islamic leaders could also lead to a reassertion of "Islamic values" to the detriment of "emancipated" women—thus the "rock and the hard place" on roads for emancipation of women in Kano.

6

Education in Kano

ALTHOUGH education presents a path of emergence for some women who live in this Islamic Hausa society, it is a way not without its problems, ambiguities, and challenges. Education does not necessarily afford a safe passage between the walls of Islam and the doors offered by women's liberation because Hausa culture and anti-Westernism counterbalance its impact. In addition, the history of Western as opposed to Islamic education in northern Nigeria in general and in Kano, in particular, has been problematic.[1]

In terms of secular education, Kano is the least educationally developed of all the states of Nigeria, a fact at least in part related to its status as a center of Islamic learning (see tables 12 and 13). Education in Kano has been heavily influenced by Islam, and historically Western education has been distrusted, if not feared. Recent advances in providing Western education for children in Kano are closely watched by Islamic leaders, and the concern for reinforcement of Islamic values is shared by religious leaders and educators alike. Mistrust of Western education and the values associated with it necessarily circumscribes the potentially liberating effects of increasing educational opportunities for women.

A HISTORICAL OVERVIEW

By the turn of the century, British military force had established European authority in the territory that became the Protectorate of Northern Nigeria. After "pacification," both the traditional rulers, the emirs, and the British

TABLE 12
Comparative Educational Development, Northern and Southern Nigeria

	Primary Schools		Primary Enrollments		Secondary Schools		Secondary Enrollments	
Year	North	South	North	South	North	South	North	South
1906	1	126	n.a.	11,872	0	1	0	20
1912	34	150	954	35,716	0	10	0	67
1926	125	3,828	5,210	138,249	0	18	0	518
1937	549	3,533	20,269	218,610	1	26	65	4,285
1947	1,110	4,984	70,962	538,391	3	43	251	9,657
1957	1,080	13,473	185,484	2,343,317	18	176	3,643	28,208
1965	2,743	12,234	492,829	2,419,913	77	1,305	15,276	180,906
1972	4,225	10,313	854,466	3,536,731	255	964	63,515	337,288

n.a. = not available

Sources: Haroun Al-Ra'shid Adamu 1973, 51; Federal Republic of Nigeria 1976, 151–52.

Primary School Enrollment Ratios, 1972

Kano State	7.7%	Western State	45.4%
North-Eastern State	9.4%	South-Eastern State	46.7%
North-Western State	9.8%	Rivers State	69.3%
North-Central State	16.3%	Mid-Western State	82.5%
Benue-Plateau State	22.0%	Lagos State	86.1%
Kwara State	27.3%	East-Central State	86.4%

Sources: Calculated from Federal Republic of Nigeria 1976, 151; Kano State 1976, 9.

colonial officers had a vested interest in establishing peace and effective government in the area. It was in northern Nigeria that the British colonial policy of indirect rule in Africa was most fully developed, which meant in effect that the British ruled with and through the traditional rulers (Lugard 1929). Hausa/Fulani culture was particularly conducive to this policy, as tact and charm traditionally were used to establish superior/inferior relationships between supervisors and inferiors, and conflict between individuals was not overtly expressed.[2] Hence, in the first decade of British rule, the dual mandate became a rather graceful minuet as both the British and the emirs sought to maintain a sense of dignity and decorum as well as control.

British educational policy as it evolved in Kano was a natural concomitant of the conception of indirect rule. In seeking avenues of cooperation between colonial authority and northern traditional rulers, the British acceded

TABLE 13
Educational Enrollments in the Northern Provinces, 1937

	I	II	III	IV	V	VI	VII	VII
	Nonadult	Islamic		III as	Elementary	V as	Middle	VII as
Province	pop. 1931	schools	pupils	% of I	pupils	% of I	pupils*	% of I
Adamawa	191,889	1,535	5,875	3.06	450	0.23	82	0.04
Bauchi	362,719	4,225	21,772	6.00	998	0.28	91	0.03
Benue	389,405	643	5,186	1.33	296	0.08	84	0.02
Bornu	389,583	4,231	29,832	7.66	903	0.23	151	0.04
Ilorin	202,919	1,116	15,639	7.71	568	0.28	120	0.06
Kabba	173,304	284	4,526	2.61	283	0.16	70	0.04
Kano	672,345	10,421	49,123	7.31	1,178	0.17	131	0.02
Niger	137,963	1,124	5,905	4.28	538	0.39	98	0.07
Plateau	178,144	250	2,787	1.56	203	0.11	41	0.02
Sokoto	676,138	7,168	38,170	5.65	2,098	0.31	123	0.02
Zaria	662,812	5,841	31,470	4.75	1,101	0.17	219	0.03
TOTAL	4,037,221	36,838	210,285	5.21	8,616	0.21	1,210	0.03

*Government schools only

Source: Bray 1981, 44.

Note: Daura and Katsina Emirates, formerly in Kano and Zaria Provinces, were combined to form a separate province in 1934. Figures here are adjusted to include both with Zaria.

to the wishes of the Hausa/Fulani emirs in allowing Christian missionaries and Christian mission work (including education) in their territories only with their approval. This policy effectively banned Western education from states such as Kano, and as a consequence, very few men and virtually no women received Western as opposed to Islamic education. What education was available was to be offered in government-sponsored schools.

In actual fact there was little, if any, government-sponsored education in the colonial state, and, for all practical purposes, education was a virtual monopoly of the Christian missionary societies. Until 1898, no Western education whatsoever existed in Nigeria other than mission education. As late as 1942, missions controlled ninety-nine percent of the schools and commanded more than ninety-seven percent of total student enrollment (Coleman 1960, 113). Thus, by 1945 the vast majority of literate Nigerians owed all or part of their education to mission schools. In this context, education was synonymous with mission or Christian education, and thus, the association of "education," "Western," and "Christian" on the part of Muslim leaders was not an inaccurate perception of reality. The consequence of this set of facts on school enrollment and levels of education is particularly dramatic in Kano, as table 13 indicates.

The concessions made by the colonialists to the Muslim leaders in the north in effect prohibited Christian churches from expanding their work from southern to northern Nigeria. The impact of this policy is brought home by the fact that as late as 1954, only one northern Nigerian possessed a university education.[3]

In 1908 the governor of Northern Nigeria appointed Hans Vischer, a Swiss national with British citizenship, as assistant resident in Kano and charged him with developing an official education policy for Northern Nigeria and in particular a plan for providing a minimum level of Western education for Muslims (Graham 1966, 66). For the first six months of his appointment, Vischer toured three other colonies in which an effort was being made to build a minimum level of Western education upon a preexisting Islamic base—Egypt, Sudan, and Ghana. In October 1909, Vischer founded the first of three schools in Kano City—the so-called Nassarawa schools. This first school was for the sons of chiefs; a year later a second was begun for the children of *mallams,* who were to be trained there to supply the teaching staff of the first school and/or to serve as clerks as needed by the Native Authorities; shortly thereafter, a craft school designed to attract "the right class of native artisans" was begun (*Quarterly Report: Education Department* [Quarter ending June 30, 1910], Archives, Kaduna #3666, 1910, cited in Whitaker 1970, 341). The Nassarawa Sons of Chiefs School served as a prototype for similar schools established later in other provinces as the second school produced teachers for them. By December 1911, there were 80 *mallams* in the *mallam* school, 102 students sent by traditional rulers in the Sons of Chiefs elementary school, and 97 men in the craft school.[4] There were no female pupils (Ogunsola 1974, 16). The staffs of the three schools consisted of Vischer and three *mallams* (Bray 1981, 37).

In addition to this special effort to provide a minimum education to sons of traditional rulers and *mallams,* the thrust of Vischer's "educational experiment" was to build upon the foundation of Islamic schools already existing. In 1913 there were 19,073 such schools with 143,312 students in Northern Nigeria (Hilliard 1957, 157–58). Vischer maintained that "the system of education should endeavor to educate without, if possible, in any way damaging their racial feeling or separating them from their parents or their surroundings." There was to be "no tyranny of foreign school examination . . . the technical instruction is intended to produce efficient artisans not dependent on European machinery" (Ogunsola 1974, 17). Vischer insisted that local crafts be offered in the schools of Northern Nigeria to the exclusion of "modern machinery" at a time of the extension of the railway throughout Nigeria and the establishment of British commercial firms throughout the country. This education policy did not prepare northern Nigerians to take the West African School Certificate (WASC) exams, "while the government department with which Vischer himself was associated would not employ Nigerians unless they had it" (Ogunsola, 71). Thus, mission-educated southerners with the WASC were recruited to fill the posts of the expanding colonial state, engendering among northerners the very feelings of inferiority in regard to their education that the Vischer education guidelines were designed to avoid.

In this connection, Carl Miller, a missionary who had sought early permission to operate a school in Kano, later noted that "many years ago I pleaded for full instruction in English, not only as a subject, but as a vehicle of instruction, realizing that English must certainly become the language both of literature and of commerce in the near future. It was in vain" (Ogunsola, 30). Instead, a few Western subjects were taught to a few sons of the emirs and other selected local elites. In Kano, the "three elementary centres for vernacular teachers" (Nassarawa schools) provided a three-year course in general education. The medium of instruction was Hausa, and graduates were certified proficient to teach an elementary school syllabus in Hausa in other government schools subsequently to be established.

Although Vischer left Nigeria at the outbreak of World War I and the schools he founded were later closed, his educational philosophy was expressed in the Education Ordinance of 1916, which stressed that northern schools should be well-grounded in the culture of the people. Vischer's objectives were also embodied in the 1921 decision to create Katsina College, the only full secondary school in the north prior to 1952, into which (in principle) traditional rulers' children were recruited. By the 1950s northern leaders themselves were expressing concern about differences between the educational levels of the north and the south and recognized the necessity for northerners to acquire Western as well as Islamic learning. Girls were still not provided education nor was the subject discussed, except in terms of training in hygiene and nutrition.

Between 1916 and independence in 1960, various education ordinances altered administrative arrangements and the relationships between the government and the various forms of schools (mission, voluntary or proprietary, and government), as well as the forms of grants-in-aid given to each sector. But the one important, consistent feature of Nigerian education remained the significant role of mission schools in the south and their absence in the north. The missions continuously pressed to establish schools in the north, but the colonial administration opposed any such operations. Article 13e of the Educational Ordinance of 1916 had stated that "no grant shall be made to any school or training institution which is a Mission or other Christian school or training institution situated in a District of the Northern Provinces in which no Mission or other Christian school or training institution is established at the commencement of the Ordinance" (Ogunsola 1974, 24).

As a result of the Vischer policies, by 1926 only 5,210 students in the northern provinces attended schools offering any English instruction; in the mission schools of the south, 138,248 students received English instruction. Since the population of the northern region was approximately one and one-half times that of the two southern regions, the disparity was even more severe than the simple numbers indicate (see table 12). In addition to the increasingly severe educational gap between north and south (table 12), there were also marked imbalances within the northern region (table 13). Although the absolute figures for Kano look impressive, particularly when Islamic schools are taken into account (table 13), enrollment in Western elementary schools, at a mere .02 percent of the school-age male population, lagged behind that of other provinces.

After World War I, Sir Hugh Clifford, the governor of Nigeria, complained:

> After two decades of British occupation, the Northern Provinces have not yet produced a single native . . . who is sufficiently educated to enable him to fill the most minor clerical post in the office of any government department. . . . The African staff of these offices throughout Northern Provinces are therefore manned by men from the Gold Coast, Sierra Leone and the Southern provinces of Nigeria. . . . Education in the North has

> been practically confined to the vernacular and the Arabic has been allowed to become the almost exclusive perquisite of the children of the local ruling classes, and has for its main object the equipment of these children with just sufficient knowledge of reading, writing and arithmetic to enable them in after life to fill posts in one or another of the various Native Authorities (Solaru 1964, 73).

Nearly every proposal for government (as opposed to mission) education in the north called for a positive relationship between governmental and Islamic educational systems. Mistrust of Western education was compounded by the views of the colonial officers themselves, who wanted to avoid in the north the "denationalization" they saw in the south. They believed that "southerners who in fact couldn't equal the accomplishments of the Europeans became frustrated, and out of this frustration organized opposition to the colonial regime" (Hubbard 1975, 155). By supporting and reinforcing, rather than challenging Islamic culture in the north, they hoped to avoid this anticolonial feeling.

Thus Lugard's and Vischer's acquiescence to and even promotion of the view that Western education was alien and would contaminate Islamic ideas had very serious consequences for both men and women in the north. Also, the privileged position of the *kadis* and *mallams* in the educational system of Kano suggested—and continues to suggest—that education could not overtly challenge Islamic teachings.

ISLAMIC EDUCATION: KANO AND ITS CONTEXT

Islamic education had its beginnings in Nigeria with the establishment of the Muslim dynasty in Bornu in A.D. 1085. Islam was firmly rooted in Kano by the late fifteenth century, when traders journeying across the Sahara helped forge small centers of Islamic literacy (see chapter one). A school of higher Islamic learning (*madrasa*) was established in Kano by the early seventeenth century and eventually offered Islamic law, theology, philosophy, and Qur'anic exegesis. After the arrival of the British in Kano in 1903, a new official elite was established, the *kadis* (*qudis*), who were recognized as scholars of Islamic law. The first of these (and most subsequent holders of the title) were graduates of al-Azhar in Egypt, the world's largest Islamic university. The tradition begun by *madrasas* and the Qur'anic schools established a literate alternative to Western education that is generally preferred by the traditional leaders. (Table 14)

TABLE 14
Enrollments in Selected Kano City Qur'anic Schools, 1972

		Boys	Girls	Total
1	Mal. Mikailu	30	36	66
2	Mal. Musa Tadde	70	30	100
3	Alh. Abdullahi	100	50	150
4	Alh. Limamin Rimi	20	15	35
5	Mal. Hamza Mohammed	60	40	100
6	Mal. Idi Mohammed	15	20	35
7	Mal. Dalhatu	35	25	60
8	Alh. Rabiu Dikko	30	20	50
9	Mal. Abdu	50	30	80
10	Alh. Isa	111	93	204
11	Mal. Dahiru	24	14	38
12	Mal. Ali	40	20	60
13	Alh. Tsoho	10	10	20
14	Alh. Gwani	28	12	40
15	Mal. Isa Maidal'ilu	36	20	56
16	Mal. Audu	8	7	15
17	Mal. Abubakar	90	70	160
18	Alh. Kasim	104	53	157
19	Mal. Sule	70	60	130
20	Alh. Sule	80	70	150
21	Mal. Hamza	50	35	85
22	Mal. Muhtari	50	7	57
23	Alh. Hassan	95	85	180
24	Mal. Musa	45	35	80
25	Mal. Abdu	205	202	407
26	Alh. Ahmadu	150	50	200
27	Mal. Umaru	30	20	50
28	Mal. Ahmadu	50	—	50
29	Mal. Bello	36	20	56
30	Mal. Hashim	20	—	20
31	Mal. Nuhu	10	—	10
32	Mal. Idi	10	8	18
33	Mal. Mohammed Unguwargini	40	50	90
34	Mal. Shehu Lamido	10	10	20
35	Mal. Dahiru K/Dama	100	50	150
36	Mal. Mohd. Indabawa	10	15	25
37	Mal. Dahiru Indabawa	15	10	25
38	Mal. Mohd. Gombe Unguwargini	11	7	18
39	Mal. Abubakar Gwangwazo	40	40	80
40	Mal. Adamu Indabawa	40	20	60
41	Mal. Tijani T/Wazirci	60	40	100
42	Mal. Dalhatu T/Wazirci	30	20	50
43	Alh. Audi Sagai	30	30	60
44	Mal. Hamidu Lokon Makera	30	40	70

TABLE 14 *(continued)*

		Boys	Girls	Total
45	Mal. Abdul rauf Gwangwazo	50	50	100
46	Mal. Salisu Lokon Makera	40	35	75
47	Mal. Yusuf Lokon Makera	35	20	55
48	Alh. Shehu Mai Gula	100	—	100
49	Mal. Abubakar L. Makera	30	—	30
50	Alh. Sani Diso	50	—	50
51	Alh. Abubakar L. Makera	30	20	50
52	Mal. Mohd. Sule Diso	40	20	60
53	Mal. Aminu L. Makera	50	30	80
54	Alh. Haruna Kwalsura	75	36	111
55	Alh. Nasiru Kabara	50	30	80
56	Alh. Tanko Hausawa	52	67	119
57	Mal. Musa Mandaware	50	20	70
58	Mal. Hassan Magashi	50	60	110
59	Mal. Ibrahim Magashi	30	10	40
60	Mal. Mohd. Pasilu Magashi	20	20	40
61	Mal. Musa Kabara	30	—	30
62	Mal. Musa Kabiru	100	70	170
63	Mal. Datti	60	40	100
64	Mal. Ibrahim	30	35	65
65	Mal. Inuwa	30	35	65
66	Mal. Shehu Diso	41	40	81
67	Mal. Mohammed	40	30	70
68	Mal. Balarabe	100	30	130
69	Mal. Haliru	120	20	140
70	Mal. Zubairu Hausawa	50	20	70
71	Mal. Sule	35	4	39
72	Mal. Yahaya	40	20	60
73	Mal. Garba	100	40	140
74	Mal. Abubakar	30	10	40
75	Alh. Hassan	100	30	130
76	Alh. Salibu	50	30	80
77	Mal. Rabiu	20	30	50

Source: Nuhu 1972, 81.

Islamic schools emphasize the importance of maintaining the Islamic traditions as a way of life; and, as others have observed, there has been little change in the content or methods of Islamic teaching from the sixteenth century. Islamic education is largely Thomistic in approach; spiritual and literary authority, rather than intellectual curiosity, are emphasized. Theology and law are the basic disciplines, and preserving the delicate balance of truth rest-ing on divine revelation and interpretation is the predominant concern. Islamic education is noncompetitive, and examinations are considered a foreign invention; there are neither entry nor exit requirements. The student's educational status is determined by the reputation of the teacher he studied with, not by his own performance. There are no teaching materials to bridge the gap between the teacher's knowledge and the wider world of knowledge (Hiskett 1975, 97; Hassan 1975, 124; Gibb and Bowen 1957, vol. 1, pt. 2, 139–61). Predictably, Islamic education alone has not been adequate for developing the skills necessary to function in the modernizing culture of the Nigerian state. Northerners have not been able to compete with more broadly educated southerners in the civil service or the private sector.

The first level of Islamic education essentially involves memorizing the *Qur'an*. The ability to recite large parts of the *Qur'an* signifies completion of basic Islamic learning. Study at more advanced levels (*makarantum ilmi*) centers on learning the *hadith*, or the records of the sayings of the Prophet. The *hadith* (or prophetic traditions) record what Muhammad did and said as a private person to his companions when he was not revealing the direct words of Allah. The *hadith* thus expands upon the *Qur'an* and, like it, omits no aspect of life. A *hadith* may concern marriage, divorce, or inheritance, and is a primary source of Islamic law (Sharia) on these subjects; or, it may concern government, and as such, is a source of Islamic constitutional theory (*Fiqh*). The *hadith* enshrine the authority of the Prophet through "indirect revelation" and are the subject of much literate Hausa verse (Hassan 1975, 136–37). As all law is "revealed" or "given" either in the *Qur'an* or in the *hadith*, there is no distinction between sacred and secular law; one who pursues Islamic education and memorizes the *hadith* as well as the *Qur'an* may ultimately specialize in *Fiqh* and become a *kadi* (or magistrate in a Sharia court). Specializations in Islamic education thus are: *Tafsir* (Qur'anic exegesis) or the study of events and the allusions in the *Qur'an*, *Hadith* (prophetic traditions), and *Fiqh* (jurisprudence or Sharia law). Other areas of study in what have become Islamic universities include theology (*tauhid*), astrology, Arabic grammar and literature, and mysticism.

In Kano, children enter Qur'anic school between the ages of four and six and immediately set about learning the *Qur'an*, beginning with the first chapter and proceeding straight through the book. Learning is by memory and rote rather than discussion and understanding. Fixed sections of the *Qur'an* are recited by the teacher and repeated by the students as the texts are learned by heart. Students squat on the ground forming a semicircle, memorizing the *Qur'an* by "reading" their verses in a singsong fashion and swaying their bodies back and forth. Students learn to write the Arabic alphabet as well as to chant large portions of the *Qur'an*. The letters of the alphabet are written on a large slate (*allo*), and children practice copying them in the sand or on their own *allo,* hence the designation *makarantum allo* or "board schools" is used to distinguish such schools from the *makarantum boko* or "book schools" that characterize Western education. Traditionally, students support their teachers, or *mallams,* by begging for alms (*sadaqa*) once a week.[5]

The prestige of a given school depends upon the learned reputation of the family from which the *mallam* is descended (Hassan 1975, 130–32). The mallams are considered to be the "custodians of the Islamic tradition," which essentially means they are responsible for teaching the young to recite the *Qur'an* (Hassan, 119–20). The social status of *mallams* is high, but generally their educational achievements are low by Western standards. The school facilities are a roof, a prayer mat, and a piece of slate. Scores of these schools may be seen all over Kano, existing today in the same form as they have for hundreds of years.

Boys attend classes for several years, while girls usually attend classes for shorter periods of time. Those students who perfect their knowledge of the *Qur'an* (i.e., can recite most of it by heart or *sauke kurani*) may go on to higher learning (*makarantum ilmi*), the study of *Tafsir, Fiqh, Hadith, Tauhid,* or Arabic. At this stage students choose their own teachers and progress as they wish. This highly individualized aspect of Islamic learning is considered to be one of its great strengths, allowing students to seek out great teachers much as the early Greeks did. Students expand their knowledge by buying commentaries on the *Qur'an* and visiting other ulema (learned men); since knowledge is revealed rather than discovered, originality is not rewarded. Students enter, attend, and leave the *makarantum ilmi* at will. As in the Qur'anic schools no specific academic qualifications are needed for admittance; it is believed that the *makarantum ilmi* should accommodate all who wish to enter and are serious about their studies.

For Muslim leaders, the function of education is to transmit Islamic doctrine, not to inspire inquiry or new interpretations: education consists in relating religious knowledge for the good of society. According to the Grand Kadi of Kano, there is no dichotomy between rationality and religion—both use knowledge, the scientific method, and scholastic analysis to understand Islam better. "Through education we find out more about the laws of Allah" (Interview #15, Kano, April 21, 1982). Education in the Western sense of teaching ways of thinking and pushing back the frontiers of knowledge is alien and threatening. A *hadith* is quoted to the effect that "what Allah has not made obvious, do not pry into." Muslim leaders fear that the introduction of Western education fosters an attempt to establish control over the minds of the people.

An effort to combine the Western tradition of learning with the Islamic tradition of memorizing was made in the establishment of the School for Arabic Studies and Higher Islamic Learning (SAS) in Kano in 1947. SAS built upon the foundation of the Shahuci Judicial School, established in 1928 by Emir Abdullahi Bayero to broaden the training of Sharia court employees. In SAS, in the 1950s, the curriculum was broadened to include teacher training as well as the study of Islamic law. Subjects were taught in the traditional way, but in a more structured manner. The SAS term was extended to five years of set courses, with a common core for the first four years and specialization in either legal or teacher education in the fifth year. In the 1960s the teacher's course became similar to that in other Grade II teachers' colleges, with the exception that Islamic history was substituted for Nigerian and European history and Arabic for geography. In 1974 a new component was added to provide emergency training of teachers in preparation for Universal Primary Education (Interview #52, Kano, December 22, 1984).

SAS was the first Arabic secondary school in Kano and was for boys only. The first such school for Kano girls, the Women's Arabic Teacher's College, was not opened until 1978. These schools were established, in part, to begin to train teachers who could introduce Arabic and English literacy to the Qur'anic schools, thus redressing the enormous imbalance in education between north and south.

It must be said, however, that even in the north, Kano was an extreme case. As an example, as late as 1954 there was only one boy from Kano in a postprimary institution (the Junior Secondary School in Kunci) (Bray 1981, 45). Kano parents' lack of interest in Western education reflects both suspicion of it and their (correct) perception of its relative unimportance in establishing social status. An official report noted that Kano and Sokoto were "full of persons who by Western European standards are only semi-literate, but have yet managed to become very wealthy" (Nigeria, Northern Region 1958, 8). As M. G. Smith (1965, 139) has pointed out, occupation tends to be hereditary, and education was notably absent from any list of determinants of social status in Hausa society even as late as the mid 1960s. Clearly, one reason the government had problems inducing parents to send their children to school was that until very recently education seemed irrelevant to the attainment of wealth and influence in Kano.[6]

By 1956 the British administrators in Kano were themselves apologizing for the general lack of educational attainment on the part of Kano citizens. "In fairness to Northern schools . . . it should be recognized that education in Kano Province is in a class of its own" (Nigeria Northern Region, 1958, 17). As independence approached, northern leaders became more consciously concerned about the educational imbalances, not only between the north and south, but within the north itself. Mallam Aminu Kano, in particular, made educational reform a cornerstone of his quest for political leadership. Mallam Aminu worried about both the education of girls and the aversion of Muslims to Western education. It was in part to convince some of the religious leaders in Kano of the benefits of Western education that he founded a school for five- and six-year old boys in his home. Here he sought to demonstrate that, by learning according to Western methods, a child could in one year recite the *Qur'an* better and learn more Arabic than he could attending Qur'anic school for five years (Feinstein 1973, 142). The school opened in 1950 with thirty boys; enrollment doubled the next year. In that year instruction in the English language, elementary arithmetic, and the English alphabet was introduced. The school was considered a great success, but because Aminu Kano's politics were anathema to the traditional ruling class, both its pupils and teachers were harassed, and after a few years the school ceased to function (Feinstein 1973, 143; Hassan 1975, 178–80). A school for girls founded in 1952 survived until Mallam's death in 1983—partly because it did not attempt to introduce Western education but rather focused on crafts, nutrition, and health care (Interview #46, Kano, April 18, 1982).

The 1960s witnessed a renewal of interest in schools such as Aminu Kano's school for boys, which came to be referred to as Islamiyya schools. The premier of the north, Sir Ahmadu Bello (the Sardauna of Sokoto), appointed a special ministerial committee to study appropriate educational reform in the northern region, and more especially to examine once again ways to build upon traditional Islamic education. The committee toured the Sudan, Libya, and the United Arab Emirates and finally recommended, in 1964, that selected Qur'anic schools "should be organized into classes in accordance with age, year of entry and standard of learning and that the curriculum should be diversified to include arithmetic, reading and writing as well as Koranic study" (Haroun Adamu Al-Rashid 1973, 56). Assistance was recommended for special inspectors who would also oversee the maintenance of standards. Almost immediately several Kano businessmen established such schools.

Initially, in Kano City the Islamiyya schools were a large component of the UPE system. By 1975, sixty-three were established under a wide range of proprietorship, from philanthropic individuals such as Alhaji Ahmadu Dantata to the Jama'at Nasril Islam (the Young Muslims' Congress) (see list, table 15). By 1980, however, ten had ceased to function, and it is likely, given the downturn in the Nigerian economy, that more will lose their patrons. Those schools that remain are under the supervision of the Ministry of Education and coexist today with the government-sponsored primary schools.

Alhaji Ahmadu Dantata established the prototype for such schools, the Dantata Islamiyya School, in 1964. The Dantata family constructed the classroom buildings and provided the basic furnishings; students purchased

TABLE 15
Islamiyya Schools in Kano State, 1977

1	Ulumuddini Biniyal Islamiyya, Kano
2	Ma'ahad Sheikh Nasiru Islamiyya, Kano
3	Yan Awaki Islamiyya, Kano
4	Yolawa Islamiyya, Kano City
5	Madrasatul Islamiyya, Hadejia
6	Kazaure Town Islamiyya
7	Zubairiyya Islamiyya, Galadanci
8	Dala Islamiyya, Kano City
9	Shamsud-Dini Islamiyya, Bici
10	Ibyawa Ulumid Din, Bici
11	Gobirawa Islamiyya
12	Mahmud Haido Islamiyya, Fagge
13	Nur-el Islam, Ringim
14	Jahun Islamiyya
15	Dambatta Islamiyya
16	Lawal Islamiyya, Gwarzo
17	Ma'ahad-el-Islam, Dandago
18	Maikwaru Islamiyya, Fagge
19	Nakota Islamiyya, Gumel
20	Nural Failati Islamiyya, Ringim
21	Bici Hagagawa Islamiyya
22	Nagogo Tshowar Gwaram Islamiyya
23	Elleman Islamiyya, Hadejia
24	Maigatari Islamiyya
25	Nurul Huda Islamiyya, T/Wada, Kano
26	Madinatul Ahbab Wattalameez, Fagge
27	Abbas Modern Islamiyya, Gwale
28	Kwa Islamiyya
29	Gidan Liman Islamiyya, S/Dinki
30	Danbazau Islamiyya, Kano City
31	Mambaiya Islamiyya, Kano
32	Saudawa Islamiyya, Kano
33	Gagarawa Islamiyya
34	Dandarama Islamiyya, Hadejia
35	Nural Islam, Jahun
36	Manladan Islamiyya, Kano
37	Tarauni Islamiyya
38	Kofar Nassarawa Islamiyya, Kano
39	Madrisatu Ta'allemul Al'sigar, Dandogo
40	Madrasatu Daril Ma'arif, Kano
41	Kila Islamiyya
42	Elleman West Islamiyya, Hadijia
43	Bakin Kasuwa Islamiyya, Hadejia
44	Madrasatud-Din Islamiyya, Dakata
45	Yakasai Islamiyya, Kano

TABLE 15 *(continued)*

46	Kunya Islamiyya
47	Misbahul Muniri Islamiyya, Mallum Maduri
48	Fityanul Islam, Gwammaja
49	E'Ela Uddeen Islam, Dandogo
50	Madasasatul Fukarai, Kano
51	Arzai Islamiyya
52	Kura Islamiyya
53	Gobirawa Islamiyya
54	Zangon Gabas Islamiyya
55	Lakwaya Islamiyya
56	Tudun Nufawa Islamiyya, Kano
57	Gezawa Islamiyya
58	Miftahu Rashid Islamiyya, Kano
59	Manadaware Islamiyya, Kano City
60	Dadin Duniya Islamiyya
61	Sa'adatul Islamiyya, Rijiya Hudu
62	Jama'atul Islamiyya, Bebeji
63	Islamiyya, Dandalin Turawa

Source: Kano State 1978.

their own *Qur'ans* and uniforms. While the Ministry of Education paid salaries of English and math teachers, the Dantata family paid the salaries for teachers of Islamic and Arabic studies. Students do not take the WASC exams and hence can proceed only to the School for Arabic Studies or the Arabic Teachers' College for further studies (Yassar 1983, 2–4). Graduates cannot meet university admission requirements except to the Islamic section of the Faculty of Arts and Islamic Studies at Bayero University (Yassar, 5). They are admitted to this faculty to prepare for teaching careers in state-supported secondary schools. Hence, attendance at an Islamiyya school and an Arabic teachers' college provides an alternate route to a university education in Kano State.

In 1976 the Galadanci Education Review Committee of Kano State[7] recommended that one Islamiyya school be established in every quarter of Kano City. Some two years later, the Islamic Education Center was established in the Ministry of Education and given the responsibility of inspecting and registering all Islamiyya schools that met ministry standards. By 1983, thirteen private schools, boasting 203 teachers and 10,277 pupils, were accredited as Islamiyya Primary Schools (Gana 1983, 1). Girls constituted over fifty percent of the enrollment in the Islamiyya schools,[8] but all teachers were male. Thirty-six of these teachers were interviewed in 1983, and *all* believed that

Western education "made girls behave immorally" (Gana, 44). Although some efforts at standardization have been made, no common syllabi have been developed and no attendance records are kept. Like the traditional Qur'anic schools, the Islamiyya schools give no formal certificated examinations, although many pupils do continue their studies at the SAS, the judicial schools (*madrasas*), or the Arabic Teachers' College by providing testimonials from their teachers. In accordance with the Galadanci Committee recommendations, graduates of these schools may enter the School of General Studies at Bayero University in order to take the remedial courses necessary for them to pursue university degrees, which are usually taken either in the Faculty of Education or the Faculty of Arts and Islamic Studies, which prepare teachers for the Islamiyya schools as well as for state secondary schools.

In several ways, the most significant educational developments in Kano have occurred at the university level. Provision of tertiary education began with the establishment of a Department of Islamic Studies as a branch of Ahmadu Bello University (Zaria) in 1960. In 1963, this program, renamed Abdullahi Bayero College, offered degree courses in Islamic Studies, Arabic, and Islamic Religious Knowledge. This signified the establishment of Islamic studies at the university level in Nigeria, giving the subject and the graduates respectability in the emerging new educational sector; this in turn ensured that there could be representatives of traditional Islamic learning engaged in the construction of a modern university, thereby guaranteeing a particularly conservative cast to university education in Kano. In 1976, Abdullahi Bayero College gained greater autonomy from Zaria by becoming a full university college, and it finally became an independent federal university in 1977, when it also admitted the first women students from Kano State. In that year also, the Department of Islamic Studies at Bayero University was mandated to retrain *mallams* teaching in the *makarantum ilmi* and to upgrade their skills so that they could teach in the new state schools created in response to the introduction of UPE during the 1970s and 1980s.

Thus, the early concern of the British, echoing Vischer's sympathies, to absorb or build upon the Qur'anic system already existing in Kano, finally bore fruit in the late 1970s and early 1980s. When state-supported schools were finally created on a large scale in the 1970s, they included a syllabus for Islamic Religious Knowledge (IRK) during which the *Qur'an* is recited. The inclusion of IRK as part of the curriculum in the secular school sector and the state support for the Islamiyya schools continues to assure that some form of Islamic education will be preserved in Kano.

Nonetheless, throughout the postindependence years, religious and traditional leaders in Kano have continued to express reservations concerning Western, as opposed to Islamic, education.[9] The fear of Western education and the emphasis on Islamic principles are particularly relevant when education for girls is considered. Hiskett has illustrated, through translations of verse, Hausa poets' reflections of northern leaders' fears that Western education especially corrupts women—even though, in point of fact, there are apparently very few cases of actual "immorality" on the part of educated Hausa women (Hiskett 1975, 103). Nonetheless, the anxiety expressed is genuine; it is feared that Western-educated women will adopt Western ways, leave *kulle,* and cause the disintegration of the Muslim family.[10] Women are viewed as the preservers of culture, and there is continuing concern that education should not undermine this function.[11]

The first girls school, St. Louis School for Girls, was established in 1951 in Kano for the daughters of southerners resident in the city. As late as 1953–54, Kano was the only province still submitting a "nil" figure for the numbers of girls indigenous to the state enrolled in school (Nigeria, Northern Region 1954, 33). The first Muslim Hausa girls from Kano attended St. Louis in 1977. It is illustrative of the dramatic nature of educational change in Kano in the past decade that in 1980, the government of Kano State took over supervision of this school and decreed that eighty percent of the student body be composed of Hausa girls indigenous to Kano State (meaning, in effect, Muslim girls). Meanwhile, in 1978 both men's and women's Arabic teacher's colleges were established to prepare teachers of Islamic Religious Knowledge (IRK) and Islamic history for teaching in primary and secondary schools (Hiskett 1975, 146).

THE INTRODUCTION OF MASS EDUCATION

In January 1974, the Nigerian head of state, General Yakubu Gowon, announced during an official visit to Sokoto that Universal Primary Education would be launched across Nigeria the following year. At the time of the Gowon announcement, only about five percent of Kano City children were in school, while ninety-eight percent of the children in the *Sabon Gari* (or "Strangers' Quarters" just outside the city where southern Nigerians were required to live) were in school (*West Africa,* February 11, 1974). The Kano State Government immediately began a flurry of activity, rapidly establishing schools and appointing a committee headed by Shehu Galadanci to devise a plan for the implementation of UPE in Kano State by 1976.

With the introduction of Universal Primary Education in Nigeria in 1976, the Kano State Government launched a massive education drive, beginning with the establishment of primary schools (grades one through three) in each of its twenty-nine local government areas. Between 1968 and 1978, nine secondary schools were established in Kano State with a total enrollment of 4,095 (out of a total secondary school-age population of approximately two million). As we have seen (chapter five), after the return to electoral politics and civilian rule in 1979, the People's Redemption Party (PRP) in Kano State made education one of its top priorities. By 1983 the PRP established 3,032 primary schools, 43 secondary schools, 24 teacher training colleges, 3 technical and vocational schools, and 2 commercial colleges (see table 17).[12] Several hundred teachers from India, Pakistan, and the Philippines, together with several score Canadian CUSO (Canadian University Service Overseas or the Canadian Peace Corps) were contracted to staff these schools until sufficient numbers of indigenous teachers could be trained. When Kano State was created in 1968, approximately 36,000 boys and 13,000 girls were in school (Interview #50, Kano, January 1, 1985); by 1978, 659,928 children were in school (see table 16). The dramatic effort to produce teachers to teach in the UPE schools is indicated by the rapid increase in enrollment in the teachers' colleges in the state and the creation of ten new teacher training institutions between 1973 and 1976 (see tables 16 and 17). It should especially be noted that the pressures brought by UPE were much greater in Kano than in any other state, first, because it had the lowest initial enrollment rate, and second, because it had the largest population of any state in Nigeria. This was reflected in both the qualifications of the teachers recruited and the number of emergency training courses; in 1978 the entire intake of students into the teachers' colleges had failed their WASC (Kano State 1978). Underskilled students graduating from these schools were given Grade II Teachers' Certification, which permitted them to teach in lower elementary schools. In spite of some concern about low standards and overall quality, however, the commitment of resources and the determination to launch UPE in Kano State were impressive (see table 18).

In 1980, an Agency for Mass Education was established by the Kano State PRP Government and, in April of that year, this agency established a Women's Division in order to develop literacy programs for women in Kano. Thirty women initially enrolled in the Kano City Women's Center; the year following, enrollment in the central City Center was 320 women, and by 1982 over 700 women were attending fourteen classes in this center, while three other such centers had been established in Kano City (at Goron Dutse, Fagge, and in Gwagwarwa), which together enrolled 440 women.[13] By 1983, an additional thirty centers, enrolling over 10,000 women, were established in the twenty-nine local government areas. They offered courses in basic literacy in Arabic, Hausa, and English, simple arithmetic, Islamic Religious Knowledge, and in some cases, knitting, sewing, and cooking (*Triumph,* April 1, 1982).

TABLE 16
Student Enrollments by Type of Institution for the Years 1978/79–1982/83

The following charts give evidence of the enormous strides made in providing education of both males and females in Kano under the PRP government.

Years	Male	Female	Total
Primary school enrollments			
1978/79	469,570	190,358	659,928
1979/80	601,219	253,420	854,639
1980/81	726,753	299,677	1,026,430
1981/82	843,514	356,828	1,200,342
Secondary (grammar) school enrollments			
1978/79	13,453	2,227	15,680
1979/80	15,713	2,515	18,228
1980/81	24,133	3,441	27,574
1981/82	27,941	4,330	32,271
1982/83	57,781	6,983	64,756
Teachers college enrollments			
1978/79	15,395	1,524	16,919
1979/80	15,008	1,727	16,735
1980/81	24,133	3,441	27,574
1981/82	20,226	2,422	22,648
1982/83	22,930	3,793	26,723
Technical/vocational center enrollments			
1978/79	1,439	—	1,439
1979/80	1,790		1,790
1980/81	3,897		3,897
1981/82	4,298		4,298
1982/83	5,230		5,230
Commercial school enrollment			
1978/79	951	326	1,277
1979/80	1,231	309	1,540
1980/81	2,338	384	2,722
1981/82	2,449	395	2,844
1982/83	3,404	422	3,825

Source: Figures from Ministry of Education, Kano State Government, obtained April 14, 1983.

All women attending classes in the Kano City Centers in 1982 were or had been married (fully 83 percent by age fifteen and 100 percent by age twenty) (Bature, Usman, Mahmud 1982). All currently married women were

TABLE 17
Educational Expansion, Kano State, 1940–1983

Year	Primary	Secondary grammar	Secondary commercial	Secondary technical and vocational	Grade II teachers' colleges
1940	20	1	—	1	1
1945	31	1	—	1	1
1950	58	1	—	1	1
1955	74	2	—	1	1
1960	146	5	—	2	3
1965	222	6	—	2	5
1967	241	7	1	2	5
1969	251	10	1	3	5
1971	519	15	1	3	6
1973	532	18	1	3	9
1974/75	616	19	1	3	15
1975/76	678	19	1	3	19
1979/80	701	21	1	3	19
1982/83	3032	43	2	3	24

Source: Kano State 1977–1983.

required to bring written permission from their husbands in order to be admitted to the courses (Interview #26, Kano, February 28, 1983). Sixty-one percent said they were "sent" by their husbands to the centers because "the *Qur'an* says that women should be educated,"—the heart of the PRP campaign to encourage men to let their wives and daughters go to school (Interviews #23, Kano, February 25, 1983, and #26, Kano, February 28, 1983). While 10,000 adult women in classes is a small percentage of the overall population of ten million people in Kano State, the high visibility of the program and the enthusiastic endorsement of it by both political and religious leaders suggest its potential significance.

GIRLS AND EDUCATION IN KANO

As noted, after the introduction of UPE in 1976 and the return to civilian rule in 1979, the PRP government in Kano State oversaw the dramatic increase of the numbers of girls in school (see table 16). Shortly after installa-

TABLE 18
Kano State Government Expenditure on Education at Current Prices 1968/69 to 1975/76 (in naira)

Year	Total	Capital education	%	Total	Recurrent education	%
1968/69	1.14	0.31	27	16.10	1.78	11
1969/70	5.79	1.15	20	23.69	2.36	10
1970/71	17.88	2.25	13	29.65	3.25	11
1971/72	23.44	3.28	14	32.91	5.02	15
1972/73	27.31	4.03	15	34.61	6.66	19
1973/74	29.08	3.95	14	30.38	8.37	28
1974/75	53.49	9.61	18	38.92	10.27	26
1975/76	98.93	36.39	37	77.55	22.00	28
1976/77	148.58	73.53	49	130.07	51.51	40
1977/78*	257.41	99.90	39	198.39	101.21	51
1978/79*	102.65	25.00	24	118.61	50.07	42
1979/80**	100.00	26.14	26	129.32	33.00	26

Source: Bray 1981, 94.

*approved estimates

**estimates

tion of his government in 1979, Governor Abubakar Rimi proclaimed "My government is equally aware that no profound change could take place in a society where women are relegated and marginalized from the helms of socio-economic and political life of any society. It follows then that any serious mass education programme should make women its focal point. . . . Parents and husbands or guardians are therefore urged to send their wives and daughters to school. . . . Critics of women [*sic*] education should stop deceiving themselves and others by opposing women's education from the religious point of view, because God will in the hereafter question them for distorting his words" (Aishatu Salihu Bello 1983, 13).

Getting girls into the classrooms was a crucial step, but only a first step. Because of the low level of Western education, the problem of finding qualified teachers was and continues to be substantial, especially for girls' secondary schools. This is reflected in extraordinarily high failure rates for Kano State secondary school girls in national examinations. The problem is compounded by a general lack of concern about such high failure rates in Kano State schools in general, and it is especially pronounced in the case of girls, for whom the value of education is still seen as limited, particularly in the rural areas.[14]

TABLE 19
Pass Rate on West African School Certificate (WASC) Exam

School	Year	# Pass	# Fail	% Pass	Year	# Pass	# Fail	% Pass
Dala	1980	14	348	3.8	1981	12	196	5.7
WTC	1980	14	104	11.0	1981	14	114	5.7
GGSS	1980	28	513	5.0	1981	0	172	0.0
Kazaure	1980	10	192	4.9	1981	5	201	0.02

Source: Yuguda 1983, 4.

Note. WTC is the Women's Teacher's College and GGSS is the Girls' Secondary School (Gwagwarwa). Dala, WTC, and GGSS are in Kano City, while Kazaure is a town approximately fifty miles to the north of Kano.

A look at the pass rates on the WASC (West African School Certificate) exams in three government secondary schools in Kano City and one rural school in Kano State for the years 1980 and 1981 is illustrative.

Two-hundred-seventeen students and eighty-three teachers in three of these four schools (Dala, Women's Teachers College, and Kazaure) were surveyed in regard to the high failure rates recorded (Aishatu Salihu Bello 1983; Yuguda 1983). Sixty of the 217 students (or 27.7 percent) were already married, and all the others were engaged. All these students and teachers believed that there was no good reason to be concerned about the poor performance of girls because their husbands would support them regardless of how well they did in school. Also indicative of a lack of motivation is the fact that ninety-three percent of the students noted that their parents believed that Islam enjoins females to stay home and live in seclusion after marriage. A large majority, 190 or eighty-eight percent, indicated that their parents did not encourage them to study and 138 (or eighty-eight percent) of those girls not married indicated that their parents would not allow them to pursue further studies in any event. Another observer noted that female students in the secondary schools feel that "it is a waste of time to study hard and strive for good result since they will only end up in their husbands' houses" (Gana 1983, 47). Since all students are promoted whether they pass or fail, many girls take their WASC exams without ever having passed a single subject (Gana, 47; Interview #53, January 5, 1985). Two principals interviewed (at Dala and Kazaure) asserted that although English is the official language of instruction in Kano State, the actual language of instruction in the primary schools is Hausa, as it is in the Islamiyya schools from which many of the rural students come. In the secondary schools, many of the expatriate teachers cannot speak

Hausa and the students cannot speak English; hence students cannot learn. In the secondary schools, exams too are in English. Both principals stressed the necessity of upgrading primary education if girls were to do better at the secondary level (Interviews #53 and 54, Kano, January 5, 1985). But, since both parents and students expect girls to marry and have children, there is no particular motivation to succeed in school. Beliefs, values, and customs of the society all militate against girls' taking their studies seriously. Girls who later want to teach can do so regardless of whether they have passed any subjects or succeeded in the WASC exam.

Both Hausa and Islamic culture stress modesty and uncompetitiveness, especially for girls and women. This fact, together with the emphasis on early marriage and the overall importance of marriage for women, greatly affects girls and their attitudes toward education. To gain a more comprehensive picture of societal attitudes toward girls and education the author interviewed an American-educated woman who had been principal in both an urban secondary school in Kano City and a rural secondary school in Kano State. In addition, university students surveyed 103 teachers and 319 students in three secondary schools, and 430 literate and illiterate parents in both urban and rural areas.[15]

On cultural matters there is no discernible difference between girls in urban as opposed to rural schools. The difference in the mental and emotional health of the students in the two settings is pronounced, however. Overall, students in the two urban schools (Dala and WTC) appeared more future-oriented and achievement-oriented than their rural counterparts at Kazaure, although their more "modern" aspirations toward careers generally were tinged by the contradictory desire for a traditional marriage as well. Their ambivalence suggests the influence of the large numbers of expatriate teachers and NYSC (National Youth Service Corps) teachers from other parts of Nigeria serving in Kano City schools. It is perhaps also significant that the very existence of these aspirations contradicts the values of Hausa culture, which stress complete submission to the will of Allah and the acceptance of fate. In contrast, the rural students adhered to the belief that whatever happened must be accepted and did not believe they had any control over their fates—as in fact, for the most part, they did not. Hence, rural girls were more inclined to believe that nothing depended on their own effort.

In the rural school, a large proportion of the teachers were Hausa. In the urban school, where teachers were predominantly non-Hausa, adjustment to the school situation was very difficult for most students; the principal likened the reactions of her urban students to those of soldiers in combat who give evidence of nervous irritability, overreaction to the merest provocation, and a loss of identity and self-esteem (Interview #55, Kano, January 5, 1985).

Many Hausa children, like this young girl, are raised for some years by relatives of their natural parents. This girl lived with her older sister and her husband. She attended elementary school for a few years, but when she went back to her natural parents she was soon married.

She felt that in the rural setting, the threat of failing or of being expelled from school did not affect the girls, who for the most part did not want to be there in the first place and saw education as irrelevant to their future roles as wives and mothers. The urban girls, she emphasized, felt both ambivalent and confused about such matters.

In another study, an urban girls' secondary school principal commented that "the Hausa girls on the first day sit almost motionless on their beds doing nothing, showing general apathy with little interest in their surroundings . . . often become mute, talking to no one and will not answer questions" (Abdullahi 1980, 99). This principal noted that bedwetting is frequent among the younger urban students, but is nearly nonexistent for rural students, suggesting greater psychological stress among the urban students. To illustrate, she noted that on several occasions in the late 1970s the urban students became "quite hysterical" and claimed to have seen "spirits of the dead" during the night. They were clearly affected by the great change in environment and the isolation from the protective walls of their mothers' compounds. She notes "there were five suicide attempts while I was principal, all involving an overdose of drugs which were brought from home." During this time also, fifteen girls a day requested to go to the hospital. The girls in one dormitory set fire to their mattresses, burning the dorm to the ground (Abdullahi, 105). In the principal's perception, the girls suffered from feelings of alienation, helplessness, and failure (Abdullahi, 114). In short, they could not internalize the Western values presented in the classroom; torn between two sets of norms, they succumbed to stress. In rural areas where there were fewer non-Hausa, the teachers described their students as much less traumatized by the experience of living away from home. There were few instances of unacceptable behavior, and the girls themselves seemed happy to be away from home for a few years before marrying.[16]

In the urban school the students tried to speak English because so many of their teachers could not speak Hausa. In the rural school, in contrast, the teachers tended both to speak and teach in Hausa, even though the official language of instruction in all secondary schools in Kano State (as in Nigeria as a whole) was English. The importance of this fact, vis-à-vis the high failure rates in Kano State, is seen when the scores of girls in the St. Louis Secondary School for Girls are contrasted with those of the government schools discussed above. As noted, St. Louis was founded in 1951 for the daughters of non-Hausa parents resident in Kano. In 1976, all sixty-seven girls at St. Louis taking the WASC passed; in 1977 and 1978, when fifty-six and sixty-six girls were examined, 95 percent passed. The scores began to come down in 1980 after the state government decreed that eighty percent of St. Louis students must henceforth be indigenous to Kano State. That year the pass rate fell to eighty-five percent, and by 1981 it had fallen to sixty-eight percent (Umar 1981, 5). The better prepared students were the twenty percent non-Hausa girls admitted under the quota system. It is reasonable to attribute the gap between Hausa and non-Hausa girls to ability in the use of the English language. Of the 235 students taking the WASC exams at the end of the fifth form in 1981 (roughly the equivalent of an American high school education), all but 2 of the 25 non-Hausa students (eighty-eight percent) passed the exams, whereas only 136 of the 210 Hausa girls (sixty-four percent) taking the exam passed, even with the twenty percent bonus points added to their scores for being from an "educationally disadvantaged state" (Interview #56, Kano, January 5, 1985).

When the author visited Kazaure in 1982, the rural students appeared to be at ease and easily engaged in animated conversation in Hausa, much in contrast to students in classes visited at the Dala Girls Secondary School in Kano City. Classes seemed to be free-floating, with the teachers giving little guidance and placing little pressure on the girls to settle down to their lessons. Clearly, school as an academic institution had little relevance for the lives of these girls. And, indeed, no candidates for the WASC examinations in this school obtained a passing score in 1982. For most of them, according to the principal, school was a "waste of time and a good social center where they can meet their friends and do interesting things together before going to live in their husbands houses" (Interview #55, January 5, 1985).

By their senior year (1982), fifty percent of the Hausa students who had entered Form I at St. Louis had left, eighty percent of these for academic reasons. Ninety percent of those who remained passed the WASC, but the passing score for residents of Kano State was only twenty-five percent. In Kazaure, ninety percent of the students remained to complete their Fifth Form, but less than ten percent passed the examination that would allow them into a postsecondary institution or the Bayero University School of General Studies, a kind of remedial program that attempts to prepare students from Kano State schools for university work. As noted elsewhere, "These girls are not threatened by academic failure, because they want to lead traditional lives with marriage and children and see no reason why they should not" (Abdullahi 1980, 97).

At home, girls are too busy with domestic chores to study, even were the atmosphere conducive to it. However, the lack of privacy, the inability to appreciate the virtues of studiousness, and the constant stream of people in and out of compounds make it virtually impossible for a girl to pursue school work at home even were she so inclined. This is a problem in Hausa society in general. Of 319 female secondary school students surveyed, eighty-eight percent indicated that their parents did not encourage them to read and eighty-seven percent claimed that their parents did not encourage them to study (Aishatu Salihu Bello 1983; Yuguda 1983). Of 144 students at Dala Government Girls Secondary School in Kano, 40 (27.7 percent) were married and all the others were betrothed. Ninety-three, or eighty-nine percent of those not married, said their parents or husbands-to-be would not allow them to continue their education, no matter how well they did in school. A large majority of the eighty-three secondary school teachers (seventy-eight percent) related the high failure rates of girls to the fact that they would never have to work, as their husbands would provide for them; so, education was more of a social interlude before marriage than an experience related to any practical application (Yuguda 1983).

The failure rates and the lack of concern about them suggest that while education is now viewed as an asset for girls before marriage, it does not offer options in addition to marriage. The dramatic indications of stress caused by cultural disorientation among urban students suggest that education alone is not a panacea for the cultural factors inhibiting women's emancipation in Kano. However, where illiteracy rates are high, as in Kano, and female illiteracy even higher, female education is the single most sensitive indicator of women's changing social status; as the PRP stressed, it is not so much an engine of change as a necessary precondition. In terms of numbers affected, educational developments have been rapid and far-reaching in Kano State in the past decade. Their impact on the lives of women is just beginning to be felt; the long-term effects on women's perceptions about themselves and their life prospects will interact with deeply ingrained cultural prescriptions to determine what changes, if any, will affect women's emancipation from the confines of domestic life to public roles. At present, while education succeeds in expanding theoretical horizons, as indicated by "aspirations" data in table 10 of chapter five, the practical realities of girls' lives as dictated by the culture and the marriage system have not changed. Girls themselves do not take their studies seriously, partly because they either are or soon will be married and they do not expect the nature of marriage to change.

7

Paths of Emergence

Education

EDUCATION AND CHANGE

In order for education to be an effective catalyst for change in the lives of women and the roles they play in the public and private domains, there must be complementary changes in male perceptions of appropriate roles and new patterns of interaction between men and women. If women are to have new freedoms, men may be forced not only to give up certain expectations and privileges, but to entertain a fundamentally different view of themselves. If women are to have a voice in matters that concern them, men may have to concede that their own opinions are not always beyond question or compromise. While education makes economic independence possible, a salary in and of itself does not liberate a woman from the restraints imposed by the sociology of her culture. Information about the attitudes of both men and women towards women's education and its implications for marriage and employment thus is crucial in seeking to understand the potential of education as a path of emergence for secluded Hausa women.

Some relatively early indications of the likely long-term impact of Western education on Hausa girls arise from the work of Jean Trevor in Sokoto, a city to the northwest of Kano (Trevor 1975). Trevor taught in Sokoto in 1953; in 1970, she returned to see what had become of her students. Of the 100 students she was able to follow up, 11 had died during childbirth. Two had married men whose careers as civil servants took them away from Sokoto for long periods of time; they claimed to be "very happy" and expressed the hope that their husbands would not be posted back to Sokoto lest relatives force them to take additional wives and to confine all their wives to *kulle.* They described their marriages as "modern" and reported that their husbands encouraged their careers as teachers and showed personal interest in the progress of their school-aged children.

Trevor asked her 89 surviving former students what use they had made of their schooling and whom, in retrospect, they believed they had wanted to please at various times in their lives. She found a high correlation between what girls claimed to have wanted at age twelve and what they did later. Those who said "I wanted to please my family" married early and lived in seclusion, while those who said they wanted to please their teachers sought marriages that would permit them to teach.

One pupil had urged her parents to agree to her marriage at thirteen to a much older, illiterate man who had three wives already, believing that he would indulge her more because of her age and would not hinder her from continuing her education. Another girl who followed a similar strategy found that it backfired; having married a commoner because he would let her teach, she found that he beat her cruelly for acting "grand"; she left him and her five children to return to her parents, and subsequently entered an arranged marriage and agreed to live in *kulle.* A few women whose husbands were more indifferent tried to work, but tension mounted as family and job responsibilities collided—entertaining, visiting relatives, keeping up with the constant round of naming ceremonies, weddings, condolence calls, etc. necessarily required an otherwise blank calendar. Trevor observed that houses where educated wives lived in seclusion were much calmer than houses where they did not; but her former pupils, even in *kulle,* were interested in the outside world and were teaching their children a less traditional outlook. They patiently bore what they described as frustration, trusting that things would be different—that is, better—for their daughters. Of Trevor's ex-pupils, only one rebelled, lives independently, and works on her own (Trevor 1975, 257).

Interviews in Kano a decade later suggest that a woman can apparently be contented as a good *kulle* wife, yet think and treat her children in a "modern" way, thereby avoiding marital confrontation while providing a stimulus for change. Even the most traditional women in the emir's palace, who would not think of breaking society's mores themselves, believed their daughters would not live as they had—nor did they want them to. These women said that times were changing and there was nothing anyone could do about it (Interview #24, February 26, 1983; #25, March 19, 1983).

Change is often subtle, rather than dramatic. Of fifty educated women indigenous to Kano interviewed by the author, about ten percent had married men of lower social status in order to be able to teach. These women claimed that husbands of their own class would have lost face if their wives had worked. Therefore, with their families' help and consent, they married men more professional but of lower status, such as teachers or university professors. This development is in itself indicative of change; also significant was the fact that young men who had been educated abroad could quickly see the advantage of a double income, at least initially when they were establishing a more modern life style and trying to meet familial demands; several doctors, the secretary to the state government, and the managing director of the state newspaper, all of whom studied abroad, encouraged their educated wives to work (two as teachers and one as a medical doctor).

Not all educated women want to work, however. Of the fifty interviewed, five lived in seclusion and liked it, particularly when the other wives were also educated (and so made good company). When extreme circumstances required, however, these women believed their educations provided them with options unknown to their mothers.

The *Qur'an* makes it clear that the husband is responsible for supporting his wife, never she him. If he should become incapacitated or impoverished, he becomes the responsibility of his children, his parents, or his brothers and sisters. Ordinarily a woman is never responsible for or expected to support a man. At Bayero University two wives (twenty-six and thirty-one years old) of a faculty member paralyzed in an automobile accident decided to become self-supporting while remaining at home and keeping the family together rather than enter new and separate marriages. To this end, they took in sewing, did some teaching and tutoring in Arabic, and bought a car for shopping. Though they were clearly breaking with many traditions, they were generally admired on the University campus and thought remarkable for remaining with a man who could not support them. Both their families, however, regarded the situation as troubling and pressured the women to remarry, leaving their husband's care to his own family as tradition would dictate.

Forty-nine of the fifty women expected their daughters to go to school. They felt that school would make them more assured, less afraid of gossip and evil spirits, and more independent of mind; moreover, it would enable them, if the need arose, to support themselves and their children rather than remain in a "cruel marriage." All wanted their daughters to marry, and all believed that happiness and religious blessing comes with marriage. None believed it essential their daughters do well in school—"only that she finishes." Once again it was clear that education was an end to itself; the quest for knowledge was secondary. They themselves claimed to have stable marriages (unlike traditional women, they believed) that belied the male stereotype of educated women. These women were emphatic in insisting that they wanted to live in their own culture and had no desire to become Westernized—which they described as being neurotic, competitive, materialistic, and "bad" to old people. They wanted to move toward self-determination, but did not want to upset familiar roles. In spite of the conservative bent of many of the beliefs expressed, it is clear that these women are part of a movement away from tradition.

Evidence of the new, "modern" spirit, albeit on a small scale, was illustrated in the life of one woman, a grandmother at age twenty-nine. She talked of having taken the "Hausa path" first, marrying at age twelve and bearing six children in seven years. Now, she asserts she cannot be criticized for taking the "British path": having earned her Standard II certificate in adult literacy classes for women at a women's center (the Gidan Galadima) and been divorced from her husband, she is attending the Women's Teachers College in Kano. She plans to be a teacher and not to remarry (Interview #49, December 26, 1984). She was the only one of the fifty women interviewed to so clearly see herself as on a "new road."

A more common attitude is recorded in the survey of 572 male and 114 female university students at Bayero University; 81 of the women thought life would be easier for their daughters than for them. When asked whom they wanted their daughters to marry, "A good man whom she likes" was the most frequent response of female students (seventy-eight percent); in contrast, male students thought wealth or position were most important to young women and their families (seventy-five percent). No students conceived of life outside marriage as a desirable option.

This survey nonetheless produced some data suggesting that change—slow rather than dramatic, but none the less highly significant—was in the offing. Views were solicited on the expansion of female education, the situation of educated women, the impact of education on marriage, the participation of women in the work force, and on women's participation in politics.

Students have marriage and family life expectations that they have acquired through observation and personal experience, and they have acquired attitudes and expectations regarding what is appropriate and inappropriate for husbands and wives in different domestic situations. They are interested in the process of social change and the effects of education on social life. They make it possible to make a preliminary assessment of the effects of an independent variable (education) on the direction of social change.

Female students at Bayero were from better-educated and more well-to-do families than were male students. Forty-three percent of the ninety-two Muslim girls had gone to school in western Nigeria, particularly in Kwara State, and spoke Yoruba as a first or second language; fifty percent came from the lower north rather than from Kano State. Twenty percent (twenty-three) of the female students were Christian and had attended Christian schools. One-third of the Muslim girls had also attended Christian schools, again reflecting both the rather high percentage of Muslim Yoruba girls among the female students and the requirement that St. Louis Secondary School for Girls reserve eighty percent of its seats for Kano State girls. In contrast, ninety-three percent of the male students were from Kano State and were graduates of government secondary schools or teacher training colleges in the state. In terms of the population of Kano State, Hausa girls were underrepresented, as were Muslim girls who had not attended a Christian secondary school. Thus, the very poor performance of Hausa Muslim girls in Kano State secondary schools, discussed in chapter six, is clearly reflected in the university enrollment figures.

Since 1976, when the concerted campaign for girls' education was begun, Muslim families have appeared somewhat less opposed to Western education or education for girls; most girls claimed that their families were supportive of their educations. The greatest obstacle to Muslim girls' education remains the fear among parents that it will "spoil" them; thus, while opposition to education per se is unusual, an insistence on early marriage remains. Ninety percent of the Muslim female students rank "pressure to marry young" as the primary obstacle to girls pursuing their education, whereas only fifty percent of Christian girls cited this as an obstacle, and apparently, in the case of Christian girls, they are not referring to themselves, but to girls in general and especially in the north where the survey was taken. For Christian girls an equally important obstacle in the way of education appears to be financial. (Only one student, a Christian female, cited religion as the main obstacle to girls' education (see table 20).)

TABLE 20
Bayero University Survey: "What is the main obstacle to girls' education?"

	Female Students (114)		Male Students (572)		Totals (686)
	Christian (22)	Muslim (92)	Christian (34)	Muslim (538)	
Belief it will "spoil girls"	0	7	13	81	101
Cost	11	0	13	180	204
Conservatism	0	1	4	96	101
Pressure to marry young	10	82	2	116	210
Need for girls to do *tala*	0	1	0	49	50
Religion	1	0	0	0	1
Men's jealousy	0	0	0	0	0
Fear	0	0	0	0	0
Other	0	0	2	17	19
TOTALS	22	92	34	538	686

Source: Bayero University student survey conducted by author, 1983.

More than any other factor, education postpones the age of marriage for girls whose families have allowed them to continue in school. Still, at the university level a majority of female students is married (only four of the twenty-two Christian girls in the survey, but eighty-two of the ninety-two Muslim girls were married). Cultural differences underscored by religion are evident in the fact that the Muslim girls believed that progressive fathers were the most important factor in furthering their education, whereas Christian girls credited their mothers' interest as the decisive factor. Christian girls also cited their mothers as important financial contributors to their education, whereas for Muslim girls, fathers and husbands are virtually the only means of support; they also believed that having educated sisters is important—perhaps because it suggests a family strongly supportive of female education, even though sisters do not often contribute financial support (table 21).

TABLE 21
Bayero University Survey
"Who supported (paid for) your education?"

	Female Students (N = 114)	
	Christian	Muslim
Father	2	61
Mother	14	0
Brothers	2	0
Husband	0	30
Sisters	1	0
Uncles	1	1
Government	0	0
Mission	2	0

"Who encouraged you most in your education?"

	Female Students (N = 114)	
	Christian	Muslim
Educated sisters	0	10
Educated brothers	0	0
Mother	18	0
Father	4	75
Husband	0	7

Source: Survey by author, 1983.

Also indicative of strong cultural predispositions in regard to relations between the sexes is the fact that fifty percent of the Muslim girls preferred single-sex schools at the primary school level for children, and seventy-five percent of them believed single-sex institutions at the secondary level were essential, lest girls develop "moral" problems later in life. Both Muslim and Christian girls overwhelmingly stated that they expected that their daughters would attend university. Male students were even more strongly in favor of single-sex education and much less committed to university education for their daughters (table 22).

Muslim male students overwhelmingly felt that women were not "exploited." Interestingly—and perhaps reflecting the concerted emphasis of Islamic leaders on the importance of education for girls—they felt that no preference should be given to boys in education. On the other hand, eighty-seven percent of the Muslim girls stated that it was important to change the status of women in Nigeria, particularly in the north where women are espe-

TABLE 22
Bayero University Survey

	Yes	No
A. "Do you support coeducation in primary school?"		
Christian female students (22)	20 (91%)	2 (9%)
Muslim female students (92)	41 (50%)	41 (50%)
Christian male students (34)	23 (68%)	4 (12%)
Muslim male students (538)	435 (81%)	86 (16%)
(No answer = 34)		
B. "Do you support coeducation in secondary school?"		
Christian female students (22)	18 (82%)	4 (18%)
Muslim female students (92)	23 (25%)	69 (75%)
Christian male students (34)	21 (62%)	11 (34%)
Muslim male students (538)	101 (19%)	435 (81%)
(No answer = 4)		

C. "To what level will you educate your daughter?"

	Female Students (114)		**Male Students** (572)	
	Christian (22)	**Muslim** (92)	**Christian** (34)	**Muslim** (538)
Primary school	0	0	0	230 (43%)
Secondary school	0	15 (16%)	7 (21%)	221 (41%)
University	22 (100%)	77 (83%)	27 (79%)	80 (15%)
(No answer = 7)				

Source: Survey by author, 1983.

cially disadvantaged. Both groups thought that educated women were happier than uneducated women, because they had more freedom and could attain a greater degree of personal fulfillment. But, a significant subgroup of Christian girls (thirty-one percent) thought that traditional women were happier because there is too much conflict in modern life (table 23).

In spite of changing views on the importance of education, then, traditional attitudes are still a predominant component of the value system. Rising levels of education suggest a more articulate and informed society in Kano in the years to come, but patterns of interaction between men and women may not be challenged. Women will be more enlightened concerning their daily lives, more articulate about their problems, and more effective in securing public policies which address these problems so long as they do not overtly challenge those factors which structure the relationship between the sexes.

While the concerted emphasis on the importance of sending girls to school by the PRP government had dramatic impact, a boy was still much

TABLE 23
Bayero University Survey: The Status of Women

	Agree	Disagree	No Opinion
"Women are exploited and disadvantaged in northern Nigeria and their status should be improved"			
Muslim male students (n = 538)	103 (19%)	435 (81%)	
Christian male students (n = 34)	20 (59%)	10 (29%)	4 (12%)
Muslim female students (n = 92)	80 (87%)	12 (13%)	
Christian female students (n = 22)	20 (91%)	1 (4%)	1 (4%)
"In education preference should be given to boys over girls"			
Muslim male students (n = 538)	80 (15%)	451 (84%)	7 (1%)
Christian male students (n = 34)	20 (59%)	14 (41%)	
Muslim female students (n = 92)	40 (43%)	52 (57%)	
Christian female students (n = 22)	5 (23%)	17 (77%)	

"Which women are the happiest?"

	Christian Female Students (n = 22)	Muslim Female Students (n = 92)
Urban educated women	15 (68%)	40 (43%)
Rural educated women	0	10 (11%)
Urban uneducated women	0	5 (38%)
Rural uneducated women	7 (31%)	7 (8%)

Source: Survey by author, 1983.

more likely than a girl to go to school and advance in educational attainment. Traditional reluctance to send girls outside the home remained much in evidence. In the rural areas of Kano State, the ratio of boys to girls in school was four to one in 1980; in the city, the ratio was three to one. In secondary schools, the ratio was five to one in the state (Kano State 1982); at the University, it was ten to one (Bayero University 1980–82, 3). By 1982, classes in the Kano municipal area were mandated to enroll a standard forty students, twenty-six boys and fourteen girls (Interview #57, Kano, January 5, 1985).

To supplement the student survey, several men of traditional status were interviewed. These men emphasized that they were not opposed to a high level of education for women per se, but only to the corruption of character and resulting societal instability promoted by Western education. Interviews with a leading Islamic educator in Kano highlighted concerns that girls' education beyond the primary school level would interfere with the widespread belief that girls should be married shortly after the onset of puberty (Interview #15, Kano, June 21, 1982). His views were echoed by both students and parents. The Grand Kadi of Kano expressed deep admiration for knowledge; but while he believed that girls should be educated, he feared lest educated girls would not give full attention to "their proper roles as wives and mothers." "Women's place is in the home training children to be obedient Muslim citizens" (Interview #15, Kano, June 21, 1982). He contended that the "moral threat of work outside the home threatens the peace of the home." Interestingly, however, the Grand Kadi allowed his own daughters to attend secondary school and one (Fatima Gwarzo) is a medical practitioner.

According to the Madaki of Kano (one of the four highest traditional title holders), the status of women fell once men became concerned with the establishment of their own power rather than with religion. The Madaki stressed that education for women was important, but asserted that the best way for most women to become educated beyond primary school is to marry scholars and learn privately from them (Interview #55, Kano, July 7, 1983). He repeated the often-heard assertion that the Shehu himself may have been more liberal than contemporary Muslim leaders in Kano, and indeed, there is ample justification for this contention. Dan Fodio criticized Islamic society in Kano at the time of the jihad for ignoring women's education, accusing men of "leaving their wives, their daughters and the captives morally abandoned, like beasts, without teaching them what God prescribes" (from *Mur al albab,* quoted in Hodgkin 1960, 194–95). The Shehu's daughter Mariamu reported the battles of the jihad in Arabic, while his daughter Nana (Asma) wrote poetry. The Shehu's brother Abdullahi is reported to have said that education took precedence over seclusion (Abdullah Ibn Muhammad 1960, 86–87, quoted in Hiskett 1963, 438), although it was he who first advised that the best way for a woman to receive an education was to "marry a scholar, and do not argue too cleverly or he will stop teaching you" (Hiskett, 439).

In this vein, a man generally perceived as very progressive on religious matters, former Grand Kadi of Northern Nigeria Abubakar Gummi once remarked that men should see that women are educated "according to their own natures. Some may prefer science and the law to domestic subjects and we should encourage their minds to grow by studying them. This does not mean that they should practice these subjects professionally when they are adults because they should marry, and then their first responsibility will be to safeguard the peace and piety of the home and develop their children's sensitivity and moral character. But we have a duty to see that their own minds and personalities develop too, or their contribution will be less" (Trevor 1975, 255). In fact, all of Gummi's daughters too attended postsecondary institutions.

Hence, while traditional leaders now stress the importance of education for girls, they continue to believe that such education should consist of literacy and domestic science. The culture continues to discourage individuality and competitiveness between girls. Islamic leaders concur in stating that girls should marry young so that they will not know much of the world (although divorce rates for young girls in first marriages are very high).

While there is little enthusiasm for Western education under any circumstances, less concern is aroused when boys rather than girls are the focus. The Grand Kadi explained that "men are bred to lead, therefore they need Western skills." During the colonial period, sons of hereditary leaders were given special attention for this very reason, and traditional leaders concurred with the British on this point. Thus, men may adapt to cultural change, but women, as the preservers of culture, must reflect tradition and continuity.

It is thus hardly surprising that in Kano at Bayero University as elsewhere sex stereotyping of occupations is beginning to occur. During 1975/76, sixteen percent of the University student population was female (Federal Office of Statistics Economic Indicators, vol. 12, cited in Kisekka 1980, 39). At Bayero, 62 of the 98 women matriculating for the 1982/83 term entered the faculties of Arts and Islamic Studies or Education, while 8 women and 140 men entered the Faculty of Science, 3 women and 38 men entered the Faculty of Law, and no women and 45 men entered the Faculty of Technology. The other 25 women were in the social and management sciences (Bayero University 1983). However, it is interesting to note that in other Nigerian universities, the national statistics imply that approximately half of female students were not pursuing stereotypical courses, which suggests a correlation between Islam and sex stereotyping (Pitten 1980, 890), although it should also be noted that options concerning all courses of study are more limited at Bayero University than they are at other universities.

Most children in Kano State receive some Qur'anic education, the boys usually attending several hours a day and the girls less. Rural parents, in particular, mistrust Western education as something alien and unnecessary for girls who will marry, while urban mothers can see that education can protect a girl from having to endure an unsatisfactory marriage. A university student too felt that women's education was indeed important, because "If the marriage should fail, they will have the independence of mind and the skills to support themselves and their children until there is another marriage and the children can be placed" (Interview #56, Kano, December 26, 1984). Rural mothers are concerned that their girls spend their early years trading, rather than studying, lest they fail to accumulate sufficient dowries. Urban mothers, particularly in Kurawa and Gwagwarwa, are beginning to believe that education can be, in effect, a part of the dowry, a part of the assets a girl takes into marriage. Both rural and urban men know and recount the government theme—that education for girls is important because it is the women who will raise the children—and respect education insofar as it teaches them Islamic Religious Knowledge (IRK), hygiene, and nutrition (the tools of a superior mother); more academic subjects are not taken seriously by parents or students, and generally girls do not succeed in passing them.

The fact that some women are beginning to see education as a buffer to marriage is significant, although it might be argued that some parents hope a daughter can be prepared for a career in order that they themselves will not be burdened with providing for an educated daughter when and if her marriage fails. At the same time, because families are obligated to provide support in such an event, many women do not feel the need to use their education to establish economic independence. More especially, the severe community censure of an independent woman and the great suspicion of the moral character of unmarried women helps explain the inability of school girls to think of a career as an alternative, rather than a possible adjunct to, marriage. This same mind-set accounts for the efforts of divorced, educated women to remarry at the first opportunity. At the University, at least three female students who were married in 1981 had been divorced and remarried by 1983. While in 1981 they had condemned polygamy, in 1983 each had become the third wife of her new husband. As there are few examples of women who have clearly broken with tradition, the present generation of college and secondary school students are potential pioneers whose futures will be monitored with interest by men and women alike.

Just as men from families of high traditional status have been the first to receive Western education, women in secondary schools and the university in the 1980s are more likely than their male counterparts to come from middle- and upper-class families. Male students tend to represent the entire range of Nigerian society, from poor peasant to ruling elite, whereas only two percent of the Hausa Muslim girls come from homes that would be considered less than middle-class (see table 24). Thus, all the girls, but only fifty-six percent of the Muslim males in the university survey expected their own daughters to be educated beyond primary school. This unanimity of opinion among female students indicates that change is beginning to occur in the aspirations of upper-class girls, if not in actual life styles and choices. The percentage

TABLE 24
Bayero University Survey: Education and Occupation of Students' Parents

	Islamic School**	Primary School	Post Primary School	Post Secondary School
Highest Level of Students' Fathers' Education*				
Muslim male students (538)	510 (95%)	25 (4%)	3 (.05%)	0
Christian male students (34)	0	21 (62%)	10 (29%)	3 (8%)
Muslim female students (92)	5 (5%)	28 (30%)	58 (63%)	1 (1%)
Christian female students (22)	0	2 (9%)	5 (23%)	15 (68%)
Highest Level of Education of Students' Mothers				
Muslim male students (538)	538 (100%)	0	0	0
Christian male students (34)	0	12 (35%)	17 (50%)	5 (15%)
Muslim female students (92)	92 (100%)	0	0	0
Christian female students (22)	0	10 (45%)	11 (50%)	1 (5%)

Occupation of Students' Fathers

	Farmer	Trader	Civil Servant	Traditional Authority	Teacher Doctor Lawyer Banker	Laborer
Muslim male students (538)	120 (22%)	70 (13%)	78 (14%)	190 (35%)	55 (10%)	25 (5%)
Christian male students (34)	0	9 (36%)	15 (44%)	0	10 (29%)	0
Muslim female students (92)	2 (2%)	5 (5%)	50 (54%)	20 (22%)	15 (16%)	0
Christian female students (22)	0	0	7 (32%)	0	15 (68%)	0

Source: Survey by author, 1983.

*Levels indicate attendance, not completion

**Includes attendance at Islamiyya school or Qur'anic school of girls continuing their education beyond primary school declines rapidly in comparison to the figures for boys, but the proportion is steadily increasing and this is in itself important. As the number of educated women rises, so does the possibility that a few women will insist on seeking personal fulfillment through careers.

The content of the daily press in Kano suggests a growing public recognition that women's creative energies must be developed through education if Nigeria is to make maximum use of its human resources.

> Speaking on the importance the ministry attaches to the crucial role of women in the society, it was disclosed that this is in recognition of the potentials of women as instruments for constructive change and orderly development of the society (*Daily Times*, August 15, 1982).

> It was also discussed that the Federal Government is building more secondary schools for girls in all the states of the Federation to enable them go on to further education. There are also dynamic programmes being adopted to eradicate illiteracy among women since the government is of the opinion that illiteracy among women constitutes the major obstacle to their participation in the economic and social development of the country (*Punch*, November 26, 1982).

Nevertheless, male resistance to changes in domestic roles is enormous.

> But it needs to be noted that most of the women who are decent are not those who threw their bras into the gutter and chanted sterile equality slogans on women liberation trails. [*sic*] They are not the "soul sisters," but mostly housewives, mothers and grandmothers (*Concord*, February 1, 1983).

> How true that old quip—'The hand that rocks the cradle also rules the nation.' Today in Nigeria the moral discipline of children is a feminine responsibility. And so as the housewife carries out her complex role of child bearing, house chores and job, she is supposed to use all the resources at her disposal including affection, rewards and punishments in the right mixture in bringing up the child. An overdose as well as an underdose of these ingredients could be disastrous. . . . Observers of the Nigerian scene are quick to relate juvenile delinquencies to laxity on the parts [*sic*] of women. . . . With the craze for wealth and materialism, many housewives rear children, do house keeping, hold office jobs and sometimes trade. As a result, such women are left with little time to show affection to their children or correct the erring kids. . . . A young woman

> who idles hours to and from lectures wasting smiles on strange men for lifts may not be in good moral standing to educate her kids (*Concord,* February 21, 1983).

It has been asserted that higher education is the most potent force stimulating a reassessment of women's roles (Dodd 1973). Secondary and university education are credited with expanding women's horizons, thus encouraging them to look for fulfillment not only in the home but outside it, equipping them with the skills and inclination for employment, and reducing childbearing and lessening its burdens. While this may accurately describe education's impact on middle- and upper-class urban Hausa women, it also describes attitudes and practices widely regarded as Western and unacceptable, particularly by religious leaders and by both men and women in rural areas.

Despite this indictment, it is in fact the case that educated women in Kano are as religious as uneducated women. They may be less fatalistic, feel more responsibility for their actions, and feel they have more ultimate control over their lives, but they do not challenge their religion and its prescriptions to marry, obey, and seek greater knowledge of Allah. However, their attitudes towards their children often diverge from the traditional. Among the dozen or so educated women married to university lecturers, only one is practicing traditional *kunya* ("first-child avoidance" or giving the child to relatives and avoiding all interaction with it including ever referring to it by name). While several have given care of their first children to sisters or mothers-in-law, they keep in touch with them, talk with them, and are keenly interested in how they are being raised and educated. These women help their children learn to think and to expect and respond to change; they value the greater self-determination they feel they have as educated women. They often make conscious choices against traditional practices such as *kulle* and *kunya* while continuing to function traditionally in regard to marriages, naming ceremonies, and the like. Educated women who have lived abroad with their husbands are appalled at the loneliness and isolation of women in the West and want to avoid any such development in their own culture.

Alternatives to marriage to not exist. Women's options within marriage (to seek education, to work) are slowly changing, but the structure of marriage itself is not. There is some evidence that educated women are likely to marry later and are beginning to postpone motherhood a few years, but they have just as many children and in closer succession than do uneducated women. (They are able to have their children closer together than is traditionally sanctioned because they do not nurse as long as most women—up to three or four years—and they do not observe the lactation taboo.) As of 1983, no program of family planning existed in Kano, and educated women, like their

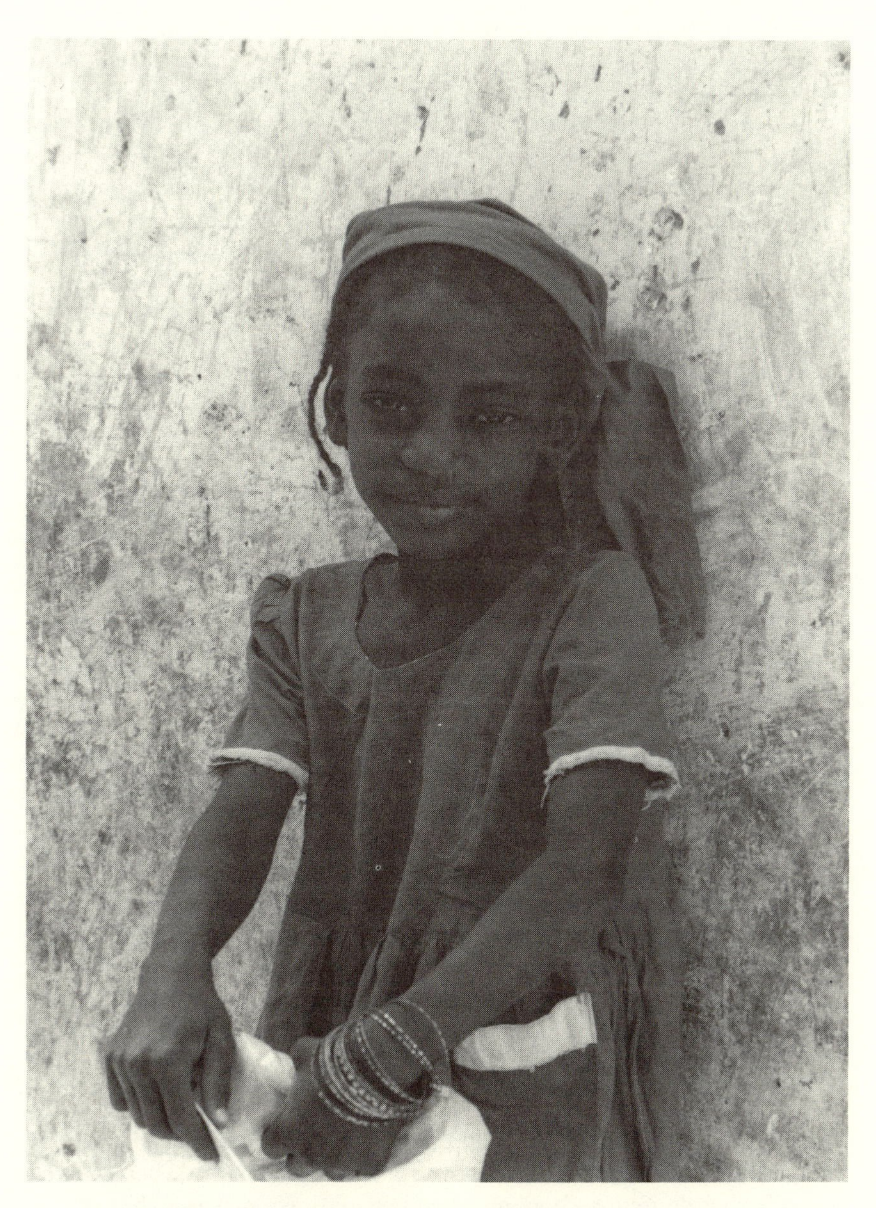

The daughter of a university teacher and a primary school teacher, this girl, in her school uniform, often visited her grandparents in the old city. Young women like this will provide the answers to the questions raised in this book about the long-term effects of education on women's lives.

uneducated sisters, wanted to bear as many children as Allah would give to them. Having children, not careers, was central to their lives. Women still feared and expected that many of their children would not reach adulthood and consequently bore as many as possible to assure that one or several would look after them in old age. Among educated women there was some recognition of the advantages of spacing children, but not any evident desire to limit their number. All women interviewed in the course of this study believed that children bring "joy" and were shocked by the notion that some women in other parts of the world might choose to forego them. Nevertheless, as of 1985, the military regime had begun to acknowledge publicly that Nigeria needed a policy for planned population growth (*New Nigerian,* January 4, 1985; May 10, 1985; *Punch,* May 7, 1985). Perhaps once again a military government will introduce a dramatic public policy affecting women. Hence, in this sense it is men, rather than women, who are likely to provide means by which women can change their lives.

The development of education has gained many young girls far more freedom to leave the confines of their or their husbands' homes than was acceptable even ten years ago. Further, the consequent association of girls with girls from families to whom they are not related and to teachers from foreign cultures has exposed them to influences from which they would have been entirely sheltered ten years ago. But, it must be remembered that very little that challenges fundamentalist Islamic beliefs will be tolerated. Education, even at the university level in Kano, is primarily an exercise in the communication of Islamic values. At Bayero, objectivity, constructive criticism, and the open communication of ideas is not encouraged; Islamic beliefs about women and their roles are not directly challenged.

EDUCATION AND MARRIAGE

In spite of very dramatic increases in the numbers of girls enrolled in primary schools, it is still a fact that few women obtain access to higher education, primarily because of parental pressure to marry young and the widespread belief that only elementary levels of education are appropriate for women. And once a girl marries, her continued education becomes her husband's, not her parents' decision and responsibility. A girl may ask her parents to consider her desire for schooling when negotiating a marriage, but the decision is never hers alone to make; and, even though the husband-to-be may agree, he may also change his mind once the marriage is consummated, as the following letter indicates:

c/o A. Abubakar Mijinyawa
P.O. Box 3021
Kano

The Faculty Board,
Faculty of Social and Management Sciences,
Bayero University,
Kano

Dear Board,

Refering to my application for re-admission, to Part II for the 1983/84 session, whereby you requested me to tell you the family reasons which I said could not allow me to continue with my studies at the appropriate time, I do hereby write.

The fact is that, after my Part I I had to get married, before which we made an agreement with my husband that he will allow me to continue with my studies. After the wedding, when the time to resume school came he refused to allow me to attend lectures after I registered. Since that time I have been begging him but the matter was not settled until this time.

So, I hereby appeal to the Board to please help me finish my studies since the interest has not die away in my mind by considering my case.

Yours sincerely,

(signed)

Such cases are not ususual.

One girl made extraordinary efforts to be admitted to a master's program at Bayero with the strong support of her family and was finally admitted. After she began her studies and was doing well, her husband decided that she was away from home too much and demanded that she quit. In the end he announced the ultimatum that she either quit her studies or be divorced by *talaq*. Some members of her family actually urged her to remain at the University; but, afraid of being divorced and having to make new marriage arrangements, she bowed to her husband's wishes and now lives in *kulle tsari,* much to the distress of her friends and the supportive members of her family (Interview #56, Kano, December 26, 1984).

University women expect that their daughters will both receive university education and marry men of their own choosing. But even university women agree that men should be dominant in marriage regardless of whether they themselves or members of their families arrange the marriage (see table 25).

TABLE 25
Bayero University Survey: Education and Marriage

1. Who should decide who a daughter should marry?
2. Who should decide when a daughter should marry?
3. Who should decide to what level a girl will be educated?
4. Who should decide whether a wife will work?

Question	Husband alone		Husband and wife together		The wife alone		The girl herself		The girl and her parents		The girl and her husband-to-be	
	M	F	M	F	M	F	M	F	M	F	M	F
1	201	28	20	10	0	0	6	5	8	15	8	7
2	115	83	89	15	0	0	0	0	329	15	39	18
3	91	2	85	2	0	0	6	21	225	82	107	7
4	118	20	325	20	99	19	0	5	0	0	30	50

N = 686, (F = 114, M = 572)
(Does not account for "other" or no answer)

Source: Survey by author, 1983.

Since marriage is so essential in Hausa society, parents are most concerned about factors which might affect the marriageability of their daughters. Marriageability of Hausa girls allowed to continue in school is adversely affected by the long delay before cohabitation (consummation is often delayed until after the girl finishes school), the higher brideprices of educated girls, and the extent of traditional gifts required for such marriages. Many men express the opinion that all of this is "too much trouble." Further, educated and uneducated men both assert that educated wives are harder to manage, that they may reject purdah, and in general threaten the male right of dominance (table 26). There is a profound belief that independence for women breeds disobedience. The Prophet said that the perfect woman is one whose "sight gives you pleasure and who obeys your order without contradiction" (Haddad 1980, 69); the potential disobedience of women who may not need men for support is seen as threatening to male superiority and is believed to be condemned by the *Qur'an.*

Even the majority of male university students had little desire to marry women educated to their level. Both educated and prosperous men acknowledged that they sometimes enjoyed the company of educated women, but are unlikely to want to marry one. "Although educated men want educated

TABLE 26
Attitudes Concerning Educated Women

Category	Agree	Disagree	No Opinion
"Higher education makes Hausa women better wives."			
Male University Students (100)	34	47	19
Female University Students (100)	84	7	9
Educated Men (100)	51	3	26
Uneducated Men (100)	19	60	21
"An educated Hausa woman does not show proper respect to her husband."			
Male University Students (100)	79	15	6
Female University Students (100)	20	75	5
Educated Men (100)	73	24	3
Uneducated Men (100)	84	14	2
"The personal behavior of educated women is inappropriate."			
Male University Students (100)	13	72	15
Female University Students (100)	82	13	6
Educated Men (100)	34	55	10
Uneducated Men (100)	87	11	2
"Educated women are more likely to mix with men or enter *karuwanci.*"			
Male University Students (100)	10	83	7
Female University Students (100)	5	90	5
Educated Men (100)	20	80	20
Uneducated Men (100)	81	18	1
"Do educated women have difficulty in marrying?"			
Male University Students (100)	60	27	14
Female University Students (100)	42	56	2
Educated Men (100)	66	19	14
Uneducated Men (100)	78	14	8

"At what level of education do you want your husband or wife to be?"

	Uneducated	Primary	Secondary	University
Male University Students (100)	3	6	84	7
Female University Students (100)	0	0	6	94
Educated Men (100)	21	62	16	0
Uneducated Men (100)	86	14	0	0

Sources: Data collected by Mohammad Jabo, Sani Mohammad, Bikisu Ismail; also Ayuba Zakirai Musa 1981, pp. 135–150; see note 1 to Chapter seven.

wives to grace their households, they do not necessarily share the idea of education being intrinsically valuable. Men wish their wives to be good looking, and smartly dressed, but, at the same time, they have a stereotype of educated women as troublesome, critical, demanding, insubordinate, neglectful of husband and children" (Musa 1981, 32). Many men believed educated women to be semi-prostitutes because they mixed with men and went out unaccompanied (see table 26).

Many men who supported the political ideal of women's education were less enthusiastic when it came to their own daughters, sisters, or wives. They feared that girls in school would not be pliant, obedient, and content in *kulle,* or that they could not attract good husbands or would be divorced by them for being too "pushy," or might even enter prostitution (table 26; Interview #23, Kano, February 25, 1983). Given the enormous emphasis on marriage and the almost nonexistent place for unmarried women in the society, this male attitude presents a formidable challenge to notions of female emancipation.

Surveys indicate that men and women both expect educated women to be difficult and therefore likely to be divorced by their husbands (Musa 1981). However, there is not yet any evidence to indicate that educated women are divorced more frequently than noneducated women. When Trevor compared divorce rates in the families of her students she discovered that 61 of the 100 uneducated women had had three or more marriages, but that sixty-nine percent of the educated women in these families were still in their first marriage, indicating that the marriages of educated women are in fact more stable (Trevor 1975, 270).

Rural mothers largely believe that education is wasted on girls, although they send their daughters to school for fear that their husbands will be fined if they fail to comply with the law (Ibrahim Ismaila Mohammad, Sani Mohammad, Garko, see note 1). Somewhat reassured by the information that girls will study primarily Islamic Religious Knowledge and the fundamentals of literacy in Arabic, English, and Hausa, they are still concerned lest these new educational ventures upset other traditional practices. Like the men, they fear that secular education beyond primary school is too risky—girls may lose their virginity, feel dissatisfied with life, and commit adultery (Yusuf Garbo Adamu 1981; Dan'tsoho Muhammad 1980; Musa 1981; Rimi 1983). It is widely believed among rural women that schooling is likely to make girls discontented, defiant and immoral, and too easily tempted by Western attitudes. Further, because the schooled and the unschooled live together, the alien attitudes of the educated may engender widespread discontent.

Urban women also relate all experiences, including education, to marriage. Both Islam and Hausa cultures teach wives to be submissive, to be humble, and to obey their husbands. Control over women is established early, and the practice of parentally arranged marriages assures that girls do not remain unmarried from preference. Women and girls themselves almost universally evidence intense desires for a family and extoll the rewards of children, regardless of class, education, or place of residence. Women without children are pitied. Persons who pass childhood and are not married and do not have children are not considered adults. This has long been the case in Hausa society (Mary Smith 1964, 42; Yeld 1966, 114–16).

In Schildkrout's sample of 109 children, fifty-seven percent of the girls and nine percent of the boys did not attend school and were engaged in street trading (Schildkrout 1984). Girls and their mothers felt it imperative that dowries be earned before puberty; from age five or six girls spend most of their time in this pursuit, and perhaps half of all girls of school age in Kano are kept home for it. When girls go to school, the burden of dowry accumulation shifts to men; men who want educated wives must provide large courting gifts that will be used for dowry or *kayan daki;* men with sisters, daughters, or others under their care whom they want to be educated feel an obligation to provide money to purchase the *kayan daki* necessary for them to be proper brides. The expenses can be considerable, as in the case of one family on the Bayero Campus. The professor involved had in effect sponsored the education of his niece whose father was dead and who was now a student at the University. On her own she had met a businessman and wanted to become his fourth wife; although he did not approve, her uncle sanctioned the marriage. The family felt it would be disgraceful to let the girl marry without making what they considered minimal provisions, especially since this was her first marriage. The expenses thus involved were N1000 for a bed, N500 for cloth, and N800 for eight brass pots, in addition to the bill for a large wedding reception with ample prepared food—altogether about one-quarter of the average professor's annual salary. Such expenses are not unusual; in order to arrange a marriage with an educated man, a father may send his daughter to school to increase her brideprice, thus ensuring himself of some compensation for his contribution to her education and dowry. Thus, both men and women, whether living in urban or rural areas, continue to focus on marriage as the only "opportunity" for women. Education may change the timing or the nature of the negotiation, but it does not change the end result.

Educated men and women disagree on one major issue, however. Informal discussion points to a significant, virtually universal divergence on the matter of polygamy. Almost all men either have or plan to have more than one wife. Men assert that it is only educated women who advocate monogamy, but this is not the case. No women, educated or uneducated, who were interviewed on the matter endorse polygamy, although many feel they have good relations with their co-wives. "What can you do, that is the nature of men, so you might as well make the best of it." That almost all women find the situation lamentable is illustrated by the fact that it is the custom for a first wife's friends to come and sit with her when her husband announces his intention to marry a second wife. At the university, the friends of a woman whose husband is preparing to take another wife gather in order to calm the wife's anger, dissuade her from any rash action that might cause her husband to divorce her, offer sympathy and comfort, abuse the husband, and criticize the new wife assuring the first wife that she is desirable and superior in every way to the new, usually younger and therefore "foolish" one. Eventually, educated women, who are able to hold paying jobs, may well leave a marriage rather than tolerate the presence of a second wife. However, as polygamy is reinforced by both Islam and Hausa culture, education by itself has a lot to overcome. Women may desire monogamy, and educated women may even demand it, but they are always at the risk of a husband's taking a second wife. Women's allies on this point are other women; a few educated women are beginning to organize, as indicated by the fact that all major Nigerian women's organizations advocate the prohibition of polygamy through law. This is one area in which women's political voice may be distinct in the future.

EDUCATION AND FEMALE EMPLOYMENT

In spite of its importance, acquiring an education is only the beginning of the challenge of expanding roles for women. This is particularly so for women looking towards careers, since the cultural imperatives of Islam militate against them.

The qualified woman aggressively seeking employment will stumble over a variety of obstacles. For example, regulations at Bayero University allow a married female faculty member to continue in employment only so long as her husband maintains a good character (Bayero University 1983). On at least two occasions non-Nigerian female faculty members were asked to move off campus because the University administration disapproved of their husbands, both of whom were from other sections of Nigeria. In both cases, the University Staff Union (the faculty union) persuaded the administration to reconsider; but in at least one of the cases, the University simply let the woman's contract expire, thus making the issue of University housing moot. University employment itself is preferentially offered to men; if a married couple are both to be employed, the wife is invariably offered the lower-ranking position even if her qualifications are superior to her husband's. Several such cases came

A nine-year-old school girl from Kurawa delivering cooked food to a neighbor's house after school. While girls who attend school rarely participate in street trading, they continue to help with errands, many of which involve helping secluded women communicate with the world outside the compound.

to light in the early 1980s, when expatriate female professors were asked to take positions of lower rank in order to be employed at the University at all, while their husbands were offered ranks equal to or higher than those they had held abroad. Married Nigerian women must submit written permission from their husbands before they can be employed.

As late as 1966, only one percent of northern girls attended even primary school; thus for the overwhelming majority of women, work outside the home was not an option (Pitten 1980). By 1976, six of the forty girls in Schildkrout's sample in Kurawa had some primary education—one had reached primary six, and two were in teachers' training colleges—while in Kofar Mazugal none of the forty-eight girls was in school. In 1982, all the girls in the

Kurawa study were in school, several families had daughters in secondary school, and several women teachers lived in the ward. In Kofar Mazugal only one girl was in school because mothers still needed their daughters for *talla* (street trading); clearly, however, the pattern was changing and the expectation was that most girls would soon go to school, at least for the first few years of primary education (Schildkrout 1984). University students overwhelmingly endorsed education for their daughters, although only twenty percent of the male students expected them to continue to university, while eighty-seven percent of the female students expected their daughters to continue and, with their husbands' consent, to work (table 22c).

Papers presented at a "Women in Development Conference" in 1979 suggest that educated Hausa Muslim women do desire a more equal share in decision making as well as full control of their salaries (Nevadomsky 1980, 851). On the other hand, there is a strong willingness to subordinate their own aspirations to those of their husbands and to defer their own pursuits to follow their husbands. In a study of 125 women, only seventeen percent disagreed with the statement that "whether educated or not, a married woman should always subordinate her interests to those of her husband" (Nevadomsky, 853).

While educated women and some men support higher levels of education for women, uneducated men and women still fear it as a challenge to social norms and particularly to the authority of men (Interview #56, Kano, December 26, 1984). One woman related that her uncle educated one of his daughters through to the university, whereupon she rebelled against the marriage her family had arranged for her and took a job with national television in Lagos, where she still lives unmarried. As a result of this experience, the uncle is insisting that all the other girls in the family cease their educations after secondary school and go to their husbands' houses, where they will live "properly." His authority in this matter is not challenged (Interview #56, Kano, December 26, 1984).

Some research suggests that men and women admire different qualities in women at the present time. When uneducated men were asked to rank women in terms of respect, they placed the emir's wives first and primary school teachers and midwives last. On the other hand, uneducated women ranked primary school teachers on top and the emir's wives at the bottom, "because they are shut in and have no power to do anything positive, only grumble" (Trevor 1975, 260).

Men generally do not regard women with careers as "successful." In fact, the Hausa term for "modern women," *matan zamani* is a euphemism for prostitute. Career women who do not marry or who divorce and support themselves are regarded as a disgrace to their families, having challenged religious and social mores. In addition, shame is often associated with nonprofessional female employment, for it indicates to the common people that the husband cannot support his family or is unwilling to do so.

Clearly, women rate other women with some independence highly, and those few women who are able to support themselves and to live outside of marriage (and not in *karuwanci*) are admired and envied. Already, in Kurawa the few women teachers go out, leaving their children with their co-wives, and are respected. These women are not against *kulle* for themselves or their daughters, however, for it provides security and companionship and household help. There are few incentives for women to work unless they are internally motivated since their economic well-being is assured within the kinship structure; few personal freedoms are gained by outside employment, and working may present difficulties in negotiating a marriage.

At present the financial contribution of educated women to their families is small. But women in public roles are providing role models not available to them when they were growing up, and are thus creating a unique experience in socialization for the coming generation; the author's survey of secondary school students indicates that their motivations and aspirations are broader than their mothers'. Educated women who live in large households influence the direction of social change, just as the Islamic scholars assert women should. Indeed, it may well be that the main contribution of educated women is to educate the young.

REFLECTIONS ON EDUCATION

Secondary and university education in and of itself cannot change the life prospects or the public and domestic roles of secluded Hausa Muslim women. Underemployment and unemployment are severe problems in Nigeria; in Kano even university graduates are beginning to have difficulty in finding appropriate positions. Women generally are considered for employment only if no qualified male candidate presents himself; according to a dean at Bayero University, several critical positions have been open for years because the only qualified candidates have been women (Interview #51, Kano, December 22, 1984). Unless the Nigerian economy experiences a recovery or significant expansion, most educated women will have no choice but to marry and pursue their domestic responsibilities more or less in seclusion. More educated women are beginning to live in *kullen zuci* rather than *kullen tsari,* but essentially women's lives continue to be almost wholly focused on their families and compounds rather than the public sphere. Their life decisions are still made by husbands and male relatives. In order to change the extent of male domination, women will need more than education—they will need a market for their skills and the social standing to participate in it.

Another primary consideration in opening opportunities and expanding life choices for women is the extent to which men's psychological dependence on female seclusion and submission will produce resistance to women's involvement in nondomestic employment, even without the added stress of competition for jobs between the sexes. To date we have no data on this sensitive question; what can be said is that many men appear more willing to see changes for their daughters than for their wives.

It is also important to note that while research on other Islamic societies has emphasized that Islamic women are in many ways more independent of men than are Western women who have not experienced seclusion or life in a female world (Del Vecchio Good 1978, 485; Fallers 1982, 225; Papanek 1973, 312), observation in Kano suggests that when secluded women step into public roles, they remain deferential to men; they retain a sense of independence from men, but are unable to assert their own interests in the face of male opposition. Nonetheless, as teachers, midwives, or bureaucrats, they interact with a wide variety of people. And, their influence among women is considerable. At home, young professional women interact with co-wives, relatives temporarily in town from rural areas, women of all ranks from extended families, and others who may be in their compounds for a wide variety of reasons. Women's reticence at work is not reflected in their lively interaction with other women. In their own world, women's views and perceptions are changing. How muted this changing consciousness is will be dependent in large measure on changing men's attitudes—a much more problematic matter.

While levels of education for girls and women are rising dramatically in Kano, attitudes toward marriage and family and appropriate behavior for women do not seem to be changing. Therefore, women seek "female appropriate" employment, i.e., work of which husbands and fathers approve. Because of a great and increasing need for women teachers to teach girls and women physicians to treat women patients, and because these two fields can be juggled around family needs, teaching and medicine are considered appropriate careers for women.

Because Islamic writing on the subject of sex roles often stresses "complementarity," which essentially means that women obey and serve men and more specifically that men will not cook or concern themselves with domestic tasks, working Hausa Muslim women in Kano are finding themselves concerned with the same problems as Western women—child-care arrangements and the pressure of the double day in the workplace and in the home. The difference in Kano is that women do not feel that confrontation with men or discussions about a different allocation of responsibilities are likely to be fruitful; in fact, they do not see such reallocation as legitimate within an Islamic culture.

Nonetheless, however slow, there is change. While educated girls may feel their lives are very much like their mothers', in fact they are not. Choices are expanding, even if most women are not yet taking conscious advantage of them. Women increasingly do have access to higher education; employment opportunities do exist for some women; women can vote; and, should there be a return to civilian rule, they can run for office. Aminu Kano's long campaign for expanding education and giving women the right to vote contributed significantly to the development of political consciousness among women in Kano. There are women activists, both on the campuses and in the professions, who are waiting for a return to politics. The heads of the women's wings of the former political parties and the former women commissioners have now had exposure in the world of politics. Even though politics are now banned, education is increasing, radio and television are expanding awareness, and books and magazines are available that show alternative ways of life. The military government in Kano State announced in January 1985 that it had established a science secondary school for girls at Kura, thus opening the possibility of wider career choice for women.

To predict that change engendered by education will be slow is not to deny that pressure for such change exists. The interplay between these pressures and entrenched cultural norms will often be contradictory and unpredictable. Women's education, although having some impact and effect, is working against a dominant culture in which female subordination is central. Hausa mores, Islamic teachings, men's attitudes, and the association of women's liberation with Westernization circumscribe the dimensions of possible change. The cognitive and emotional dissonance created by expanding educational levels on the one hand and strong culturally imposed norms of subservience on the other leaves an opening for charismatic and ideological leadership to tap a wellspring of female support. Under such circumstances, dramatic changes could occur. In the absence of such a development, all indications are that women will rationalize their subordination in the public components of culture while nurturing their own evaluations of the merits of that culture in their own private domain.

8

Paths of Emergence
Resistance and Change

ON ISLAM AND CHANGE

As we have noted, Muslims in Nigeria often assert that Islam is not just a religion, but a "total way of life." Because Muslims are not an absolute majority in Nigeria, the Sharia is seen as the symbol of their minority rights and identity. Islamic identity in Kano is as great as, if not greater than, Nigerian national identity, and Islamic culture is seen as being morally superior and international in scope; anyone who "believes" is a member of this community. Muslims claim that the uniformity of Islamic culture produces social similarities regardless of "race, color, language or place of birth" (Khurshid 1974, 12). To this end, the *Qur'an* is cited: "O mankind, be conscious of your duty to your Lord, who created you from a single soul, created of like nature, his mate, and from the two created and spread many men and women" (*Qur'an* 4:1).

Devout Muslim women in Nigeria assert that Islam gives equality to women in all that matters—in their relationship to Allah. They also observe that because women are offered protection and support, they are privileged above women in other religions and cultures (Interviews #12, Kano, March 12, 1982; #16, Kano, October 25, 1982; #17, Kano, October 28, 1982; #21, February 24, 1983; Lemu and Heeren 1978). In addition, they emphasize that while men rule the world, women rule in the home. The home and its extended family networks provide women with an alternative world in which they function relatively autonomously. "Master of the world at large, the man acts in his home as one who recognizes the rule of his wife in this domain and respects it" (Nasr 1966, 113).

Many women believe that significant reform is possible within Qur'anic teachings. Reformers assert, for instance, that the Prophet meant to encourage Muslims to abandon polygamy by requiring that in the event of second, third, and fourth marriages, all wives be treated equally (*Qur'an* 4:3); they maintain that since, according to the Prophet himself, it is in fact impossible for a man to treat wives equally—"You shall never be able to do justice among women, no matter how much you desire" (*Qur'an* 4:128–29)—this is an indirect but emphatic prohibition of polygamy. Polygamy already has been prohibited in many Islamic countries: Turkey in 1926, Jordan in 1951, Syria in 1953, Morocco in 1958, Iran in 1959, and Pakistan in 1961.

The right of women under the *Qur'an* to inherit property is also seen as being most significant in allowing reform, as it provides the foundation for financial self-sufficiency (Interview #32, Kano, May 13, 1983). It is also seen as important in the development of sophistication relating to marriage alliances; Kano women point out that while in Western societies marriage is primarily a sacrament, in Muslim societies it is a contract, a civil agreement, reached through negotiation (Interview #32, Kano, May 13, 1983.) Finally, while women "have rights similar to those of men . . . and men are a degree above them" (*Qur'an* 2:228), it is stressed that this is "only a degree above them . . . one degree, not 100 degrees!" (Lemu, 1983, 5).

On the other side, radical university students and self-proclaimed Marxists engaged in the debate concerning the place of women in society stress that references to "equality" in Qur'anic law are purely formal in nature and are negated by other directives, supplementary stipulations, and limitations.[1] Under the strictures of the Sharia, they claim, it is virtually impossible for a woman to make any life decision (when to marry, whom to marry, how many children to have, to go to school, to go to work, etc.) without the permission of a man—her father, her brother, her husband, her son, or her guardian. And, while Muslim law urges moderation in disciplining women, it explicitly allows physical beating in the last resort as punishment for disobedience. "As for those women from whom you fear disobedience, admonish them and boycott their beds and beat them" (*Qur'an* 4:34).

In contrast to both the conservatives and radicals, the majority of university students in Kano who advocate reform accept the idea that matters affecting women's status may be raised only if they are addressed in the *Qur'an* or derived from interpretations of the *Qur'an* or the sayings of the Prophet. Thus, all innovations affecting women must contend not only with local custom and belief but also with the Sharia or holy law. And, while guarantees of support, protections of property, rights of inheritance, and the concept of a marriage contract represented improvements in the lives of women in the seventh century, they do not quite so clearly provide the foundation for equality and liberation in the twentieth century. Islamic teachings on modesty and interpretations of them that have led to the seclusion of women in their homes (*kulle*) have necessarily also excluded women almost completely from public affairs and engendered in them a sense of lowered general status and a reduced sense of their rights. In the years since the life of the Prophet Muhammad, a woman's world has become more and more narrowly confined to her home, her children, and her private relationships (Boulding 1976, 384–91, 718).

Islamic law grants equality between the sexes only in one area—before Allah. Even here, there is no unanimity among schools. The Sunni schools of Hanafi, Shafi'i, and Hanbali Sharia make no distinctions between the rights of men and women to deal with their own property. All become adults at puberty; all females over age fifteen are free to deal with their property as they see fit, and husbands cannot interfere. However, *Maliki* law in Nigeria is interpreted in such a way that the right to control property is not granted until a woman's guardian specifically states that she is capable of dealing with it (Interview #14, Kano, May 17, 1982); nor may a wife dispose of more than a third of her property without the consent of her husband. Women cannot conclude their own marriage contracts or act as marriage guardians for their daughters (Hinchcliff 1975, 255–56; Interview #37, Kano, May 14, 1983).

Powerful anti-Western feeling compounds this long-entrenched conservatism. As the concepts of an Islamic state and an Islamic revolution spread, adopting the veil and living according to Islamic teachings are seen as nationalistic responses and reactions against the West and its denigration of Islam. "It must, therefore, be pointed out that the role of a Muslim woman in this country must be governed by what Islamic culture demands and not by what the so-called advanced societies or other non-Muslim societies do" (*New Nigerian,* March 5, 1982). Since the family and the proper roles of women are so central to Islam and the *Qur'an,* any deviation is seen not only as sinful, but also as succumbing to the forces of "Western imperialism."

> It must be realized that any solution to this social problem must come from the correct teaching of Islam rather than by emulating activities of non-Muslim societies where we have already witnessed the contribution of feminists in destabilizing societies (Shehu Umar Abdullahi, undergraduate lecture, Bayero University, June, 1982).

Therefore, demands for women's "liberation" can be and often are seen as rebellion against Allah and his ordained order for the world and an embracing of a hostile Western culture. Thus, men assert and educated women generally concur that any notion of women's "liberation" is alien, primarily

Western, and un-Islamic. Both men and women appeal to the faithful to protect Islam from such "Western" influences by rejecting any such discussions. "It must be realized here that culture in Islam includes the correct relationship between males and females" (*New Nigerian,* March 5, 1982). Liberation for a woman in the Islamic context is to be free to be "herself" (i.e., to fulfill the role she is given by her "nature") and to fulfill the "destiny" for which God has created her.

> Islam is always practical and realistic and that is why the difference is made clear in the area of physical condition. Islam allots strenuous work and rough outdoor life to men and regards home as the first concern of women. The effort of some women to do man's strenuous activities has only produced women alcoholics, neurotics and heart patients. We cannot possibly change nature (Abdullahi, ibid., 1982).

Liberation is not freedom from responsibility to give obedience to men or freedom from the restriction of the faith; rather, it provides protection from the corruption and alienation of the West. It is not surprising that few Islamic women have undertaken the challenge of promoting "liberation" in the Western sense.

Both religion and custom, then, pose formidable restraints to reform of legal inequalities suffered by women in predominantly Islamic societies such as Kano's. Because of the nature of Islamic law and the comprehensiveness of Islamic beliefs concerning women and their proper roles and behavior, efforts at reforming the position of women through law are handicapped. The mere legal imposition of new family codes may not be effective in changing norms and behavior; new laws evidencing too great an inconsistency with Islamic law will likely be ignored, or modified, or adopted in form but not in fact. In the Islamic parts of the USSR, for example, laws dealing specifically with the family or with women's rights have not been effective in changing practice, for even in a secular state Muslims believe they themselves must live according to Islamic law (Massell 1974). Since the prescriptions and sanctions of that law are considered to be divine revelation and thus not subject to manipulation by secular authorities (not to speak of foreign or alien forces or notions) (Levy 1965, ch. 6), the content of an acceptable program of women's emancipation is problematic.

Nevertheless, in Nigeria a feature of radical politics in the Islamic north has long been the pledge to upgrade the status of Islamic women. In other Muslim countries, secular governments have introduced reforms that supersede Islamic prescriptions, opening possibilities that most women do not yet pursue. Reforms to restrict child marriage and polygamy, to extend a wife's right to dissolve a marriage, and to curtail *talaq* were enacted into law in Turkey in 1915, in Sudan and Egypt in 1917, in India and Pakistan in 1939, and in Syria, Tunisia, Jordan, Lebanon, Iraq, Iran, and Morocco in 1961. However, no Islamic country has yet attempted to prohibit wife-beating for "disobedience," to establish equal inheritance laws, or to encourage "affirmative action" in education and employment for women. Thus, the efforts of the People's Redemption Party (PRP) in Kano to make a material difference through advocating education and encouraging women's entry into politics are unique and radical.

Culturally imposed problems are no less difficult to overcome than those posed by religion. Regulations establishing the subordinate status of women are reinforced by values most women themselves consider legitimate. By and large, women in Kano have no conception of themselves as requiring or desiring "liberation" in the Western sense. The price to be paid is high, and even the most educated women realize this. Women will not voluntarily agitate for "liberation" other than in the Islamic sense—demands that their rights in Islam be honored. Efforts of women elsewhere to assert their individualism strike no cord in a society that does not much value individualism for either men or women, a society in which many people live in a small space and privacy is seldom felt or even sought after. Women do not have an internalized sense of self that would be recognizable in a Western culture; a woman thinks of herself in terms of her family—her father's family and her husband's family. Women think of themselves as "actualized" through bearing children and living in a large family group; the notion of living alone is incomprehensible to them.

Observations about women's status in Kano fit women's self-image, so there is no controversy. To say that women are unequal, secluded, or precluded from public or independent lives is to state facts most women consider not only obvious, but immutable and also right. What an outside observer would view as prima facie evidence of manifest inferiority is perceived as merely a divinely ordained difference in sex roles. Young, educated women who speak about "women's rights" want to eliminate society's worst abuses, such as easy divorce for men, male custody of children, and early and unwanted marriage, and, in some cases, polygamy. They assert that the *Qur'an* requires none of these things, that these matters are a distortion of Islam by Hausa culture and custom. At the same time, they want to retain their communal form of living and the extended family and the support it lends. For them, fundamental adherence to the teachings of Islam will provide all the change and "liberation" they want or need.

As concerned women students in Kano have pointed out, patriarchy, patrilineality, patrilocality, child marriage, polygamy, sudden repudiation, and male domination of economic and political systems could all be challenged without challenging the fundamental tenets of religion. To date, however, rather than initiate such challenge overtly, women have developed their own world coexistent with but apart from men, and in that world their own "muted" values and beliefs provide compensation for their subordination in this male-centered society (Callaway 1984).

WOMEN AND CHANGE IN KANO

Writing on nineteenth-century America, Alexis de Tocqueville made a statement that most Americans take as axiomatic: "The gradual development of the principle of equality is a providential fact. . . . It is universal, it is lasting, it constantly eludes all human interference, and all events as well as all men, contribute to its progress. . . . [It is] an irresistible revolution which has advanced for centuries in spite of every obstacle" (De Tocqueville 1946, 5). As we learn more of societies whose value systems do not derive from the European Enlightenment, we must entertain the possibility that the drive for equality in fact may not be universal. In Nigeria, "women's liberation" as we know it is not perceived as the expression of a legitimate concern about equality, but rather as a Western "monster" that will rightly be tamed by the countervailing force of Islam. Only equality as defined in Islam is legitimate, and that does not include social equality with men for women; women and men are equal before Allah, not in relation to each other.

In Europe, the gradual expansion of the merchant, commercial, and middle classes created new opportunities and experiences that slowly altered the very bases of political legitimacy and related concepts of justice and equality. New perceptions and values in economic and political spheres coupled with ever wider concepts of equality eventually led to a reevaluation of notions of male-female complementarity. The organization of the patriarchal family conflicted with what was becoming a "universal" norm of equality, and legitimated an inequality of status, power, and rewards. The gradual decline of the family as a productive economic unit altered the structure of relationships within the family and hence the economic foundation of complementarity (Boserup 1970; Engels 1972; Sacks 1974). In an Islamic society the complementarity of sex roles is not based on the structure of the economy; rather, the religion clearly defines separate spheres in which men are enjoined to work in order to support their families and women are enjoined to stay at home, sheltered from public view, nurturing them. Although Islamic fami-

A widowed woman continues to be supported by her sons, but also has the freedom to go out herself. Many older Hausa women have a hard-earned independence, although those without family support can have a difficult time making ends meet.

lies function as economic units in fact, this reality is not endorsed by the Islamic ideal.

In modern as well as traditional cultures, women's subordination to men in the home shapes their social roles and psychologies. To date, the maternal role poses a nearly universal opposition between "domestic" and "public" that is inherently asymmetrical and keeps women tied to "nature" while men advance in "culture" (de Beauvoir 1974). Does biology demand a domestic role for women, which in turn leads to the development of a "female personality" more closely bound to nature, hence less rational and less able to rise above basic drives and constraints than the "male personality"? A cultural definition of women that restricts them to "domestic" or nonpublic roles and realms is built on an affirmative answer to this question.

In what has become the classic statement concerning women's "space," Michele Rosaldo related the "universal asymmetries" in actual activities and cultural evaluations of men and women to universal, structural oppositions between "private" and "public" spheres of human activity. Women are oppressed and lacking in status and value to the extent that they are confined to domestic activities and to the extent that these activities are different or physically separate from those of men.

She too emphasizes that the differential relationship of men and women to the establishment of authority is not directly related to biology but to the fact that women bear and raise children. This activity consumes most of adulthood for most women, leads to the differentiation between domestic and public roles, and in turn shapes relevant aspects of human social structure and psychology. While the domestic sphere is composed primarily of mothers and children, the public sphere subsumes them under its authority while (until recently) excluding them from active participation. Women become almost exclusively identified with domestic arrangements and men with public institutional roles. Analyzing this basic fact of human organization contributes significantly to understanding female subordination and represents a fundamental corollary to the consequences of biology. Such understanding also provides insights into how this subordination can be overcome.

It is asserted that women gain power and a sense of value when they transcend their domestic roles either by entering the public world of men or, less clearly, by creating a separate society of their own with independent sources of power and legitimacy (Firestone 1970). There are scholars who talk of a "female sphere" where women hold forms of power not recognized by men, but which are effective for their own life situations and perspectives (Jaquette 1982, 281; Ardener 1975). Ardener has proposed that women in certain societies may be analyzed as a "muted group" (Ardener 1975, iv–x). She hypothesizes that there are some societies in which women are so suppressed in a world dominated by men that they constitute a distinct, though often nearly invisible, social entity attuned to its own values and mores. When the day-to-day world of women is muted it may actually function in counterpoint relation to that of men, giving women a perspective of their own distinct from that of men. Hausa women may appear to an outsider to be silent on concerns seemingly vital to them essentially because their values are not those of the dominant male group—i.e., male perspectives do not accommodate such values and the male perspective is the public one, therefore the only one acknowledged. Relatively inarticulate vis-à-vis men, muted women may nevertheless operate effectively within their own social world or sphere.

The hypothesis of the existence of a separate set of values, not recognized or acknowledged by men but of significance to women, helps in part to explain why women themselves often resist changes intended to "liberate" them. Women as divergent as the Hausa and the American "pro-lifers" are afraid to sacrifice what status and security they have for benefits they cannot see or understand. Feminist strategies of change that assume women can and will seize power in the public sphere if it is open to them ignore the fear such change engenders in threatening the existing "power" they feel they hold in the private sphere. It is this dynamic which in part informs the efforts described in this study to create paths of emergence for women in a deeply traditional Islamic society.

In the Western world, where financial independence is seen as fundamental to equality, the women's movement has emphasized that the ability to earn a living when necessary and thus the concomitant educational opportunities are essential to women. In the Islamic world, the concept of equality between the sexes implies no such equal opportunities. Islamic societies stress that women must be educated solely in order to study the *Qur'an* and understand its meaning. When women work, as they are beginning to do in Kano, it is to supplement their husbands' support, not to replace it. Work or career can never legitimately replace the role of wife and mother—it is not an alternative, but an added burden that can only be assumed so long as it does not interfere with divinely ordained roles. It is unclear whether in Kano, as in the West, the emergence of women from the narrow confines of household activities into the world of "productive relations" carries profound consequences for relationships between the sexes. If the experience of other societies is indicative, the potential for economic independence for women will produce demands for more equality within as well as outside of marriage. Women in Kano have economic autonomy in *kulle,* but because they are confined to the household, the benefits of that autonomy are limited. If more women work outside the home and overall economic dependency lessens, the demand that marriage be a more equal institution may grow.

Unlike the Western experience, the effect of granting the franchise to women in Kano was, at first impression, more dramatic than anticipated. Apparently, more women voted than men, and furthermore, women were widely believed to have been responsible for the election of the opposition party to power in Kano State. In the United States, documentation of the gender gap shows that women may vote differently from men on a number of issues, but it does not indicate that more women than men vote. Women's participation lags behind men's in a wide range of political activities in modern democratic societies. In voting, in the frequency of political discussion, in letter-writing, in party membership, and in holding party or political office, indicators suggest that women participate less than men (Baxter and Lansing 1983; Klein 1984; Mueller 1985); and, as men scale the levels of political authority, the presence of women becomes increasingly more rare (Gruberg 1968; Amundsen 1971; Duverger 1955; Jaquette 1974; Campbell et al. 1960). The degree to which this will be true in Kano is again problematic. Four years of women's active involvement in politics is too short a time to make predictions concerning the future. However, the nomination of a woman vice-presidential candidate, the election of a Kano State woman to a seat in the National Assembly, and the high visibility of the women appointed as commissioners suggest a level of acceptance of women in public roles in Kano that is astounding in light of the very conservative nature of Islam and its attendant socialization of both sexes.

This apparently remarkable progress has not altered the fact that in Islamic societies, a man's honor, status, and standing in the society is greatly affected by the number of wives he has and the degree of control he exacts over them. Even women politicians do not advocate female "disobedience," but rather express the hope that husbands can be convinced of the appropriateness of women's studying or working outside the home. So long as women's political activism can be seen as supportive of men's political decisions, it may continue to be endorsed. But, should women really pose challenges to male positions, there is no indication that either men or women would tolerate such heterodoxy. A central question therefore is: To what extent does Islam contribute something unique in terms of understanding the nature of equality and women's rights?

As noted, some analyses search for female power in "female spheres" and assert that women actually have power and prestige and can and do control or influence decisions made by men in and through their unchallenged position in their own sphere. Usually this power is aligned with supernatural forces that can be called into play only by women (as in Bori). These studies hypothesize or assert that women derive power and satisfaction from their association with the spirits or the supernatural and use it to gain economic advantage over men or to affect the very survival of the community. They point to myths of primordial female eminence and maintain that images of goddesses and fertility cults imply supernatural power in the hands of women (Buvinic, Yousef, and von Elm 1978; Chinas 1973; Da Vanzo and Poh Lee 1978; Lomnitz 1977; Mernissi 1975). These analyses lose cogency, however, when a distinction between power and authority is attempted. Authority is defined as legitimate power. In this context, any power women have to act effectively in their own interests is generally conceived as being illegitimate in nature—it consists of an ability to be manipulative or to disrupt through supernatural or irrational means, neither of which is a legitimate source of political or personal power in modern societies. When women have "power," it usually does not imply legitimacy. Thus, when such writers talk of female "power," they imply power on the sly, outside normal procedures or legitimate institutional arrangements. When women in Kano appeal to Bori to rectify intolerable situations for them, they are appealing to supernatural spirits beyond the reach of rational authority.

The degree to which women are respected or even revered is usually what is meant when it is said that women have "high status" in a given society. Certainly in Islam, the "high status" of women is a function of their perceived roles in producing and raising children; in recognition of these roles, protections are provided for them (*Qur'an* 17:23 and 31:8). While high status may be inferred from deferential treatment and may involve control over basic resources, high status and actual control over basic decisions do not necessarily coincide at all. In fact, it may well be that the "high status" associated with deferential treatment and "respect" precludes legitimate authority over basic decision making.

In Kano, as in most other Islamic cultures, religion and culture together reinforce a reduced status for women. When a woman's role as mother is emphasized, idealized, and prescribed in detail, women's status in all other spheres either declines or is proscribed altogether as religion becomes more entrenched. As this study indicated, the Kano State government's effort to bring about some change in the status of women through public policy has not been accompanied by any effort to challenge the cultural and religious foundation that results in extreme suspicion of women's ability to function in the "public" world. This religious and cultural foundation represents the real challenge to fundamentally improving the position of women.

No one has yet described a society in which women have publicly recognized power and authority equal to that of men. Where some women have had power even temporarily, as described in pre-Islamic Hausa states, or where a woman has occupied a powerful position, as in England or India until recently, it was the result of the temporary allocation of institutional authority to an individual woman. Even in these societies the overwhelming majority of women is excluded from crucial economic and political activities and continues to have fewer powers and prerogatives than men. Sexual asymmetry is thus a universal feature of human social life to date.

In the United States and other industrialized societies, the belief that women are endowed by a divine being with special abilities for domestic labor and the nurturing of the household has a certain potency in the structure of contemporary social values, but the economic necessities that have drawn women into the work force have been eroding the structural base upon which this division into domestic (or private) and public spheres rests. Generally, this changing structural base has meant that women, but not yet men, have dual roles. The burden of dual roles is eroding the acceptance by women of the "biology is destiny" rationalization that assigns them the major responsibility for the domestic or private sphere. In challenging the burden presented by dual roles, women are also stressing the relevance of egalitarian values. Partly as a consequence of this movement women have gained more equal legal and political rights along with increasing educational opportunities. These opportunities in turn lead women to reevaluate their primary responsibilities for homemaking and child care. Increasingly, what has long been perceived as "necessary" and "natural" about the social restrictions placed on women is being recognized as arbitrary and unwarranted if notions of human equality are accepted.

While social roles are related to but not limited by biological differences, status differentiation between public and private spheres is more complicated. Public policy typically reinforces a differentiated social order. While women's maternal and reproductive roles may receive support in social policy areas, this support often goes hand in hand with civic and legal disabilities. In Kano women were denied the right to vote until 1979. By convention basic human rights, such as deciding whether or whom to marry or to end a marriage, freedom of movement, control over property, and access to educational opportunities, are more open to men than to women because of the acceptance of these socially prescriptive norms. Differentiation based on sex in the area of basic human rights gives some indication of the dimensions of the status gap in Hausa society, and provides a clue to understanding the nature of the social order and the role social policy might play in restructuring it. These considerations are most relevant to this study because in Hausa society these rights have not been extended to Muslim women who are subject to Islamic law rather than to the provisions of the Nigerian Constitution in regard to fundamental human rights.

The place of gender in the organization of human life in most societies, the exclusive association of women with reproduction and the care of the young in these societies, and the relevance of women's reproductive role in the construction of public status all suggest that in a society such as the Hausa, the support of men in bringing about change is, a priori, critical. Such support is also problematic.

Women in many societies are beginning to recognize the extent to which private and public social bifurcation works to the advantage of men and the disadvantage of women. Women are increasingly recognizing that "separate sphere" and "separate power" or "women's sphere" and "women's power" arguments serve to justify continued male dominance and female subordination.

It is anticipated that women in Kano too will eventually address such concerns.

Although interpretations of civil and commercial Islamic codes have changed with the times, family codes and codes of personal status have not. Change is slow, more so in this area than others, and must always be justified within the context of religious interpretation of Islamic texts. Those Muslims with responsibility for such interpretations are all men; women do not become judges in Sharia courts. The legal machinery provided in the Constitution for the advancement of women's status in Nigeria cannot function in Islamic areas without religiously sanctioned support. Islamic women are on the low end of the continuum of rights and freedoms guaranteed by Sharia law. This conservatism in regard to the position of women carries policy implications for issues elsewhere defined as women's issues—population control, improved childbearing practices, rights in marriage and divorce, educational and employment opportunities, etc. Religious beliefs mesh with the desire of men to keep control in the one area not so affected by commercial and civic changes and to limit the areas in which women may legitimately seek redress.

And yet there are indications of profound changes in attitudes in areas that do not directly conflict with Islam, but which nonetheless may fundamentally affect women's roles, at least in some small but distinct sectors of the society. Parents now generally endorse the education of girls, at least through the primary level. More and more middle-class and wealthy parents are willing to postpone the age of marriage for their daughters and to consider her wishes in making marriage arrangements. Educated women are organizing to pursue their own priorities. A northern-based newspaper, *The New Nigerian,* carried the first editorial calling for population control on December 15, 1984, after a speech on the matter by the then head of state, General Buhari. It is significant that this issue has been raised by a military government, just as it was a military government that extended the right to vote to women a decade ago. As the military is above the Constitution, so also it is not bound by Islamic law.

Women do not yet envision using the vote to gain control over their bodies through birth control, nor to demand equal pay for equal or comparable work, equal credit, or even equal opportunity; what they seek is liberalization in the interpretation of those Islamic teachings that most dramatically affect them, such as those on polygamy, forced marriage, *talaq,* child custody, and continued support after unilateral divorce. Only tangentially through politics, but more directly through education, do women hope to address these matters. Just as discussions of democracy and its meaning in the West led women to question prevailing arrangements between the sexes, so religiously devoted women may begin to question the prevailing interpretations of Islamic teachings. In this undertaking they will need the support of learned Islamic men; in precisely this way Mallam Aminu Kano's role was crucial to women's progress in education and politics in Kano during the last decade. Because Islamic jurisprudence turns on interpretation of divine will, the role of religious teachers is pivotal in bringing about changes in prevailing interpretations. By the same token, reforms legislated without particular religious endorsement will probably not affect practice, particularly among uneducated women who scarcely understand their rights and protections even in Islam. In the rural areas in particular, women asserting new conceptions of rights face heavy social sanction. Even in the city, women may yearn for new options, particularly in regard to marriage, yet remain unwilling (or unable) to suffer the social consequences of demanding them.

In Kano, Ardener's concept of muted groups—subdominant groups that appear uninvolved in matters of special concern to them because there can be no accommodation of those concerns by the dominant group (Ardener 1975)—is relevant. In Hausa society, women appear relatively inarticulate vis-à-vis men and function in relation to them only in terms acceptable to the dominant (male) group; yet they hold strong and articulate views that are expressed among themselves. To a large extent, women can conduct their daily lives with an independence for which no recognition is allowed in the dominant model of the society.

Presumably, it is because of this dual existence that women can accept, with apparent contentment and professed support, the values and codes of the dominant system. Their own sense of themselves and their world derives from a complementary and counterbalancing value and support system of which they may not be completely aware. For example, an independent and successful woman may experience the social condemnation that reflects dominant (male) attitudes, but yet be admired by other women. Survey research cited in chapters four and six suggested that men and women admired different qualities in women. When men were asked to rank women in terms of respect, they ranked the emir's wives first and placed primary school teachers and midwives at the bottom. Women, on the other hand, ranked primary school teachers on top and the emir's wives at the bottom because "they are shut in and have no power to do anything." Men did not regard a woman with a career as a successful woman; in fact, the Hausa words for modern women, *matan zamani,* are a euphemism for prostitute. In contrast, women respect signs of independence in other women, and those few who are able to support themselves and to live outside of marriage (and not in *karuwanci* or prostitution) are admired.

The measures of success in the dominant and muted groups clearly are different. Thus, the fact that women are low on the scale of success according to male values is mitigated by the fact that they are successful according to the logic of their own muted model. Women's values overlap, but do not necessarily coincide with those of men. The discrepancy between women's acceptance of a reticent posture and their actual behavior is often quite marked. Women who appear shy, timid, and devoid of opinions in the presence of men become animated, opinionated, and articulate in the presence of other women. It is possible that the total segregation of men and women promotes the development of appropriate personalities for their two worlds. In religion, politics, social life, and economic activities, we have seen how separate the Hausa women's world is from the men's. This separation is underscored by clear-cut spatial arrangements whereby men and women are rarely together, even in the home.

Because men's and women's worlds are separate socially and economically, men and women often in fact operate more or less independently of each other. The male value system is tacitly accepted, and it is obvious that major decisions are made by men and that women are confined essentially to the private, domestic world. Women, however, engage in their own networks of friendship and make their own investments of time and resources in their own businesses. They live in their own world of women with minimal reference to the male-dominated world around them, and thus have an autonomy that would be envied in a less male-oriented society. Women's days are filled with personal visits, their labor is devoted to generating their own small incomes, and they exchange information not shared with men through their own family networks.

Although most women live a profoundly restricted life, they share with other women a profound degree of sociability and can tap reservoirs of mutual support should trouble come. Such sisterly support would be the envy of Western feminists. It must be observed, however, that sympathy and empathy do not change the circumstances of a mistreated woman's life or alter the arbitrary decision of a husband to divorce her, to prohibit her further education or employment, or to take additional wives. Moral and spiritual support provided by women for women has little power to alter objective circumstances. Relevant statute law as found in the Nigerian constitution is ineffective when it lacks cultural underpinnings.

Thus, while the foundation for economic independence exists, women's limited social options preclude real economic and social autonomy. In effect, reform must first attack the inner dynamics of the marriage relationship before it can alter the social position of women. This is most difficult and not predictable.

Western women's concerns about autonomy are not those of Hausa women. Hausa society as a whole is neither egalitarian nor individualistic and demands integration of the individual into his or her social role. We cannot assume that the enormous regard for individual choice and individual freedom so obvious in Western culture will develop here. The emphasis in all social life is on family relationships, family connections, obligations as defined in Islam, and the external appearance of serenity in nonfamilial relationships. Confrontation with those you know is most difficult; in the family group, women's place is central to the maintenance of harmony; outside of the family, women are not expected to call attention to themselves in any way.

In the West, emphasis on the vote has led to the increasing social integration of women and minorities. But the vote per se is irrelevant for Islamic women. Their emancipation in terms of their daily lives can only occur within the confines of what can be justified within Islamic law. The vote has been important in moving women into the public sphere, but their involvement has been permitted only as a tool of male election strategies. Women have not organized themselves around women's issues (such as divorce, child support, or family planning), but have adopted agendas (such as education and voting) set by men. While the numbers of women voting and the obviously increasing acceptance of a public role for women in Kano politics are impressive, there is every indication that women do not believe it proper to seek such roles to the exclusion of the traditional roles of wife and mother. Overwhelmingly, Western women believe birth control to be necessary for women's liberation; Islamic doctrines do not explicitly prohibit birth control, but descriptions of proper roles for women make it clear that their lives are intended to be child-centered and home-based. All Islamic societies generally advocate large numbers of children on religious grounds, and a man's virility is established by the number of children he has sired. The degree of emancipation required for both men and women to accept and practice, let alone campaign for, birth control is a long way off.

This said, it is interesting to note that unlike Islamic societies that are predominantly Arab, Hausa society permitted women to become highly visible in public life during the 1979–1983 period of civilian rule and the first two years of the 1984 military regime. In the Islamic world, women are seldom elected to public office and only a few have been appointed to high-level government positions. In Kano, a woman was elected to Parliament, and the several women commissioners who were appointed remained—despite their deficiencies and difficulties—very much in the public eye. In 1981 a new talk show was introduced in Kano State, "Kallabi Tsakanin Rawuna" (which translates literally as "head tie among the turbans"), on which women of achievement were regularly interviewed. This is not to suggest, however, that in assuming public responsibilities, women may neglect traditional ones or live unconventional lives. Women in public view must have the support of their husbands and their families or be scorned by the community. But a woman who lives by society's rules and has the support of her husband can indeed emerge from behind the walls of seclusion in today's Kano in order to play a public role. This is not to say that a majority of women have this option, or that a majority of men would approve of such roles for their wives —they would not. But those few women who do become publicly visible provide a role model for young girls, more and more of whom are now going to school and a few of whom, at least, are beginning to consider life options significantly more varied than their mothers'.

In most areas of life, progress is being made in the effort to enhance the status, social position, and life opportunities of women. At present this affects only a small minority of girls from privileged families and occurs only within very strict confines, but it suggests a direction for the future. Women are allowed and occasionally encouraged—within the confines of marriage and Islamic belief—to pursue education and employment.

But it is still the case that women attempting to pursue careers as an alternative to marriage are severely ostracized. The only two women in Kano publicly acknowledged in 1982 to have attempted this had succumbed to family and community pressures and reentered marriage between 1983 and 1985. Thus, in the one area that is most crucial to Western feminists—personal codes and family laws concerning marriage, divorce, and the conduct of behavior between men and women—there has been little progress. The age of marriage may be postponed, but marriage is still required. Education may be encouraged, but families take precedence over careers and men still make the crucial decisions in both areas. Islamic law gives men control over their wives, daughters, and sisters; and the importance of Islamic teachings and the denunciation of Western or secular law in these matters is constantly reiterated and asserted. Hence, in the final analysis, there can be no full emancipation of women, no matter how great the progress in other areas of social and political life, until Islamic codes are revised through reinterpretation. Nothing indicates that this may occur in the foreseeable future. Islamic law on the one hand and perceptions of women's liberation as alien and evil on the other, represent the challenge and opportunity of movement toward change in Kano. Women's liberation is regarded as a Western corrupting influence, and Islamic law decrees that women can never be the equal of men. In the final analysis women will no doubt continue to live their lives in ways endorsed by their husbands for many years to come. The experience of other Islamic countries illustrate the likelihood of this prediction.

WOMEN AND CHANGE IN THE ISLAMIC WORLD

The Shah of Iran decreed in 1936 that women should cease to wear the veil; education for girls was made compulsory in the 1940s. Iranian women were encouraged to enter public life, and many did. But women were still depicted primarily as sexual objects and as dependent, irrational, submissive persons in need of supervision and protection (Pakizege 1978, 216–26). The Iranian revolution has demonstrated the enormity of the gap between the legal system with its publicly sanctioned reforms and the hold of religion and custom. Only with prior acceptance of equality of rights and equality of human potential in general can a society move beyond the veil to an era of greater awareness of basic equality between the sexes.

So long as men's and women's roles are viewed as being complementary, equality based on individual merit regardless of sex is not to be expected. As women have learned in the West, until there is a revised division of labor in the home, equality outside the home is not to be looked for; so long as men are sexually free and women are not, women will be perceived as weaker and in need of protection or as inherently promiscuous and therefore in need of seclusion or surveillance. Unveiling and the granting of women's suffrage in Iran did not change women's position within the family (Haeri 1980). In Kano women continue to be divorced by *talaq,* to lose their children at a husband's whim, and to suffer the indignity of husbands' taking second, third, or fourth wives against their wishes. Family pressure and the loss of children in the case of divorce predisposes women to remain married, even if they must themselves become second, third, or fourth wives after a first divorce.

Even in the Soviet Union, efforts to force reforms for women in Islamic south central Asia were resisted. The social mores and religious values of a collective group, the Muslim community, were used to deflect and evade the controls of an overarching political community, the totalitarian Soviet state (Massell 1974, 390). If all the powers of the aggressively secular Soviet state could not effect such change, how much less likely is it that radical politics will be successful in a society where many advocate the institutionalization of an Islamic state?

If a charismatic Islamic reformer in the tradition of Usman dan Fodio or even Aminu Kano were to arise and make reform of personal codes a focus of his teachings, dramatic progress might continue. Students of modern politics from Rousseau to Weber and including, of course, contemporary comparativists, have noted the pivotal role such a person can play in deeply traditional societies. Almond and Powell observed that "one of the most important mechanisms of change in public policy in traditional systems is charismatic" (1966, 136). There is evidence, however, that in the case of women in Islamic societies, even committed and strong leaders cannot introduce lasting reforms when they contradict or appear to contradict Islamic personal law. In Tunisia, President Bourguiba emphasized the emancipation of women as a central feature of his reforms by introducing new legal codes concerning marriage, divorce, and education. In the beginning, these reforms appeared to make great headway (Tessler 1978, 141–57). But as Bourguiba declined in health the government began backing down from its emphasis on education for girls, claiming that it was too expensive, that the opportunities for graduates were limited, and that these enrollments were a cause of declining standards. As this book is being written (1985), both federal military and state governments in Nigeria are echoing these claims. In Tunisia between 1967 and 1978, there was a great decline in support for change for women. In the absence of official programs and stimuli, support vanished. As the economy weakened, the social position of men became more precarious and they began strongly to object to women's emancipation, which was cast as a symbol of the forces of alienation and increased competition for positions and status. In this case, frustration and insecurity fueled a resurgence of traditional values.

Finally, so long as Muslim societies refuse to face the challenge of population control, there is a natural limit to the degree of women's emancipation; unless both values and law change, birth control will remain unacceptable to both men and women. So long as women perceive their care and survival in old age to be dependent on children who will support them, and so long as custom awards children only to the husband in the case of divorce, women will continue to bear as many children as they are able.

Islamic societies have much higher fertility rates than do non-Islamic societies at comparable levels of economic and industrial development (Youssef 1978, 69–99). In most Islamic countries, professed respect for women is high while their personal rights are limited and monitored by husbands and/or fathers. Partly for this reason, it is important to distinguish between public policies that result in lower levels of education, less economic independence, and less participation in public life for women, and the injunctions of Islamic law that limit such choices. The latter are the more serious obstacles; social and religious constraints, not secular law per se, are the problem. Notions of decency and respect provide cultural strictures that control behavior and keep women in their proper place as chaste and obedient wives. At the moment, in Kano these strictures still draw at least public credence from women.

In Turkey coeducation in elementary and secondary schools has been crucial to changing the nature of the relationship between men and women (Del Vecchio Good 1978). In Iran coeducation was introduced only at the university level. In Kano the suspicion of coeducation is one indication of the conservative tenor of debate. Both Ataturk in Turkey and the Shah in Iran initiated reforms in the status of women. But the pervasive and overwhelming force of conservative Islamic religion overturned the Shah's prescriptions when his regime fell; in Turkey, where Islam is less militant in its presence, reform has endured. Islamic fundamentalism in Kano is more akin to that of Iran than of Turkey at comparable stages of development. Men and women still live in separate social worlds in Kano; the strong insistence of parents and the preference of university students for single-sex institutions beyond the primary level indicate a well-entrenched attitude that will not easily succumb to change. Although Bayero University is coeducational and is likely to remain so because of its status as a federal institution, the fact that most female students indigenous to Kano State are either already married or engaged militates against the easy mixing of male and female students that characterizes coeducational institutions in other parts of the world. The predominance of Islamic fundamentalists on the faculty ensures that an articulate and vocal ideology stands behind this status quo. As women university graduates enter careers and begin to identify with their new roles, a new consciousness may develop. But unless a political party emerges that is capable of rooting these new beliefs in Islamic notions of justice, they will be held by a minute minority and regarded as deviant.

GENERAL THEORETICAL CONCERNS

Feminist research seeks to explain why the full range of human potential is less available to women than to men and to understand the underlying logic of the many cultural patterns that underscore the subordination of women. A basic indicator of the status of women is the extent to which behavioral options are precluded on the basis of sex (Safilios-Rothchild 1970). Measuring training, education, and employment opportunities; marital, familial, childbearing, and sexual decisions; political and power aspirations; and geographic mobility for both women and men would make it possible to construct an equality index in order to compare the status of women across cultures. The question raised in this study was whether education and political activism would affect the culturally determined status of women in Kano. Would it initiate a reassessment of sex roles, a redistribution of the burdens of domesticity, and access to resources and opportunities? This study of Hausa culture suggests the answer is no.

The overall thrust of change for women in Kano basically reinforces rather than challenges the cultural and religious justifications that limit women to essentially domestic functions and subordinate their public roles to men's control. While education affords access to greater opportunity and political participation allows the status quo to be questioned, fundamentalist religious beliefs circumscribe the arena in which change can occur.

This study too suggests that the variety and diversity of roles and status of women in Hausa society indicate that solely biological explanations for female subordination are not sufficient. Biology limits the roles of men and women in human reproduction, but does not define social roles. Societies define appropriate roles which are then legitimated through cultural and religious beliefs. But culture and social structure determine the implication of the biological distinctions between men and women and define their statuses. It has been suggested here that when the values of a culture are informed by deeply ingrained religious norms, they are highly resistant to any change not fully justified by reference to interpretations or reinterpretations of those religious values. Religion legitimates these social distinctions. Sexual norms affect the economic roles assigned to women, and religion also underscores these roles. Islam limits female economic independence, emphasizes male honor, and underscores perceptions of women as nurturers and men as decision-makers. Women in the West have insisted on reforms in both Judaism and Christianity that de-emphasize the male bias in these religions. Thus far, Islamic women have initiated no such movement.

If, indeed, control over their own bodies necessarily precedes control over their own lives, then the beginning is only now a hope in Kano. Such matters as the opportunity to earn income, the option to come and go as one pleases, decisions about family formation, duration and size, education, health, and sexual control are not women's to make. Thus far women's participation in politics has not moved these concerns very far into the public arena. Sexual inequality did not begin with Islam, but Islamic women seem to have the most difficulty in coming to grips with it. Why is Islam stronger than Judaism and Christianity in this regard? It is suggested that the special status of Islamic law and the absence of liberalizing reform movements is central. The pockets of enlightenment that led to social movements that eventually addressed women's inequality in the historical traditions of Western societies are absent in Islamic societies. The transition from orthodox Islamic to a modern society has yet to occur.

In advanced industrial societies most women work outside the home and men are beginning to help in the home. In order for women to work, public services that provide health care, pensions, child care, and social security have expanded in order to help relieve the burden on the family. Not without considerable objection, women's primary domestic role in the family has diminished, as has men's role as the sole breadwinner. The Islamic belief that men have a divinely ordained responsibility to be sole providers of their families makes such public acknowledgments of changing roles and mores difficult if not impossible. In less traditional societies, a woman works outside the home and the state helps with some of her traditional responsibilities. As women's options outside the home widen, their education, employment, political, and cultural expression also expands. It has been suggested that this process might be analogous to similar developments for men during the industrial revolution (Olin 1976, 105–28). In communist countries, governments have assumed such responsibilities while urging women into the work force and emphasizing enforced equality. In the West, economic development and growth and the expansion of government services have been accompanied by a focus on personal liberation for both men and women. Such an emphasis has yet to develop in Hausa society.

The significance of education and women's political participation cannot be interpreted only in political and social terms, but must speak also of the relationship between men and women. In order to comprehend how male/female relationships come to be opposed in terms of interests, images, and beliefs of each concerning the other, more historical analyses of changing sex roles in societies such as this are needed. Research elsewhere indicates that societies in which authority within the domestic sphere is shared by both men and women are among those offering expanding opportunities for both sexes in the public sphere (Lamphere 1974). In Kano, the physical space itself is not shared, which precludes any meaningful sharing of responsibility.

Can the ideology of women's liberation successfully challenge the ideology of female subordination inherent in Islam? Islamic thinkers elevate the status of women as mothers, but assume underlying moral and intellectual inferiority. Muslims believe that women's status is genetically inherent, that women are naturally subordinate to men and are satisfied with their inferior place. As Sir Ahmadu Bello said, "Our women have not said they are dissatisfied" (Bello 1962, 232).

It has been emphasized that children's primary identification is with their mother, and mothers tend to treat male and female children differently, which affects female psychological development (Chodorow 1974). Children's early perceptions are internalized and supported by cultural beliefs and values. Social training and social interaction in childhood builds on and reinforces this largely unconscious development.

In Hausa society families show preference for male children and celebrate when they are born. By age six, a boy's masculine gender identification must replace his primary identification with his mother. Boys are taught to identify with things masculine and to denigrate and devalue whatever they take to be feminine. Boys identify with fathers and treat women as their fathers do. Girls identify with their mothers and in time become mothers.

In childhood, boys are children, but girls are little women. Girls begin caring for children from around age six in Kano. They begin to wear makeup, to paint their fingernails, and to wear earrings and bracelets around the same age. The only roles they foresee for themselves are those of wife and mother. Female sex-role learning is uniform regardless of social class, urban/rural residence, native ability, or the cognitive impact of school. Because of their early and complete socialization, girls are more likely to develop weak ego boundaries and be less likely to differentiate themselves from their mothers and sisters. Separation and the development of individual agendas is especially difficult for girls, partly because their mothers do not push them to differentiate themselves, but rather emphasize the importance of conformity to all social conventions, quietness, and modesty. In Kano, strong group identity and a culture that discourages individualism do not promote women's activism in the public arena that would directly challenge prevailing sexual mores.

Studies in other Islamic societies emphasize that an assault on women's subordination is an assault on the role most distinctively ascribed rather than achieved (Jane Smith 1980). An attack on women's roles is an attack on a highly interlocking set of roles, both men's and women's, with a wide spectrum of functions. To alter the concept of "woman" is to threaten to dissolve the boundaries defining maleness itself. It is not just the superordinate position of men vis-à-vis women, but male self-image, self-definition, self-esteem, and ego-identity that is threatened (Massell 1974, 401). In Islam, there is an extraordinary interdependence between male identity and family honor and the role and place of women (Miner and DeVos 1960; Gordon 1968; Bellah 1975).

The more a man's ego development is dependent on rigid distinctions between male and female roles, the greater the perception of inner stress and the less manageable are inner conflicts when such roles are threatened. "Any diminution of deference can result in immediate sensitivity, and in the use of coercion or even violence to reaffirm dominance" (Massell 1974, 403–404).

In Islamic society, change in the status of women is more threatening than anything else because it affects relations of authority and power in the most intimate part of man's life. There is not a single instance of Islamic women waging an independent campaign for women's rights and ultimately winning through a political process. If, through cooperation with men in the public arena in Kano, women's independence is increased through education and political participation, it will be a first for an Islamic society.

As a result of increasing levels of education for women, new forms of marriage, new patterns of interactions between generations, and new styles of family accommodation are being introduced. To be generally accepted, a new generation of women must come of age, women whose horizons extend beyond the confines of their homes and villages and who see evidence that they can find security and satisfaction in life with an altered perception of appropriate roles. If such altered perceptions are not supported by institutional arrangements and legal rights to which women can turn, such altered perceptions will remain muted, perhaps undermining the traditional status quo in the private sphere, but not really transforming its public expression.

Historically, in modernizing societies, changing circumstances and changing perceptions and values gave rise to social movements that questioned the prevailing arrangements and pressed for the extension of egalitarian principles into new arenas (Lapidus 1978, 1–3). A radical reconstruction of society calls for fundamental transformation of economic and social institutions that finally destroys the roots of inequality and permits construction of a new and genuinely egalitarian social order. Commitment to sexual equality is an important component of broader egalitarian impulses. But reform in Islamic societies tends to leave in place authoritarian relations between the sexes and socialization patterns that are crucial to personality formation and sex-role differentiation.

In non-Islamic societies, new political and legal norms gradually established the juridical foundations of sexual equality, while new institutional arrangements began slowly to alter the structure of pressures, opportunities, and rewards. In Western as well as Islamic societies, the traditional view contends that the origins of inequality are found in the hierarchy of nature itself. Once this stance is refuted and inequalities are identified as conventional rather than natural, the way is open for questioning female subordination. In the West, near the opening of the nineteenth century, such women as Mary Wollstonecraft and Abigail Adams pointed up the political implications of this corrected view of the origins of social inequality. They asserted that democratic values were incompatible with democratic ideas of political participation (Pateman 1983). But, for another century the political role of women was restricted to raising citizens.

Even in the West, however, women recognize their nearly universal subordination, but only rarely form organizations to advance their interests in classic interest group fashion. Rather, they internalize and rationalize their subordination (Hacker 1951; Fanon 1966; Mannoni 1967). Women tend not to politicize their concerns; their residence and intimacy with men and the consequent emergence of self-identification based on family and male interests reinforces the difficulties of perceiving, expressing, and acting on sex-based concerns.

Women in the West moved toward full participation in the state and the political system when their interests led them to perceive the impact of political power on them. The quest for female emancipation in Hausa society

While great advances have been made in education for women, this has not yet changed perceptions of roles, behavior, and relative positions of men and women. The great stumbling block is the interpretation of Islamic law, which keeps women submissive and subservient and denies them the freedom to make basic life decisions and thus, keeps their status dependent on factors beyond their control. If liberalization of women's roles is associated with the West and the West is rejected and it is Islamic law that defines women's roles, how can change in women's status be initiated? Thus both Islam and women's liberation limit the potential of women to go over the walls of seclusion or through the doors of opportunity to the emancipation made possible by education.

A more differentiated economic role for women, increasing educational opportunities, and an expanded political role must be legitimated over time through changes in cultural norms. This is a very complex process, because when status changes for women threaten male power and authority over them, as they inevitably must, there will be opposition and sexual antagonism. It is thus essential to develop a value system that legitimates or sanctions increasing equality between men and women. The degree to which such a belief system can develop in an Islamic society is problematic.

highlights in a particularly acute way the contradiction betweer
equal treatment and differential treatment; and because it touc
biologically rooted complementarity of male and female roles an
ture of the family as a fundamental social institution, this particu
of the problem of equality is indeed unique. But the fluid natu
tended polygamous family and the widespread responsibility fc
and child rearing within Hausa families means that women are
sarily so tied to their own biological children as they are in the
we come full circle in suggesting rather concretely that it is religi
ology rather than biology that limits women's options in Kano.
versies surrounding the nature of Islam and consequences of wom
tion are testimony to the distinctive problems raised by discussic
equality in this context.

In analyzing the obstacles to change and the potential f
emancipation in Kano, three factors in particular need to be tak
count: the degree to which political ideology can affect women
introduce changes in women's lives, the degree to which such cha
rationalized according to the precepts of Islamic law, and the degr
traditional social patterns are adaptable to changed sex-role exp

It is important to note, however, that political leadership i
been immensely important in undermining and radically changin
tional Muslim reaction to Western education and education for v
over three decades, Mallam Aminu Kano reiterated the central pl
reform in the political program of his political parties. Whether
litical leaders and their parties will expand upon this foundation
age higher education and more public roles for women, as well as r
of tasks and responsibilities in the home, remains to be seen. Per
female inferiority as revealed in children's songs and child-rearin
exist side by side with exhortations concerning the revolutionary p
women. The variety of responses and reactions to these opposed
only begun to be recorded. It is pertinent to note, however, that
ciety has historically proved to be very adaptable to outside forces a
by its assimilation of Fulani rule, incorporation of Islam, and accom
to British colonialism. Having developed as an orthodox and c
Islamic society, however, it has not been receptive to those forces t
appear to challenge Islam; Christian missionaries, Western educ
notions of the social (as opposed to the religious) equality of wc
all been received with great reservations if not outright hostility.
to be seen how resistent to reform the Muslim orthodox milieu is a
type of traditional society, as distinct from the historic adaptability
society itself.

Glossary

ahkam, legal injunctions of the *Qur'an*
akuya, goat
alikalya, women's judge
alkali, judges in Islamic courts
allo, large slate used for writing lessons in Qur'anic schools
almajirai, Qur'anic students who beg for alms
attijirai, class of wealthy Hausa merchants
auren silkiti, noncoresidential marriage
auren zumunci, kin marriage

babban daki, rooms of emir's first wife
bakwai, seven (in reference to the original seven Hausa states)
Bayajidda legend, the Hausa legend of origin
bazarawa (or bazawara), a single woman or a woman who is not married
bik, virgin
bokaye, Bori priests and priestesses
boko, Literally "book," refers to Western education or to the Hausa language written in Roman script
budurwa, maiden or virgin

daki, separate hut of a woman
dillalai, brokers

Fiqh, Islamic legal theory

girgim, kings list
gwauro, unmarried men

hadith, words of the Prophet as recorded by his companions
Hanafi, School of Islamic law
Hanbali, School of Islamic law

idda, mourning period
Iya, traditional woman's title
iskoki, Bori spirits

jawarci, nonmarriage, a state recognized by women but not by men
jihad, Islamic holy war, crusade
jinjiniya, female infant
jinjiri, male infant

kadis (qudis), scholars in Islamic law; judges in Sharia courts
kake, small, peanut brittle-like cakes
karuwa, woman of questionable reputation in proper society; prostitute; word men use speaking of divorced or widowed woman
karuwanci, prostitution
kawa, obligation of reciprocity among males
kayan daki, "things of the room," that part of the dowry for which the bride's mother is responsible
kudin sarauta, royal money
kuhl, separation sought by the wife through court
kulle, wife seclusion, imprisonment
kullen dinga, complete seclusion of wife; she never goes out
kullen tsari, wife seclusion in which wife may occasionally go out
kullen zuci, most lenient form of wife seclusion, "purdah of the heart"
kunya, respect; first child avoidance (in practice, a mother avoids mentioning the name of or interacting with a first born child)

madrasa, a school of higher Islamic learning
magajiya, queen mother, "speaks for women" (title of respect)
maharba, hunters
mahauta, butchers
mai unguwa, ward head
Majira, variant of *magajiya*

makarantum allo, "board" or Qur'anic school
makarantum boko, "book" or Western school
makarantum ilmi, higher Islamic learning
makira, blacksmith
Maliki, school of Islamic law observed in Kano
mallam, an Islamic learned man or teacher
manoma, farmers
maroka, musicians
masa-sana'a, craftsmen
mata, woman or wife
matan zamani, modern woman, euphemism for prostitute
miji, young man

radir suna, naming ceremony

sa, cow
Sabon Gari, strangers' quarters
sadaki, bridewealth
sadaqa, alms
Salla, days of feasting marking the end of Ramadan
sana'a, skill, work skill
sanuja, ox
sarakuna, traditional ruling class
sarauta, offices of aristocracy
sare-kia, snake slayer
sarki, king
sauke kurani, students who know *Qur'an* by heart
Shafi'i, School of Islamic law
shehu, spiritual leader
soro, entranceways to homes
Sunna, acts of the Prophet

tafsir, interpretations of the *Qur'an*
tafsir mallam-mallam, who has mastered the *Qur'an*
talaq, divorce unilaterally pronounced by husband
tala, talla, hawking or street trading: children selling cooked food for their mothers on the street
talakawa, commoner class; peasantry
tauhid, theology
thayyib, widow or divorcee
tsoho, old man

tsohuwa, old woman
tuzuru, unmarried men

ulema, learned men
umma, Muslim community
Uwar Soro, first wife of emir

wakili, groom's guardian

'yan kasuwa, small traders
'yan kwarya, women who practice Bori openly
yarinya, girl
yaro, young boy

zaure, entranceway to a house

Notes

1—The Historical Setting and the Place of Women

1. According to the last officially accepted Nigerian census, taken in 1952, Kano City was ninety-eight percent Islamic. While the overall population has grown dramatically over the past thirty years, the percentage of Muslims has not changed.

Strictly speaking the Hausa are not a tribe but rather an amalgamation of different peoples who, over the centuries, have adopted the Hausa language. Most Hausa subgroups trace their origins to Baghdad or Tripoli, and there are many myths of migration from the north across the desert into the western Sudan and then south to present day Niger and Nigeria (Palmer 1928, vol. III; Skinner 1969, 4). By the sixteenth century these various migratory groupings had become a homogeneous people speaking a common language; they are known collectively as Habe to distinguish them from the Fulani, a nomadic people who conquered the Hausa states during an Islamic holy war in the early nineteenth century. The Habe and Fulani together are often called by the collective term "Hausa." In distinguishing between the Hausa and Fulani, the term Habe is used to designate the indigenous Hausa people, while the term Hausa is used when speaking of the language of the Hausa/Fulani as one cultural group.

There is a large literature relating to the Hausa, including numerous works in Arabic and Hausa, cited in the bibliographies of Paden (1973) and Tahir (1976), works related to Hausa economy cited in Hill (1972), and items regularly noted in the journal *Savanna,* published by Ahmadu Bello University.

2. For this purpose, the work of Guy Nicolas (1975) is particularly important. The Katsinawa, upon whom his work is partly based, were the prejihad rulers of Katsina, an important Hausa state in Nigeria immediately to the north of Kano. The Katsinawa now reside in Maradi in Niger, to which they fled at the time of the jihad. They have retained many of the traditions lost or greatly altered after the jihad that most directly affected the Hausa states now in Nigeria.

3. The Daura "list" generally cited is taken from A.E.V. Walwyn's *History of Daura,* printed in Palmer (1928), p. 42.

4. According to Hogben and Kirk-Greene (1966) the *Kano Chronicle* was apparently written between 1883 and 1893, but probably represents an older record destroyed by the Fulani in their conquest of Kano during 1804–1809. They speculate that a literate traveler from the

north settled in Kano and collected oral traditions concerning the reigns of former kings. The *Kano Chronicle* is reproduced in Palmer (1928), vol. III, pp. 92–134.

5. The original English translation of *Infak al Maisuri* by E.J. Arnett (*The Rise of the Sokoto Fulani*) is difficult to obtain.

6. Palmer (1950) suggests that women in Bornu gained status and influence due to the practice of matrilineal descent, brought perhaps by the Tuareg, who are matrilineal to this day, and with whom the Bornu nobility had important marriage alliances.

2—Hausa Women in Kano Society

1. The majority of Nigerian Sunnis belong to the Sufi brotherhoods of Qadiriyya, Tijaniyya, and Mahadiyya. The smallest of these, the Mahadiyya, endorses belief in revealed reinterpretation of truth and has a significant, although relatively small, following in Kano.

2. Reproductive histories of eighty-two women with children in two Kano wards (Kurawa and Kofar Mazugal) were taken by Schildkrout in 1977. Of these, seventy-nine had children and three were "caretakers," i.e., they had been given children to foster. The seventy-nine women had given birth to a total of 164 children, or an average of 8.2 each. Women without children are assumed to be unable to conceive.

3. As of 1983 the president of the Planned Parenthood Society of Nigeria, a member of a distinguished Kano family, saw nothing disconcerting in the fact that no office of the organization existed in the city. He asserted that Kano women knew he was the president of the society and were free to come to his house and request a note from him to the appropriate doctor in the city hospital if they wanted information or birth control assistance (Interview #23, 1983).

4. Renee Pitten found, however, that a significant number of women in Katsina (a city to the north of Kano) elected to remain single and enter careers as "courtesans," an accepted but not generally approved, traditional Hausa role (Pitten 1983). It should be pointed out, men too are expected to marry. During Ramadan children in Kano City go out chanting before sunrise in front of houses containing unmarried young men—*tuzuru* or *gwauro*.

5. It was often asserted that the rationale for inequitable inheritance laws is the quite real possibility that women will need to rely on their families for support in the event of divorce or death of a husband.

6. Schildkrout interviewed eighty-two women in two wards during 1976–1978, and Callaway interviewed fifty educated women in Kano during 1981–1983.

7. Pitten has written a Ph.D. dissertation on Hausa women entitled "Marriage and Other Career Alternatives" in which the only "career" alternative discussed is prostitution.

3—Hausa Women: A World of Their Own

1. The 1954 biography of a Hausa woman, Baba of Kara, is considered a classic (M. Smith 1954).

2. The use of the terms "dowry" and *kayan daki* in Hausa often causes some confusion. Although *kayan daki* is loosely translated as "dowry," technically it is only that part of the dowry for which a bride's mother is responsible. A bride's dowry is composed of gifts from her father as well, usually consisting of furniture, linens, and cloth. The *kayan daki,* from her mother but

earned in part through her street trade (*tala*) for her mother, consists of the brass and enamel pots and bowls, dishes, china, and other breakables that are used to decorate the walls of her room after marriage.

3. In 1982–1983, surveys of 686 university students were conducted by the author, and surveys of 419 secondary school students were conducted by students working with her.

4—Politics in Kano: Bringing Women into the Polity

1. During the First Republic (1960–1966) Nigeria had a parliamentary form of government. Therefore, the title of president at this time was a ceremonial one accorded to the head of state, while a prime minister served as head of government.

2. The PRP was returned to power in the August 1983 elections, but this government was overthrown by a military coup d'état the following December.

3. Between 1982 and 1983, 686 students were surveyed at Bayero University in Kano.

4. Although after winning the 1979 elections these young radicals broke with Aminu Kano in order to pursue more "secular" political ambitions, their lack of legitimacy in the society was underscored when their self-defined "reformed" PRP (running on the ticket of the NPP) was roundly defeated by Aminu Kano's officially recognized party in the 1983 elections.

5. A sheik must be able to trace his own spiritual line directly to the founding saint of the brotherhood, and thus Ibrahim Niass traces his descent to Sheik Ahmad Tijjani, while the leader of the jihad in Nigeria, Usman dan Fodio, traces his to Abd al-Qadir Jilani (Hiskett 1973).

6. The deposed Sanusi is the older brother of the present emir, Ado Bayero, and both are sons of Abdullahi Bayero, for whom the University is named.

7. The "tradition" of political activism on the part of women in *karuwanci,* however, perhaps did express itself in the founding of the first women's party in Nigeria, the National Democratic Action Party, founded by Felice Alheri-Mortune. Although Ms. Mortune herself was a "business woman" who spent most of her life outside of Nigeria, the party's members were almost exclusively women in *karuwanci.* The party was never recognized by the Federal Electoral Commission, but it did receive front page publicity in leading newspapers—see for instance the *Sunday Times,* August 23, 1981, and *The Nigerian Standard,* October 2, 1982.

5—Paths of Emergence: Parity in Politics

1. *The New Nigerian* ran a column every Sunday written by Ibraheem Sulaiman, a lecturer in the Center for Islamic Legal Studies at Ahmadu Bello University in Zaria. A three-part series dealt specifically with "The Liberation of Women" (see *New Nigerian,* April 17, April 24, and May 1, 1983). Often, in his columns he extolled the virtues of the protections afforded women in Islam.

2. Although not a Hausa nor a Kano woman, Hajiya Hassana Hassan's anger with the NPN was well-noted in the press and discussed by women in letters to the editors (see *Concord,* October 7, and October 11, 1982). In 1979 she had headed the women's wing of the party in Bornu State and was credited with getting a large number of women registered to vote, but after the election she was removed from her position when she began criticizing the party's male leadership. In spite of several elections held by the women's wing to reinstate her, she was never again

accorded a place in the party. Having been divorced by her husband, Hajiya Hassana dedicated her life to politics. As she stated in an interview, "I can settle, I could marry again and stay in my husband's house, but they will not shut up my mouth" (*Punch,* October 8, 1982).

3. Her grandfather was a member of the Sokoto ruling family and was associated with the Mahdi, who led a Sudanic and West African reform movement at the turn of the century (Paden 1973, 171–73).

4. Alhaji Hassan Yusuf, a labor leader, was the nominal leader of the party after the death of Mallam Aminu Kano and its presidential candidate in 1983. Sabo Barkin Zuwo had been a senator during the 1979–1983 period and was the gubernatorial candidate in the August 1983 elections, which he won by a large margin. His remarks about "a government of illiterates for illiterates" were made in a talk on the "Life and Times of Aminu Kano" given at Bayero University in Kano on October 10, 1983.

5. The basic text for the theory of Mahdism is Ibn Khaldun's *Muquaddimah,* of which F. Rosenthal has produced an excellent translation.

6. The special focus and effort in regard to education could indeed be revolutionary for women. In five short years (1978–1983), female elementary students increased from 5 to 32 percent, female secondary students increased from .8 to 27 percent and female university students from 2 to 10 percent of their school populations (Kano State 1983).

6—Education in Kano

1. In this context "Western" schools refer to those providing conventional classes with classrooms, desks, certificated teachers, and blackboards, as well as textbooks and examinations. It is difficult to avoid the use of the term "Western" in referring to these schools in order to distinguish them from Qur'anic and Islamiyya schools, described below. The term Western thus includes both government-sponsored non-Islamic schools and Christian mission schools.

2. Politeness is stressed in all interpersonal relationships in Hausa society. Alhaji Shehu Shagari, Nigeria's president in 1982, alluded to this feature in an interview with *Africa* magazine when he remarked, "If a Fulani man is your sworn enemy, you will never know it" (*Africa,* October 1982, 34).

3. As noted in chapter four, the only northern Nigerian Hausa-Fulani man who had earned a university education in 1954 was Dr. A.R.B. Dikko, who had been educated in mission schools and who himself had converted to Christianity (Coleman 1960, 133).

4. It should be noted that members of the traditional ruling class (*sarakuna*) did not send their own sons to such schools, but rather sent the sons of their retainers or slaves to fill the seats in these schools. Some of the most prominent northern Nigerian politicians in the First Republic were thus educated.

5. Theoretically Qur'anic students, or *almajirai,* beg for alms after mosque on Friday; but at the present time (1983) these young boys, dressed in white, are on the streets and in all public places in Kano nearly every day from 10:00 a.m. until midafternoon begging for alms, food, or clothing. It has been alleged that this practice of young boys' supporting itinerant *mallams* through begging on the streets in the name of Islamic scholarship is so extensive only in West Africa, especially Hausaland (Abba 1984, 193).

6. Reputedly, the richest man in West Africa was Alhaji Alhassan Dantata, a Kano businessman who controlled the Nigerian groundnut (peanut) and kola trade in the 1950s before branching into myriad other enterprises. He had no Western education. Another such example in Kano is Alhaji Isiyaku Rabiu, who formed a limited company in 1952 and today heads

a group of industries with paid-up capital in excess of naira fifty million (*New Nigerian,* February 22, 1982).

7. Kano Emirate had been designated Kano State in 1968 by the military regime that divided Nigeria's four regions into nineteen states, partly in response to the tensions that had led to the attempted secession of the eastern region as the independent nation of Biafra, which in turn led to the Nigerian/Biafran war.

8. Although figures are not available, the Sarkin Bai of Kano, Muhtari Sarkin Bai, the commissioner of education from 1968 to 1974, asserts that this is so (Interview #50, Kano, January 5, 1985).

9. The majority of orthodox Muslims in Kano today belong to the Tijaniyya brotherhood, the leadership of which is very suspicious of Western education (see chapter four). The impetus for the establishment of Islamiyya schools came partly from this source. A 1972 survey by the British Council in Kano ("Education in Kano") recorded 34,293 students in 1,630 *makarantum ilmi,* while only 9,084 students were in secondary schools in the whole region (Kano: The British Council, 1972).

10. Both Mu'azu Hadejia, in "Karuwa" ("Prostitute") (in *Wakokin Mu'azu Hadejia* [Zaria: 1958]) and Hamisu Yadudu Funtuwa, in "Wakar Uwar Mugu" ("Song of Mother of Evil") (in *Wakokin Hausa* [Zaria:1957]) (cited in Brown and Hiskett 1975, 103); bitterly attack prostitutes who adopt English ways. Prostitutes are portrayed as speaking English, which implies that they are literate and have been to school (Mack 1981).

11. See M. Hiskett, "The Song of the Salihu's Miracles," in *African Language Study,* vol. XII, 1971, pp. 23–29 for accounts of restraints placed on even educated Hausa women in the late eighteenth and nineteenth centuries. See Shehu Galadanci (1971) for expressions of proper roles for educated women in the latter half of the twentieth century and Jean Trevor (1975, 252) for accounts of educated girls in Sokoto.

12. In the Nigerian system of education, teacher training colleges, technical and vocational schools, and commercial colleges are all postprimary institutions.

13. In 1983, the author visited all the women's centers in Kano City and interviewed their directors. In addition, a small survey was conducted in the City Center to gather information concerning the background of the women attending classes at that time.

14. In 1983, the following students conducted modified survey research touching on this problem in gathering material to write their M.Ed. theses for the Faculty of Education at Bayero University.

Aishatu Salihu Bello surveyed 100 educated parents for her research on "The Problems and Prospects of Mass Education with Special Reference to Women, Kano."

Lami Jibril Dokau surveyed seventy parents for his research on "Attitudes of Parents Toward Co-Education."

Halima Isyaku surveyed fifty students for her research on "The Problem of Married Educated Women in Hausa Society in Kano State."

Sa-adatu Rimi surveyed sixty parents for her research on "The Attitudes of Parents Towards Women Education in Kano Municipality."

Amina Salihu surveyed 144 students for her research entitled "A Case Study of Social Problems in a Girls Boarding School in Kano Municipal."

A'isha Indo Yuguda surveyed eighty-three teachers in her research entitled "An Investigation into the Mass Failure in Girls Secondary Schools and Teachers Colleges in Kano State."

15. I wish to thank Najah Abdul-Azeez, Hannatu Adamu, Binta Rabi'u. Nana Fatima Nagogo, Amina Audi, and Attahiru Mohammed, who administered questionnaires to the teachers and parents while researching their own third-year theses in Political Science at Bayero University in Kano during 1982–1983.

16. Secondary schools in Nigeria have traditionally been boarding schools. In 1983 the Government of Nigeria requested the states to "deboard" students in such schools as an economy measure. All girls secondary schools in Kano State were boarding schools during 1981–1983.

7—Paths of Emergence: Education

1. In 1982–1983 the author interviewed educated Hausa women and surveyed university students. Third-year undergraduate students at Bayero University interviewed Hausa men and uneducated Hausa women as a part of their own research requirements for their undergraduate honors theses.

The data base built by these students included the following:

80 illiterate women—Ibrahim Ismaila Mohammad
100 illiterate men—Mohammad Jabo
144 students and 83 teachers at Dala Girls Secondary School and 20 teachers at the Women's Teachers College, Kano—A'isha Indo Yugudu
23 illiterate mothers and 57 illiterate fathers—Sani Mohammad
35 illiterate mothers and 35 illiterate fathers—Yusuf Garbo Adamu
100 uneducated men and 100 female students—Bikisu Ismail

2. Recent articles in the American press suggest that women who choose high-powered careers sacrifice children, if not marriage. See for example Susan Fraker, "Why Women Aren't Getting to the Top," *Fortune,* April 16, 1924, pp. 40–45; Polly Hurst, "Downsliding From the Fast Track," *Philadelphia Inquirer,* May, 1985, pp. 152–99; "Women and the Gender Gap," *Newsweek,* September 26, 1983, p. 80; and "The New Dropouts: Career Women," *Philadelphia Inquirer,* March 10, 1985.

8—Paths of Emergence: Resistance and Change

1. Radical students mostly at Ahmadu Bello University in Zaria (to the south of Kano) established a new women's organization, Women in Nigeria (WIN), in 1982. In the summer of 1983 a national conference was held at the University during which several women students presented papers criticizing conservative interpretations of Islamic law by Nigerian Muslim men.

Bibliography

Abba, Isa A. 1984. "Bara by Some Almajirai in Kano City in the Twentieth Century: A Critical Assessment." *Studies in the History of Kano,* ed. Bawuro M. Barkindo, 193–206. Ibadan: Heineman Educational Books (Nigeria) Limited.

Abdullah, A., and Zeidenstein, S. 1978. *Village Women of Bangladesh: Prospects for Change.* Geneva: International Labor Organization.

Abdullahi, Ramatu A. 1980. *Self-concept and Cultural Change in the Hausa of Nigeria.* Ann Arbor, Mich.: University Microfilms.

Abell, H. C. 1962. "Report to the Government of Nigeria (Northern Region) on the Home Economics Aspects of the F.A.O. Socio-Economic Survey of Peasant Agriculture in Northern Nigeria: The Role of Rural Women in Farm and Home Life." Rome: F.A.O. (mimeograph).

———. 1967. *Socio-Economic Survey of Peasant Agriculture in Northern Nigeria: The Role of Rural Women in Farm and Home Life.* Rome: F.A.O. (mimeograph).

Adamu, Hannatu, 1982. "The Changing Role of Women in Politics: A Kano Case Study." Kano: Bayero University, Department of Political Science, B.Sc. Thesis.

Adamu, Haroun Al-Rashid. 1973. *The North and Nigerian Unity.* Lagos: The Daily Times Press.

Adamu, Idris. 1982. "Women's Political Participation in Kano." Kano: Bayero University, Department of Political Science, B.Sc. Thesis.

Adamu, Yusuf Garbo. 1981. "The Attitudes of Rural Muslims Towards Girls Education in Kano State." Kano: Bayero University, Faculty of Education, M.Sc. Thesis.

Almond, Gabriel, and John Bingham Powell. 1966. *Comparative Politics: A Developmental Approach.* Boston: Little Brown.

Amundsen, Kirsten. 1971. *The Silenced Majority.* Englewood Cliffs, N.J.: Prentice Hall.

Anka, Fatima Musa. 1982. "The Problem of Married Educated Hausa Women in Kano Society." Kano: Bayero University, Faculty of Education, M.Sc. Thesis.

Ardener, Shirley. 1975. *Perceiving Women.* New York: Halstead Press.

Armah, Ayi Kwei. 1969. *The Beautiful Ones Are Not Yet Born.* New York: MacMillan Collier Books.

Baba, J. M. 1980. "Large Scale Irrigation Development and Women's Farm Labour Participation in Hausaland: The Case of the Kano River Irrigation Project." In *Proceedings of the National Conference on Integrated Rural Development and Women in Development,* ed. Fred Omu, P. Kofo Makinwa, and A.O. Ozo, 3 vols, 1006–16. Benin: University of Benin Press.

Baldwin, T. H. 1932. *The Obligations of Princes.* Translation of *Risalat al-Maluk* by Muhammad b. 'Abd al-Maghili. Beirut.

Bardwick, Judith. 1971. *The Psychology of Women: A Study of Bio-Cultural Conflicts.* New York: Harper and Row.

———. 1972. *Readings on the Psychology of Women.* New York: Harper and Row.

Barkow, Jerome H. 1972. "Hausa Women and Islam." *Canadian Journal of African Studies* 6(2): 317–28.

Bashir, M. K. 1972. "The Economic Activities of Secluded Married Women in Kurawa and Lallokin Lemu, Kano City." Zaria: Ahmadu Bello University, Department of Sociology, B.Sc. Thesis.

Bature, Ruth, Zuwaira Usman, and Asma'u Mahmud. 1982. *Women Adult Education Programme in Kano.* Zaria: Ahmadu Bello University, Adult Education Department, Center for Adult Education and Extension Services (mimeograph).

Baxter, Sandra, and Majorie Lansing. 1983. *Women and Politics: Visible Majority.* Ann Arbor, Mich.: University of Michigan Press.

Bayero University, Kano. 1980–1982. *Annual Report.* Kano: Bayero University, Office of the Registrar.

———. 1983. Letter of Appointment to Expatriate Members of Staff.

———. February 18, 1983. Official Bulletin No. 331.

Beck, Lois, and Nikki Keddie, eds. 1978. *Women in the Muslim World.* Cambridge: Harvard University Press.

Bellah, R. N. 1975. *Beyond Belief: Essays on Religion in a Post-Traditional World.* Princeton: Princeton University Press.

Bello, Aishatu Salihu. 1983. "The Problems and Prospects of Mass Education with Special Reference to Women, Kano." Kano: Bayero University, Faculty of Education, M.Ed. Thesis.

Bello, Sir Ahmadu. 1962. *My Life.* Cambridge: Cambridge University Press.

Binder, L. 1955. "Al-Ghazali's Theory of Islamic Government." In *The Muslim World* 45:229–41.

Bivar, A. D. H., and Mervyn Hiskett. 1962. "The Arabic Literature of Nigeria to 1804: A Provisional Account." *Bulletin: School of Oriental and African Studies* 25(1): 142–58. University of London.

Boserup, Ester, 1970. *Women's Role in Economic Development.* New York: St. Martin's Press.

Boulding, Elise. 1976. *The Underside of History: A View of Women Through Time.* Boulder, Colo.: Westview Press.

———. 1980. *Women: The Fifth World.* New York: Foreign Policy Association, Headline Series, #248.

Bray, Mark. 1981. *Universal Primary Education in Nigeria: A Study of Kano State.* Boston: Routledge and Kegan Paul.

Brown, G. N., and M. Hiskett. 1975. *Conflict and Harmony in Education in Tropical Africa.* London: George Allen and Unwin.

Buvinic, Mayra, Nadia Yousef, and Barbara Von Elm. 1978. "Women-headed Households, The Ignored Factor in Development Planning." Washington, D.C.: The International Center for Research on Women (mimeograph).

Callaway, Barbara J. 1984. "Ambiguous Consequences of the Socialization and Seclusion of Hausa Muslim Women in Nigeria." *Journal of Modern African Studies* 22(3): 429–50.

Callaway, Barbara J., and Enid Schildkrout. 1985. "Law, Education and Social Change: Implications for Hausa Muslim Women in Nigeria." In *The Women's Decade, 1975–1985,* ed. Lynn Iglitzen. Santa Barbara, Calif.: ABC Clio Press.

Campbell, A., Phillip Converse, Warren Miller, and David Stokes. 1960. *The American Voter.* New York: Holt, Rinehart and Winston.

Charnay, Jean Paul. 1971. *Islamic Culture and Socio-Economic Change.* Leiden: E. J. Brill.

Chinas, Beverly. 1973. *The Isthmus Zapotecs: Women's Roles in a Cultural Context.* New York: Holt, Rinehart and Winston.

Chodorow, Nancy. 1974. "Family Structure and the Feminine Personality." In *Women, Culture and Society,* ed. Michele Z. Rosaldo and Louise Lamphere, 43–66. Stanford: Stanford University Press.

———. 1978. *The Reproduction of Mothering: Psychoanalysis and the Sociology of Gender.* Berkeley: University of California Press.

Cohen, Ronald. 1971. *Dominance and Defiance: A Study of Marital Instability in an Islamic Society.* Washington, D.C.: American Anthropological Association, Anthropological Studies No. 6.

Coleman, James S. 1960. *Nigeria: Background to Nationalism.* Cambridge: Harvard University Press.

Constitution. See Nigeria, Government of, 1979a.

Coser, Lewis. 1977. "Georg Simmel's Neglected Contributions to the Sociology of Women." *Signs* 4(2): 869–76.

Coulson, N. J., and Doreen Hinchcliffe. 1978. "Women and Law Reform in Contemporary Islam." In *Women in the Muslim World,* ed. Nikki Keddie and Lois Beck, 37–51. Cambridge: Harvard University Press.

dan Fodio, Abdullahi. 1961. *Diya al-ta-wil* (The Light of Interpretation). Cairo: Matba't al-Istiqama.

dan Fodio, Usman. 1960. *Mur al-albab.* In *Nigerian Perspectives,* ed. Thomas Hodgkin, 184–95. London: Oxford University Press.

dan Shehu, Malam Isa. 1971. "Wak'ar Shehu Karamonin." *African Language Studies* 12:77.

Da Vanzo, Julie, and Donald Lye Poh Lee. 1978. *The Compatibility of Child Care with Labor Force Participation and Nonmarket Activities.* Santa Monica, Calif.: The Rand Corporation.

De Beauvoir, Simone. 1974. *The Second Sex.* Translated and edited by H. M. Parshley. New York: Random House, Vintage Books edition.

Del Vecchio Good, Mary Jo. 1978. "A Comparative Perspective on Women in Provincial Iran and Turkey." In *Women in the Muslim World,* ed. Lois Beck and Nikki Keddie, 482–500. Cambridge: Harvard University Press.

Dengler, Ian C. 1978. "Turkish Women in the Ottoman Empire: The Classical Age." In *Women in the Muslim World,* ed. Lois Beck and Nikki Keddie, 229–44. Cambridge: Harvard University Press.

de Tocqueville, Alexis. 1946. *Democracy in America* (translation by Phillips Bradley). New York: Vintage Books.

Deutsch, Helene, 1949. *The Psychology of Women,* vol. 2. New York: Grune and Stratton.

Diamond, Larry. 1982. "Cleavage, Conflict and Anxiety in the Second Nigeria Republic." *The Journal of Modern African Studies* 20(4): 629–68.

———. 1984. "Nigeria in Search of Democracy." *Foreign Affairs* (Spring): 62(4): 905–1005.

Dodd, B., ed. 1973. *Out of School Education for Women in African Countries.* Geneva: UNESCO, No. 82/4/1973, 52–57.

Dry, D. P. L. 1950. "The Family Organization of the Hausa of Northern Nigeria." Oxford: Oxford University, B.Sc. Thesis.

Duverger, Maurice. 1955. *The Political Role of Women.* Paris: International Publishers.

el Mahdi, Sadiq. 1982. "Islam's Moral Appeal to Mankind." *Arabia: The Islamic World Review,* Vol. 8 (April): 34–38.

Engels, Frederick. 1972. *The Origin of the Family, Private Property and the State* ed. Eleanor B. Leacock. New York: International Publishers, New World Paperbacks.

Epstein, Cynthia Fuchs. 1970. *Women's Place: Options and Limits in Professional Careers.* Berkeley: University of California Press.

Fallers, Lloyd, and Margaret Fallers. 1982. "Sex Roles in Edremit." In *Mediterranean Family Structure,* ed. J. Peristiany, 88–145. Cambridge: Cambridge University Press.

Fanon, Franz. 1966. *The Wretched of the Earth.* New York: Grove Press.

Federal Electoral Commission. *See* Nigeria, Government of, 1979b.

Feinstein, Alan. 1973. *African Revolutionary: The Life and Times of Nigeria's Aminu Kano.* New York: Quadrangle.

Fika, Adamu Mohammad. 1978. *The Kano Civil War and British Overrule: 1882–1940.* Ibadan: Oxford University Press.

Firestone, Shulamith. 1970. *The Dialectic of Sex.* New York: William Morrow and Co.

Galadanci, Alhaji Shehu A. 1971. "Education of Women in Islam with Reference to Nigeria." *Nigerian Journal of Islam* 1(2) (January -June): 5–11.

Gana, Muhammed. 1983. *The Development of Western Education in Islamiyya School [sic] in Kano City from 1970–1980.* Kano: Bayero University, Faculty of Education, M.Ed. Thesis.

Gibb, H. A. R., and H. Bowen. 1957. *Islam, Society and the West.* London: Oxford University Press.

Gibb, H. A. R. 1962. *Studies in the Civilization of Islam.* London: Oxford University Press.

Gornick, Vivian, and Barbara K. Moran. 1971. *Women in Sexist Society.* New York: Basic Books.

Gordon, David C. 1968. *Women of Algeria: An Essay on Change.* Cambridge: Harvary University Press.

Graham, Sonia F. 1966. *Government and Mission Education in Northern Nigeria: 1900–1919.* Ibadan: Ibadan University Press.

Greenberg, J. H. 1966. *The Influence of Islam on a Sudanese Religion.* 2d ed. Seattle and London: University of Washington Press and Monographs of the American Ethnological Society, #10.

Gruberg, Martin. 1968. *Women in American Politics.* Oshkosh, Wis.: Academia Press.

Hacker, Helen Mayer. 1951. "Women as a Minority Group." *Social Forces* 30:60–69.

Haddad, Yvonne Yazbeck. 1980. "Traditional Affirmations Concerning The Role of Women Found in Contemporary Arab Islamic Literature." In *Women in Contemporary Muslim Societies,* ed. Jane Smith, 61–86. London: Associated University Presses.

Haeri, Shahla. 1980. "Women, Law and Social Change in Iran." In *Women in Contemporary Muslim Societies,* ed. Jane Smith, 209–34. London: Associated University Presses.

Hake, James M. 1972. *Child-Rearing Practices in Northern Nigeria.* Ibadan: Ibadan University Press.

Hanger, J., and J. Moris. 1973. "Women and the Household Economy." In *Mwea: An Integrated Rice Scheme in Kenya,* ed. R. Chambers and J. Moris. Munich: Welforum Verlag.

Hassan, Yusuf Fadl. 1975. "Interaction Between Traditional and Western Education in the Sudan: An Attempt Towards a Synthesis." In *Conflict and Harmony in Education in Tropical Africa,* ed. G. N. Brown and M. Hiskett, 118–33. London: George Allen and Unwin.

Haswell, M. R. 1963. *The Changing Pattern of Economic Activity in a Gambian Village.* London: Overseas Research Publication, Overseas Development Administration.

Heath, F. 1952. *A Chronicle of Abuja.* (English translation of M. Hassan and M. Sha'ibu Makau. *Sarkin Zazzau na Habe and Tarihi da Al'adun Habe na Abuja.*) Ibadan: Ibadan University Press.

Hill, Polly. 1972. *Rural Hausa: A Village and A Setting.* Cambridge: Cambridge University Press.

———. 1977. *Population, Prosperity and Poverty: Rural Kano 1900–1970.* Cambridge: Cambridge University Press.

———. 1978. "Food-farming and Migration from Fante Villages." *Africa* 48(3): 220–30.

Hilliard, F. H. 1957. A Short History of Education in British West Africa. London: Thomas Nelson and Sons, Ltd.

Hinchcliffe, Doreen. 1975. "The Status of Women in Islamic Law." In *Conflict and Harmony in Education in Tropical Africa,* ed. G. N. Brown and M. Hiskett, 455–66. London: George Allen and Unwin.

Hiskett, Mervyn. 1960. "Kitab al-Farq: A Work on the Habe Kingdoms Attributed to Uthman dan Fodio." *Bulletin: School of Oriental and African Studies* 23(3): 553–79. University of London.

———. 1963. *Tazyin al-Waraquat.* Ibadan: Ibadan University Press.

———. 1971. "The Song of Salihu's Miracles." *African Language Study,* vol. XII, pp. 23–29.
———. 1973. *The Sword of Truth: The Life and Times of Shehu Usuman dan Fodio.* New York: Oxford University Press.
———. 1975. "Islamic Education in the Tradition and State Systems in Northern Nigeria." In *Conflict and Harmony in Education in Tropical Africa,* ed. G. N. Brown and M. Hiskett, 134–52. London: George Allen and Unwin.
Hodgkin, Thomas. 1956. *Colonialism in Tropical Africa.* New York: New York University Press.
———. 1960. *Nigerian Perspectives.* London: Oxford University Press, 1960.
———. 1961. *African Political Parties.* New York: Penguin African Series.
———. 1972. "Mahdism, Messianism and Marxism in the African Setting." In *Sudan in Africa,* ed. Yusuf Fadl Hassan. Khartoum.
———. 1980. "The Revolutionary Tradition in Islam." *Class and Race* 21(3): 221–37.
Hogben, S. T., and A. H. M. Kirk-Greene. 1966. *The Emirates of Northern Nigeria.* London: Oxford University Press.
The Holy Qur'an. 1968. Text, translation, and commentary by Abdullah Yusuf Ali. Beirut: Dar Al Arabia.
Hubbard, J. P. 1975. "Government and Islamic Education in Northern Nigeria (1900–1940)." In *Conflict and Harmony in Education in Tropical Africa,* ed. G. N. Brown and M. Hiskett, 152–67. London: George Allen and Unwin.
Hussein, Aziza. 1953. "The Role of Women in Social Reform in Egypt." *The Middle East Journal* 7(4): 440–50.
Iglitzen, Lynn, and Ruth Ross. 1976. *Women of the World: A Comparative Study.* Santa Barbara, Calif.: ABC Clio.
Jaggar, P. J. 1976. "Kano City Blacksmiths: Precolonial Distribution Structure and Organization." *Savanna* 2(1): 11–26.
Jalingo, Ahmadu Usman. 1980. "The Radical Tradition in Northern Nigeria." Edinburgh: University of Edinburgh, Ph.D. Dissertation.
Jaquette, Jane. 1974. *Women and Politics.* New York: Wiley and Sons.
———. 1982. "Women and Modernization Theory: A Decade of Feminist Criticism." *World Politics* 34(2): 267–84.
Kabir, Zainab sa'ad. 1981. "The Silent Oppression: Male-Female Relations in Kano." Kano: Bayero University Faculty Seminar, Department of Sociology (May) (mimeograph).
Kano State. 1976. *Education Review Committee* (Galadanci Committee). Kano: Government Printer.
———. 1977. *School Directory for Kano State.* Kano: Ministry of Education.
———. 1978. *Grants to Islamiyya Schools.* Kano: Ministry of Education.
———. 1978. *Kano State Statistical Yearbook.* Kano: Ministry of Economic Development.
———. 1982. *Annual Statistics.* Kano: Ministry of Education.
———. 1983. "Education Statistics for Kano State." Kano: Ministry of Education.
Khurshid, Ahmad. 1974. *Family Life in Islam.* Leicester: The Islamic Foundation.

Kirk-Greene, A. H. M. 1972. *Gazetteers of the Northern Provinces of Nigeria: The Hausa Emirates (Bauchi, Sokoto, Zaria, Kano).* London: Cass.

Kisekka, N. N. 1980. "The Identification and Use of Indicators of Women's Participation in Socio-Economic Development in the Context of Nigeria and Uganda." Rome: UNESCO.

Klein, Ethel. 1984. *Gender Politics.* Cambridge: Harvard University Press.

Krusius, P. 1915. "Die Maguzawa." *Archiv fur Anthropologie* 14:31–40.

Lamphere, Louise. 1974. "Strategies, Cooperation, and Conflict Among Women in Domestic Groups." In *Women, Culture and Society,* ed. M. Z. Rosaldo and L. Lamphere, 97–112. Stanford: Stanford University Press.

Lapidus, Gail. 1978. *Women in Soviet Society: Equality, Development and Social Change.* Los Angeles: University of California Press.

Last, Murray. 1967. *The Sokoto Caliphate.* London: Longmans, Green & Co.

Leacock, Eleanor, 1972. Introduction to *The Origin of the Family: Private Property and the State* by Frederick Engels. New York: International Publishers.

Lemu, B. Aisha, and Fatima Heeren. 1978. *Women in Islam.* London: The Islamic Foundation.

Lemu, B. Aisha. 1983. *A Degree Above Them: Observations on the Condition of the Northern Nigerian Woman.* Zaria: Gaskiya Corporation.

Lenin, V. I. 1965. "The Tasks of the Working Women's Movement in the Soviet Republic." In *Collected Works,* 40–46. Moscow: Progress Publishers.

Levy, Reuben. 1965. *The Social Structure of Islam.* Cambridge: Cambridge University Press.

Lomnitz, Larissa. 1977. *Networks and Marginality.* New York: Academic Press.

Lugard, Sir Frederick. 1929. *The Dual Mandate in British Tropical Africa.* 4th ed. London: William Blackwood.

Mack, Beverly. 1981. *Wokokin Mata: Hausa Women's Oral Poetry.* Ann Arbor, Mich.: University Microfilms.

Macoby, Eleanor, and Carol N. Jacklin, 1974. *The Psychology of Sex Differences.* Stanford: Stanford University Press.

Mannoni, Albert. 1967. *Prospero and Caliban: The Colonizers and the Colonized.* Boston: Beacon Press.

Massell, Gregory. 1974. *The Surrogate Proletariat: Moslem Women and Revolutionary Strategies in Soviet Central Asia, 1919–1929.* Princeton: Princeton University Press.

Mawdudi, Abdul A'la. 1960. *Islamic Law and Constitution.* Lahore: Islamic Publishing Company.

———. 1976. *Human Rights in Islam.* Leicester: The Islamic Foundation.

Mead, Margaret. 1935. *Sex and Temperament in Three Primitive Societies.* New York: New American Library.

———. 1949. *Male and Female: A Study of the Sexes in a Changing World.* New York: Dell Publishing Company.

Meek, C. K. 1925. *The Northern Tribes of Nigeria.* 2 vols. London: Oxford University Press.

Mernissi, Fatima. 1975. *Beyond the Veil.* Cambridge, Mass.: Schenkman Publishing Co.

Michels, Robert. 1962. *Political Parties.* New York: Dover.

Millet, Kate. 1971. *Sexual Politics.* New York: Avon.

Miner, H. M., and G. DeVos. 1960. *Oasis and Casbah.* Ann Arbor, Mich.: University of Michigan Press.

Modibbo, Dija. 1982. "Changing Attitudes of Women Toward Purdah." Kano: Bayero University, Department of Sociology, B.Sc. Thesis.

Mueller, Carol, ed. 1985. *Politics of the Gender Gap.* Beverly Hills, Calif.: Sage Publications.

Muhammad, Abdullah Ibn. 1960. *Tazyin al-Waragat.* Translated by Mervyn Hiskett. 1963. Ibadan: Ibadan University Press.

Muhammad, Dan'tsoho. 1980. *Comparisons of Attitudes of Educated and Uneducated Adults Toward Women Education in Kano.* Kano: Bayero University, Faculty of Education, M.Sc. Thesis.

Musa, Ayuba Zakirai. 1981. *Assessment of Societal Perceptions and Attitudes Toward Marriage and Educated Hausa Women in the Northern States of Nigeria.* Ann Arbor, Mich.: University Microfilms.

Nasr, Sayyid Hossein. 1966. *Ideals and Realities of Islam.* London: George Allen and Unwin.

National Party of Nigeria. 1979. "Party Manifesto." Lagos: National Party of Nigeria.

———. 1983. *NPN Manifesto '83.* Lagos.

Nevadomsky, Joseph. 1980. "Motivation of Married Women to Higher Education in a Nigerian Setting." In *Proceedings of the National Conference on Integrated Rural Development and Women in Development,* ed. Fred Omu et al., vol. II, 848–61. Benin: University of Benin Press.

Nicolas, Guy. 1965. "Circulation des richesses et participation sociale dans une société Hausa du Niger' (Canton de Kantche)." Bordeaux: Editions du Centre Universitaire de Polycopiage de l'A.G.E.B.

———. 1975. *Dynamique Sociale et Appréhension du Monde au Sein d'une Société Hausa.* Paris: Institut d'Ethnologie.

Nigeria, Federal Republic of. 1976. *Annual Abstract of Statistics 1974.* Lagos: Federal Office of Statistics.

———. 1979. *Proceedings of the Constituent Assembly, Official Report, Vol. III, April 3–May 30, 1979.* Lagos: Government Printing Office.

Nigeria, Government of. 1979a. *The Constitution of the Federal Republic of Nigeria.* Lagos: Government Printer.

———. 1979b. *Report of the Federal Electoral Commission: 1979 General Elections.* Lagos: Government Printer.

Nigeria, Northern Region. 1958. *Annual Education Department Report.* Kaduna: Government Printer.

Nuhu, Abubakar. 1972. "Qur'anic School in Kano." Kano: Bayero University, Department of Islamic Studies, B.A. Thesis.

Ogunsola, A. F. 1974. *Legislation and Education in Northern Nigeria.* Ibadan: Oxford University Press.

Olin, Ulla. 1976. "A Case for Women as Co-Managers: The Family as a General Model of Human Social Organization." In *Women and World Development,* ed. Irene Tinker and Michele Bo Bramsen. Washington, D.C.: Overseas Development Council.

Omu, Fred, P. Kofo Makinwa, and A. O. Ozo, eds. 1980. *Proceedings of the National Conference on Integrated Rural Development and Women in Development.* 3 vols. Benin: University of Benin Press.

Paden, John. 1973. *Religion and Political Culture in Kano.* Berkeley: University of California Press.

Pakizege, Behnaz. 1978. "Legal and Social Position of Iranian Women." In *Women in the Muslim World,* ed. Lois Beck and Nikki Keddie, 216–26. Cambridge: Harvard University Press.

Palmer, Sir Herbert R. 1913–14, 1915–16. "An Early Fulani Conception of Islam." *Journal of the Africa Society* vols. 13, 14.

———. 1927. "The Bornu Girgam." *Journal of the Africa Society* 26(103)(April): 216–36.

———. 1928. *Sudanese Memoirs: Being Mainly Translations from a Number of Arabic Manuscripts Relating to the Central and Western Sudan.* 3 vols. Lagos: Government Printer.

———. 1936. *The Bornu Sahara and Sudan.* London: Murray.

———. 1950. "Review of Y. Urvoy, *Histoire de l'Empire du Bornu.*" *Africa* 20 (2, April): 161–63.

Papanek, Hanna. 1973. "Purdah: Separate Worlds and Symbolic Shelter" in *Comparative Studies in Society and History* 15(3): 289–325.

Parsons, Talcott. 1954. "The Kinship System of the Contemporary U.S." In *Essays in Sociological Theory.* New York: The Free Press of Glencoe.

Pateman, Carole. 1983. "Feminism and Democracy." In *Democratic Theory and Practice,* ed. E. Duncan. London: Oxford University Press, 204–17.

People's Redemption Party. 1979a. "Plan for Redemption: Aims and Objectives of the People's Redemption Party." Kano.

———. 1979b. "The Platform of the People: The General Programme and Election Manifesto of the Peoples Redemption Party." Published in commemoration of the First Anniversary of the founding of the PRP 21st October 1978, 21 October 1979. Kano.

Perham, Margery. 1960. *Lugard: The Years of Authority, 1898–1945.* London: Collins.

Pitten, Renee. 1979. "Marriage and Alternative Strategies: Career Patterns of Hausa Women in Katsina City." London: University of London, School of Oriental and African Studies, Ph.D. Dissertation.

———. 1980. "Sex-role Stereotypes and the Behavior of Women: The Ideal/Real Dichotomy." In *Proceedings of the National Conference on Integrated Rural Development and Women in Development,* ed. Fred Omu et al., 886–900. Benin: University of Benin Press.

———. 1983. "Houses of Women: A Focus on Alternative Lifestyles in Katsina City." In *Female and Male in West Africa,* ed. C. Oppong. London: George Allen and Unwin.

Proceedings. See Nigeria, Federal Republic of, 1979.

Rabi'u, Binta. 1981. "Political Participation and Awareness of Women in Kano." Kano: Bayero University, Department of Political Science, B.Sc. Thesis.

Raza, M. Rafique, and Segun Famoriyo. 1980. "Integrated Rural Development As a Framework for Women's Participation in Development." In *Proceedings of the National Conference on Integrated Rural Development and Women in Development,* ed. Fred Omu et al., 933–49. Benin: University of Benin Press.

Rimi, Sa'adatu. 1983. *The Attitudes of Parents Towards Women Education in Kano.* Kano: Bayero University, Faculty of Education, M.Sc. Thesis.

Robinson, C. H. 1896. *Specimens of Hausa Literature.* Cambridge: Cambridge University Press.

Rosaldo, Michelle Z. 1984. "Women, Culture and Society: A Theoretical Overview." In *Women, Culture and Society,* ed. M. Z. Rosaldo and L. Lamphere, 17–43. Stanford: Stanford University Press.

Rosaldo, Michelle Z., and Louise Lamphere, eds. 1974. *Women, Culture and Society.* Stanford: Stanford University Press.

Sacks, Karen. 1974. "Engels Revisited: Women, the Organization of Production and Private Property." In *Women, Culture and Society,* ed. M. Z. Rosaldo and L. Lamphere, 207–23. Stanford: Stanford University Press.

Safilios-Rothchild, Constantina. 1970. "Toward a Cross-Cultural Conceptualization of Modernity." *Journal of Comparative Family Studies* 6 (Fall): 17–25.

Saunders, Margaret O. 1978. *Marriage and Divorce in a Muslim Hausa Town.* Ann Arbor, Mich.: University Microfilms.

Schildkrout, Enid. 1978a. "Age and Gender in Hausa Society: Socio-Economic Roles of Children in Urban Kano." In *Sex and Age as Principles of Social Differentiation,* A.S.A. Monograph 17, ed. J. S. Fontaine, 109–37. London: Academic Press.

———. 1978b. "Changing Economic Roles of Children in Comparative Perspective." In *Marriage, Fertility and Parenthood in West Africa,* ed. C. Oppong, G. Adaba, M. Bekombo-Priso and J. Mogey, 289–306. Canberra: Australia National University.

———. 1979. "Women's Work and Children's Work: Variations among Moslems in Kano." In *Social Anthropology of Work,* A.S.A. Monograph 19, ed. S. Wallman, 69–85. London: Academic Press.

———. 1981. "The Employment of Children in Kano." In *Child Work, Poverty and Underdevelopment,* ed. Gerry Rodgers and Guy Standing, 81–112. Geneva: International Labor Office.

———. 1982. "Dependence and Autonomy: The Economic Activities of Secluded Hausa Women in Kano, Nigeria." In *Women and Work in Africa,* ed. Edna Bay, 55–83. Boulder: Westview Press.

———. 1984. "Schooling or Seclusion: Choices for Northern Nigerian Women." *Cultural Survival Quarterly* 8 (2) 46–48.

———. 1986. "Widows in Hausa Society: Ritual Phase or Social Status." In *Widows in African Societies: Choices and Constraints.* ed. Betty Potash, 131–52. Stanford: Stanford University Press.

Skinner, Neil. 1969. "The Origin of the Name 'Hausa'." *Africa* 28(3). 201–10.

Sklar, Richard L. 1983. *Nigerian Political Parties: Power in an Emergent African Nation.* New York: Nok Publishers International.

Smith, H. F. C. (Abdullahi). 1975. "The Early States of the Central Sudan." In *History of West Africa,* ed. J. F. Ade Ajayi and Michael Crowder, vol. 1, 158–201. London: Longmans.

Smith, Jane, ed. 1980. *Women in Contemporary Muslim Societies.* London: Associated University Presses.

Smith, Mary. 1954. *Baba of Karo: A Woman of the Muslim Hausa.* London: Faber and Faber.

Smith, M. G. 1955. *The Economy of the Hausa Communities of Zaria.* Colonial Research Studies, 16. London: Her Majesty's Stationary Office.

———. 1960. *Government in Zazzau.* London: Oxford University Press.

———. 1962. "Exchange and Marketing Among the Hausa." In *Markets in Africa,* ed. P. Bohannan and G. Dalton, 299–334. Evanston, Ill., Northwestern University Press.

———. 1965. "The Hausa of Northern Nigeria." In *Peoples of Africa,* ed. James Gibb. New York: Holt, Rinehart and Winston.

———. 1978. *The Affairs of Daura: History and Change in a Hausa State 1800–1958.* Los Angeles: University of California Press.

Solaru, T. T. 1964. *Teacher Training in Nigeria.* Ibadan: Ibadan University Press.

Staudinger, P. 1889. *Im Herzen der Hausalander.* Berlin, n.p.

Tahir, Ibrahim. 1976. "Scholars, Sufis, Saints and Capitalists in Kano, 1904–1974." Cambridge: Cambridge University, Ph.D. dissertation.

Tajudeen, Abdul Raheem. 1982. *Ideology and Political Parties in Nigeria's Second Republic.* Kano: Bayero University, Department of Political Science, B.Sc. thesis.

Tessler, Mark A. 1978. "Women's Emancipation in Tunisia." In *Women in the Muslim World,* ed. Lois Beck and Nikki Keddie, 141–58. Cambridge: Harvard University Press.

Tiger, Lionel. 1969. *Men in Groups.* New York: Random House.

Tiger, Lionel, and Robin Fox. 1971. *The Imperial Animal.* New York: Holt, Rinehart and Winston.

Tinker, Irene. "The Adverse Impact of Development on Women." In *Women and World Development,* ed. Irene Tinker and Michele Bo Bramson, 22–34. Washington, D.C.: Overseas Development Council.

Trevor, Jean. 1975. "Western Education and Muslim Fulani/Hausa Women in Sokoto, Northern Nigeria." In *Conflict and Harmony in Education in Tropical Africa,* ed. G. N. Brown and M. Hiskett, 247–70. London: George Allen and Unwin.

Umar, Laba'tu. 1981. "The Administration of Private Institutions: A Case Study of St. Louis Secondary School, Kano." Kano: Bayero University, Faculty of Education, M.Ed. thesis.

United Nations. 1973. New York: *Demographic Yearbook.* Tables 8 and 10. Department of Economic and Social Affairs.

———. 1974. Geneva: *Yearbook for Labor Statistics.* Table 2A, 2B. International Labor Office.

Whitaker, C. S., Jr. 1970. *The Politics of Tradition: Continuity and Change in Northern Nigeria 1946–1966.* Princeton: Princeton University Press.

Women in Nigeria (WIN). 1983. *Proceedings: Second Annual Conference.* Zaria: Ahmadu Bello University Press.

Yassar, Daiyib. 1983. "The Development of Islamiyya Schools and Their Future in Kano Municipality, 1960–1982." Kano: Bayero University, Faculty of Education, M.Ed. thesis.

Yeld, E. R. 1966. "Islam and Social Stratification in Northern Nigeria." *British Journal of Sociology* 2:124–31.

Youssef, Nadia. 1978. "The Status and Fertility Patterns of Muslim Women." *Women in the Muslim World,* ed. Lois Beck and Nikki Keddie, 69–99.

Yuguda, Indo A'isha. 1983. "An Investigation into the Mass Failures in Girls Secondary School [*sic*] and Teacher's Colleges in Kano." Kano: Bayero University, Faculty of Education, M.Ed. Thesis.

Index

MUSLIM HAUSA WOMEN IN NIGERIA

was composed in 10-point Digital Compugraphic Garamond and leaded 2 points by Metricomp;
with display type set in Abbott Old Style by Rochester Mono/Headliners;
and ornaments provided by Jōb Litho Services;
printed by sheet-fed offset on 50-pound, acid-free, Glatfelter Antique Cream,
Smyth-sewn and bound over binder's boards in Joanna Arrestox B
by Maple-Vail Book Manufacturing Group, Inc.;
with dust jackets printed in two colors
by Philips Offset Company, Inc.;
and published by

SYRACUSE UNIVERSITY PRESS
SYRACUSE, NEW YORK 13244-5160